# NORTHSTAR 3
## READING AND WRITING
### THIRD EDITION

AUTHORS
**Laurie Barton**
**Carolyn Dupaquier Sardinas**

SERIES EDITORS
**Frances Boyd**
**Carol Numrich**

PEARSON
Longman

## Dedication

To my parents, Jack and Jorane Barton,
educators extraordinaire.
*Laurie Barton*

To my husband, Luis,
and to my children, Alexander and Alyse.
*Carolyn Dupaquier Sardinas*

**NorthStar: Reading and Writing Level 3, Third Edition**

Copyright © 2009, 2004, 1998 by Pearson Education, Inc.
All rights reserved.

No part of this publication may be reproduced, stored in a retrieval system, or transmitted in any form or by any means, electronic, mechanical, photocopying, recording, or otherwise, without the prior permission of the publisher.

Pearson Education, 10 Bank Street, White Plains, NY 10606

Contributor credit: Helen S. Solórzano contributed material to FOCUS ON WRITING in *NorthStar: Reading and Writing Level 3, Third Edition.*

Staff credits: The people who made up the *NorthStar: Reading and Writing Level 3, Third Edition* team, representing editorial, production, design, and manufacturing, are John Barnes, Aerin Csigay, Dave Dickey, Ann France, Françoise Leffler, Melissa Leyva, Sherry Preiss, Robert Ruvo, Debbie Sistino, Paula Van Ells, and Christine Wilson.

Cover art: Silvia Rojas/Getty Images
Text composition: ElectraGraphics, Inc.
Text font: 11.5/13 Minion
Credits: See page 220.

**Library of Congress Cataloging-in-Publication Data**

Northstar. Reading and writing. — 3rd ed.
    4 v. ; cm.
    Rev. ed. of: Northstar / Natasha Haugnes, Beth Maher, 2nd. ed. 2004.
    The third edition of the Northstar series has been expanded to 4 separate volumes. Each level is in a separate volume with different contributing authors.
    Includes bibliographical references.
    Contents: Level 2 : Basic Low Intermediate / Beth Maher, Natasha Haugnes — Level 3 : Intermediate / Carolyn Dupaquier Sardinas, Laurie Barton — Level 4 : High Intermediate / Andrew English, Laura Monahon English — Level 5 : Advanced / Robert F. Cohen, Judy L. Miller.
    ISBN-13: 978-0-13-240991-9 (pbk. : student text bk. level 2 : alk. paper)
    ISBN-10: 0-13-240991-7 (pbk. : student text bk. level 2 : alk. paper)
    ISBN-13: 978-0-13-613368-1 (pbk. : student text bk. level 3 : alk. paper)
    ISBN-10: 0-13-613368-1 (pbk. : student text bk. level 3 : alk. paper)
    [etc.]
    1. English language—Textbooks for foreign speakers. 2. Reading comprehension—Problems, exercises, etc. 3. Report writing—Problems, exercises, etc. I. Haugnes, Natasha, 1965– Northstar. II. Title: Reading and writing.
    PE1128.N675 2008
    428.2'4—dc22

                                                                            2008024492

ISBN 10: 0-13-613368-1
ISBN 13: 978-0-13-613368-1

Printed in the United States of America
1 2 3 4 5 6 7 8 9 10—CRK—13 12 11 10 09 08

# CONTENTS

# WELCOME TO NorthStar
## THIRD EDITION

*NorthStar*, now in its third edition, motivates students to succeed in their **academic** as well as **personal** language goals.

For each of the five levels, the two strands—*Reading and Writing* and *Listening and Speaking*—provide a fully integrated approach for students and teachers.

## WHAT IS SPECIAL ABOUT THE THIRD EDITION?

### NEW THEMES

**New themes** and **updated content**—presented in a **variety of genres**, including literature and lectures, and in **authentic reading and listening selections**—challenge students intellectually.

### ACADEMIC SKILLS

**More** purposeful **integration of critical thinking** and an enhanced focus on **academic skills** such as inferencing, synthesizing, note taking, and test taking help students develop strategies for **success** in the **classroom** and on **standardized tests**. A **culminating productive task** galvanizes content, language, and **critical thinking skills**.

➤ In the *Reading and Writing* strand, a new, **fully integrated writing section** leads students through the **writing process** with engaging writing assignments focusing on various rhetorical modes.

➤ In the *Listening and Speaking* strand, a **structured approach** gives students opportunities for **more extended and creative oral practice**, for example, presentations, simulations, debates, case studies, and public service announcements.

### NEW DESIGN

Full **color pages** with more **photos**, **illustrations**, **and graphic organizers** foster student engagement and make the content and activities come alive.

### MyNorthStarLab

**MyNorthStarLab**, an easy-to-use **online learning and assessment program**, offers:

➤ Unlimited access to reading and listening selections and DVD segments.

➤ Focused test preparation to help students succeed on international exams such as TOEFL® and IELTS®. Pre- and post-unit assessments improve results by providing individualized instruction, instant feedback, and personalized study plans.

➤ Original activities that support and extend the *NorthStar* program. These include pronunciation practice using voice recording tools, and activities to build note taking skills and academic vocabulary.

➤ Tools that save time. These include a flexible gradebook and authoring features that give teachers control of content and help them track student progress.

# THE NORTHSTAR APPROACH

The *NorthStar* series is based on **current research in language acquisition** and on the **experiences of teachers and curriculum designers**. Five principles guide the *NorthStar* approach.

## PRINCIPLES

**1   The more profoundly students are stimulated intellectually and emotionally, the more language they will use and retain.**

The thematic organization of *NorthStar* promotes intellectual and emotional stimulation. The 50 sophisticated themes in *NorthStar* present intriguing topics such as recycled fashion, restorative justice, personal carbon footprints, and microfinance. The authentic content engages students, links them to language use outside of the classroom, and encourages personal expression and critical thinking.

**2   Students can learn both the form and content of the language.**

Grammar, vocabulary, and culture are inextricably woven into the units, providing students with systematic and multiple exposures to language forms in a variety of contexts. As the theme is developed, students can express complex thoughts using a higher level of language.

**3   Successful students are active learners.**

Tasks are designed to be creative, active, and varied. Topics are interesting and up-to-date. Together these tasks and topics (1) allow teachers to bring the outside world into the classroom and (2) motivate students to apply their classroom learning in the outside world.

**4   Students need feedback.**

This feedback comes naturally when students work together practicing language and participating in open-ended opinion and inference tasks. Whole class activities invite teachers' feedback on the spot or via audio/video recordings or notes. The innovative new MyNorthStarLab gives students immediate feedback as they complete computer-graded language activities online; it also gives students the opportunity to submit writing or speaking assignments electronically to their instructor for feedback later.

**5   The quality of relationships in the language classroom is important because students are asked to express themselves on issues and ideas.**

The information and activities in *NorthStar* promote genuine interaction, acceptance of differences, and authentic communication. By building skills and exploring ideas, the exercises help students participate in discussions and write essays of an increasingly complex and sophisticated nature.

# THE NorthStar UNIT

## ❶ FOCUS ON THE TOPIC

This section introduces students to the unifying theme of the reading selections.

> **PREDICT** and **SHARE INFORMATION** foster interest in the unit topic and help students develop a personal connection to it.
>
> **BACKGROUND** AND **VOCABULARY** activities provide students with tools for understanding the first reading selection. Later in the unit, students review this vocabulary and learn related idioms, collocations, and word forms. This helps them explore content and expand their written and spoken language.

---

UNIT
9

# Is Our Climate Changing?

## ①FOCUS ON THE TOPIC

### Ⓐ PREDICT

*Look at the photograph of the Earth. Discuss the questions in a small group.*

1. What are some ways in which the Earth is changing?
2. How responsible are humans for changes on the planet?
3. Are these changes making the world better or worse?

163

---

### Ⓑ SHARE INFORMATION

*Write **A** (agree) or **D** (disagree) next to each statement. Discuss your answers with a classmate.*

_____ 1. The Earth goes through warming and cooling periods, and the warming period happening now is just part of those natural changes.

_____ 2. The weather has become more dangerous in recent years.

_____ 3. The hole in the ozone layer[1] is causing climate change.

_____ 4. New fuels will solve the problem of pollution.

_____ 5. Some people are frightening us with "global warming" so they can make money from it.

---
[1] **ozone layer:** a layer of ozone above the Earth that prevents harmful radiation from the sun reaching the Earth's surface

### Ⓒ BACKGROUND AND VOCABULARY

**1** *Look at the pictures and read the texts. Pay special attention to the boldfaced words.*

**How Greenhouse Gases Cause Climate Change**

Most of the sun's heat hits the Earth and **escapes** back into space. Some is trapped by the **atmosphere** and warms the Earth.

**Fossil fuels** (coal, gasoline) are burned and **carbon dioxide** ($CO_2$) is released. Released $CO_2$ and other **gases** are called greenhouse gas **emissions**.

Greenhouse gases make the atmosphere thicker. As the sun's heat hits the Earth, more and more of the heat is trapped and warms the Earth. As $CO_2$ increases, so does the temperature. This shows that there is a **link** between $CO_2$ and temperature. This connection is **evidence** that climate change is caused by humans.

164   UNIT 9

# ② FOCUS ON READING

This section focuses on understanding two contrasting reading selections.

> **READING ONE** is a literary selection, academic article, news piece, blog, or other genre that addresses the unit topic. In levels 1 to 3, readings are based on authentic materials. In levels 4 and 5, all the readings are authentic.
>
> **READ FOR MAIN IDEAS** and **READ FOR DETAILS** are comprehension activities that lead students to an understanding and appreciation of the first selection.

---

## ② FOCUS ON READING

**A  READING ONE: Our Climate Is Changing ...**

*Read the article adapted from a New Zealand government brochure.*

**Our Climate is Changing and It is Going to Keep Changing**

**Climate Change**

1   It's getting hotter. Our climate is changing, so you'd better get used to it. It's changing because of what we humans do and the **gases** we have put into the **atmosphere**. We have already put so much gas into the atmosphere, the climate will keep changing for a long, long time. Some of the changes may be good (at least in the short term) and some may be bad. But change is a near certainty.

2   We have known for 25 years that the atmosphere was changing. The most obvious **sign** was an increase in **carbon dioxide** ($CO_2$), the gas we breathe out and the gas produced when we burn **fossil fuels** such as coal and gasoline. This is the same gas that is absorbed by plants to make food. Before 1900 the amount of carbon dioxide in the atmosphere was 270 to 280 parts per million (ppm). Now it has grown to 380 parts per million. In the same time, the world has become steadily hotter. It is this **link**, this connection, that tells us that carbon dioxide is causing the warming. This **evidence** is powerful proof that humans, not nature, are causing climate change.

**Not Just Hotter**

3   Since the atmosphere is getting hotter, it is also getting more **energetic**. This means that in some places it will be windier, in some places wetter, in some places drier. In some places it may even be cooler. That's why we talk about "climate change" rather than "global warming." Although on average it will be warmer, it won't necessarily be warmer everywhere.

**Can We Stop It?**

4   No. We can slow it, but we can't stop it for a long, long time. We have already made the greenhouse gas **emissions** that will keep the atmosphere changing for decades to come. If we could keep the world's greenhouse gas emissions from growing, the temperature would continue to grow as fast as it is growing now. If we could cut emissions by half, the world would still keep getting hotter for a hundred years or more. But if we act soon, we can make sure the changes can be managed and kept to a minimum, and we can **adapt** to them.

*(continued on next page)*

---

### ❮ READ FOR MAIN IDEAS

*Write **T** (true) or **F** (false) for each statement.*

_____  1. Tony Hawk is ashamed of his occupation.

_____  2. He wants all his skateboard tricks to be perfect.

_____  3. His classmates liked him because of his skateboarding ability.

_____  4. His parents thought that skateboarding was a waste of time.

_____  5. He had a smooth and flowing style.

_____  6. He earned a lot of money before the age of 25.

### ❮ READ FOR DETAILS

*Write one-sentence answers to the questions. Then compare answers with a partner.*

1. What did Tony Hawk achieve at the 1999 Summer X Games?
   _____

2. How much time did he spend practicing his most famous trick?
   _____

3. When did he begin skateboarding?
   _____

4. Where did he learn to ride a skateboard?
   _____

5. What kind of problems did he have in school?
   _____

6. Who saw Tony's tricks in a Tarzan movie?
   _____

### ❮ MAKE INFERENCES

*Decide which of the statements can be inferred from Reading One. Check (✓) the correct answers. Refer to the reading to find support for your answers. Compare your answers with a partner.*

_____  1. Baggy skater clothes weren't popular at Tony's first school.

_____  2. Tony didn't try difficult tricks at first.

_____  3. Tony's parents married late in life.

_____  4. The principal at Tony's first school didn't support his skateboarding.

_____  5. Tony got excellent grades at his second school.

_____  6. At Tony's second school, he was popular with the other students.

---

Following this comprehension section, the **MAKE INFERENCES** activity prompts students to "read between the lines," move beyond the literal meaning, exercise critical thinking skills, and understand the text on a more academic level. Students follow up with pair or group work to discuss topics in the **EXPRESS OPINIONS** section.

**READING TWO** offers another perspective on the topic and usually belongs to another genre. Again, in levels 1 to 3, the readings are based on authentic materials, and in levels 4 and 5, they are authentic. This second reading is followed by an activity that challenges students to question ideas they formed about the first reading, and to use appropriate language skills to analyze and explain their ideas.

**INTEGRATE READINGS ONE AND TWO** presents culminating activities. Students are challenged to take what they have learned, organize the information, and synthesize it in a meaningful way. Students practice skills that are essential for success in authentic academic settings and on standardized tests.

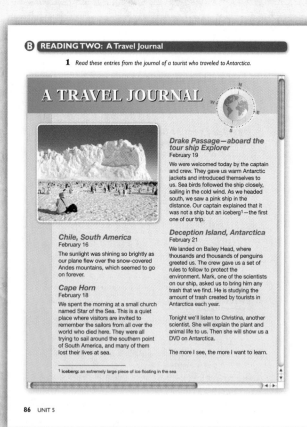

**B READING TWO: A Travel Journal**

**1** *Read these entries from the journal of a tourist who traveled to Antarctica.*

## A TRAVEL JOURNAL

**Drake Passage—aboard the tour ship Explorer**
February 19

We were welcomed today by the captain and crew. They gave us warm Antarctic jackets and introduced themselves to us. Sea birds followed the ship closely, sailing in the cold wind. As we headed south, we saw a pink ship in the distance. Our captain explained that it was not a ship but an iceberg[1]—the first one of our trip.

**Chile, South America**
February 16

The sunlight was shining so brightly as our plane flew over the snow-covered Andes mountains, which seemed to go on forever.

**Cape Horn**
February 18

We spent the morning at a small church named Star of the Sea. This is a quiet place where visitors are invited to remember the sailors from all over the world who died here. They were all trying to sail around the southern point of South America, and many of them lost their lives at sea.

**Deception Island, Antarctica**
February 21

We landed on Bailey Head, where thousands and thousands of penguins greeted us. The crew gave us a set of rules to follow to protect the environment. Mark, one of the scientists on our ship, asked us to bring him any trash that we find. He is studying the amount of trash created by tourists in Antarctica each year.

Tonight we'll listen to Christina, another scientist. She will explain the plant and animal life to us. Then she will show us a DVD on Antarctica.

The more I see, the more I want to learn.

[1] iceberg: an extremely large piece of ice floating in the sea

**C INTEGRATE READINGS ONE AND TWO**

**STEP 1: Organize**

Below is a list of characteristics and a Venn Diagram. Put characteristics that describe Tony Hawk in the left circle, characteristics that describe Ashley Lindermann in the right circle, and those that describe both athletes in the middle part where the two circles overlap.

**Characteristics**
Competitive
Dedicated
Desire to be the best
Need to feel in control
Life of pressure
World seems scary
Family is supportive
Family adds pressure
Obsession leads to success
Obsession leads to anorexia
Obsession helps to escape pain

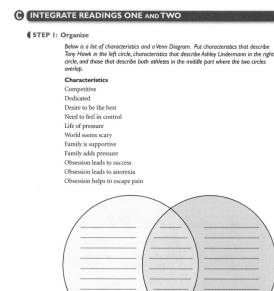

Tony Hawk            Ashley Lindermann

# ③ FOCUS ON WRITING

This section emphasizes development of productive skills for writing. It includes sections on vocabulary, grammar, and the writing process.

> The **VOCABULARY** section leads students from reviewing the unit vocabulary, to practicing and expanding their use of it, and then working with it—using it creatively in both this section and in the final writing task.
>
> Students learn useful structures for writing in the **GRAMMAR** section, which offers a concise presentation and targeted practice. Vocabulary items are recycled here, providing multiple exposures leading to mastery. For additional practice with the grammar presented, students and teachers can consult the GRAMMAR BOOK REFERENCES at the end of the book for corresponding material in the *Focus on Grammar* and Azar series.

---

## ③ FOCUS ON WRITING

### Ⓐ VOCABULARY

❰ REVIEW

*Read the paragraph about traditional courtship. Then, decide if the sentences below are related to courtship (**C**), the wedding ceremony (**W**), or married life (**M**), and mark them appropriately. Share your choices with the class.*

> **Courtship** refers to the period of time when a man and a woman get to know each other before marriage. In some cultures, they spend time together alone. In other cultures, they spend time together with friends and relatives. During this time, a couple may decide whether or not to marry.

___W___ **a.** Members of the community are invited to watch the couple promise to love each other **faithfully** with an **everlasting** love.

_____ **b.** The man **surprises** the woman with flowers to show his **romantic** feelings for the first time.

_____ **c.** The husband and wife disagree about the best way to **raise** their two sons.

_____ **d.** Friends and relatives throw rice at the couple to make a wish for their **fertility**.

_____ **e.** When a woman's boyfriend asks her to marry him, she is happy she won't have a **broken heart**.

_____ **f.** The husband and wife hope that their marriage will **produce** healthy children.

_____ **g.** A man and a woman are attracted to each other and choose to spend time together because of such **characteristics** as good looks, intelligence, and kindness. Little by little, each person discovers more about the other's **background**.

_____ **h.** Important words are spoken by a person in a position of **leadership**.

_____ **i.** The woman happily tells her mother that she is **pregnant**.

_____ **j.** The man realizes that the woman will be an excellent **spouse**.

_____ **k.** The husband and wife are **proud** of their children's achievements.

---

### Ⓑ GRAMMAR: Simple Past and Past Progressive

**1** *Read these sentences based on Frank Abagnale's story. Look at the boldfaced verbs. What is the difference between the verb forms? Notice the words in italics. How are the meanings of* when *and* while *different?*

- Frank Abagnale **was hiding** in France *when* a flight attendant **reported** him to the authorities.
- *When* he **met** the doctor who helped him, they **were** both **renting** apartments in the same community.
- *While* the FBI **was searching** for him, he **was enjoying** himself in California.

| SIMPLE PAST AND PAST PROGRESSIVE | |
|---|---|
| **1.** Use the **simple past** tense to talk about actions, states, and situations in the past that take place at one point in time. The simple past tense of regular verbs is formed by adding *-d* or *-ed* to the base form of the verb. | He finally **passed** the law exam. |
| **2.** Use the **past progressive**, also called **past continuous**, to describe a continuous nonstop action that was in progress at a specific time in the past. Examples of specific time expressions include: *yesterday, last night, at that time*. The past progressive is formed like this: *be* (past) + verb + *-ing*. | *At that time*, he **was working** at a law firm. |
| **3.** Use the **past progressive** with the **simple past** tense to talk about an action that was interrupted by another action. Use the simple past tense for the interrupting action. Use *when* to introduce the simple past tense action. | He **was living** in France *when* a flight attendant **saw** him. |
| **4.** If you put the *when* clause first, you must put a **comma** at the end of the clause. | *When* the flight attendant **saw** him, he **was living** in France. |
| **5.** Use the **past progressive** with *while* to describe two actions in progress at the same time in the past. The **simple past** can also be used in the *while* clause without changing the meaning. | He **was enjoying** himself in California *while* the FBI **was searching** for him. |
| | He **was enjoying** himself in California *while* the FBI **searched** for him. |

The **WRITING** section of each unit leads students through the writing process and presents a challenging and imaginative writing task that directs students to integrate the content, vocabulary, and grammar from the unit.

- Students practice a short **pre-writing strategy**, such as freewriting, clustering, brainstorming, interviewing, listing, making a chart or diagram, categorizing, or classifying.

- Then students organize their ideas and write, using a **specific structural or rhetorical pattern** that fits the subject at hand.

- Students then learn **revising techniques** within a sentence-level or paragraph-level activity to help them move towards **coherence and unity** in their writing.

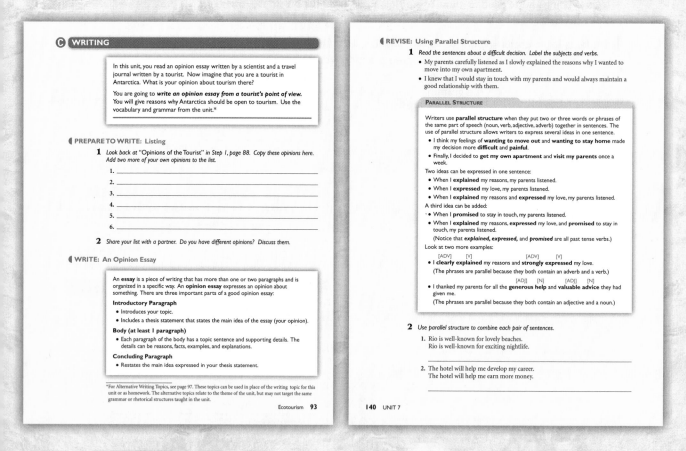

**C  WRITING**

In this unit, you read an opinion essay written by a scientist and a travel journal written by a tourist. Now imagine that you are a tourist in Antarctica. What is your opinion about tourism there?

You are going to **write an opinion essay from a tourist's point of view.** You will give reasons why Antarctica should be open to tourism. Use the vocabulary and grammar from the unit.*

**PREPARE TO WRITE:** Listing

1  Look back at "Opinions of the Tourist" in Step 1, page 88. Copy these opinions here. Add two more of your own opinions to the list.

1. _____
2. _____
3. _____
4. _____
5. _____
6. _____

2  Share your list with a partner. Do you have different opinions? Discuss them.

**WRITE:** An Opinion Essay

An **essay** is a piece of writing that has more than one or two paragraphs and is organized in a specific way. An **opinion essay** expresses an opinion about something. There are three important parts of a good opinion essay:

**Introductory Paragraph**
- Introduces your topic.
- Includes a thesis statement that states the main idea of the essay (your opinion).

**Body (at least 1 paragraph)**
- Each paragraph of the body has a topic sentence and supporting details. The details can be reasons, facts, examples, and explanations.

**Concluding Paragraph**
- Restates the main idea expressed in your thesis statement.

*For Alternative Writing Topics, see page 97. These topics can be used in place of the writing topic for this unit or as homework. The alternative topics relate to the theme of the unit, but may not target the same grammar or rhetorical structures taught in the unit.

Ecotourism  **93**

**REVISE:** Using Parallel Structure

1  Read the sentences about a difficult decision. Label the subjects and verbs.
- My parents carefully listened as I slowly explained the reasons why I wanted to move into my own apartment.
- I knew that I would stay in touch with my parents and would always maintain a good relationship with them.

**PARALLEL STRUCTURE**

Writers use **parallel structure** when they put two or three words or phrases of the same part of speech (noun, verb, adjective, adverb) together in sentences. The use of parallel structure allows writers to express several ideas in one sentence.
- I think my feelings of **wanting to move out** and **wanting to stay home** made my decision more **difficult** and **painful**.
- Finally, I decided to **get my own apartment** and **visit my parents** once a week.

Two ideas can be expressed in one sentence:
- When I **explained** my reasons, my parents listened.
- When I **expressed** my love, my parents listened.
- When I **explained** my reasons and **expressed** my love, my parents listened.

A third idea can be added:
- When I **promised** to stay in touch, my parents listened.
- When I **explained** my reasons, **expressed** my love, and **promised** to stay in touch, my parents listened.
  (Notice that *explained, expressed,* and *promised* are all past tense verbs.)

Look at two more examples:
   [ADV]  [V]     [ADV]   [V]
- I **clearly explained** my reasons and **strongly expressed** my love.
  (The phrases are parallel because they both contain an adverb and a verb.)

       [ADJ]  [N]    [ADJ]  [N]
- I thanked my parents for all the **generous help** and **valuable advice** they had given me.
  (The phrases are parallel because they both contain an adjective and a noun.)

2  Use parallel structure to combine each pair of sentences.

1. Rio is well-known for lovely beaches.
   Rio is well-known for exciting nightlife.

   _____

2. The hotel will help me develop my career.
   The hotel will help me earn more money.

   _____

**140**  UNIT 7

In the final phase of the writing process, students **edit** their work with the help of a **checklist** that focuses on mechanics, completeness, enhancing style, and incorporating the vocabulary and grammar from the unit.

**ALTERNATIVE WRITING TOPICS** are provided at the end of the unit. They can be used as *alternatives* to the final writing task, or as *additional* assignments. RESEARCH TOPICS tied to the theme of the unit are organized in a special section at the back of the book.

# COMPONENTS

## TEACHER'S MANUAL WITH ACHIEVEMENT TESTS

Each level and strand of *NorthStar* has an accompanying Teacher's Manual with step-by-step **teaching suggestions**, including unique guidance for using *NorthStar* in secondary classes. The manuals include time guidelines, expansion activities, and techniques and instructions for using MyNorthStarLab. Also included are reproducible unit-by-unit achievement **tests** of **receptive** and **productive** skills, **answer keys** to both the student book and tests, and a unit-by-unit **vocabulary** list.

## EXAMVIEW

*NorthStar* ExamView is a stand-alone CD-ROM that allows teachers to **create and customize** their own *NorthStar* tests.

## DVD

The *NorthStar* DVD has **engaging**, **authentic video clips**, including animation, documentaries, interviews, and biographies, that correspond to the themes in *NorthStar*. Each theme contains a three- to five-minute segment that can be used with either the *Reading and Writing* strand or the *Listening and Speaking* strand. The video clips can also be viewed in MyNorthStarLab.

## COMPANION WEBSITE

The companion website, www.longman.com/northstar, includes resources for teachers, such as the **scope and sequence**, **correlations** to other Longman products and to state standards, and **podcasts** from the *NorthStar* authors and series editors.

## MyNorthStarLab

PEARSON LONGMAN mynorthstarlab | AVAILABLE WITH the new edition of *NORTHSTAR*

*NorthStar* is now available with **MyNorthStarLab**—an easy-to-use **online** program **for students and teachers** that saves time and improves results.

➤ **STUDENTS** receive **personalized instruction** and **practice** in all four skills. Audio, video, and test preparation are all in **one** place—available **anywhere, anytime**.

➤ **TEACHERS** can take advantage of many resources including online **assessments**, a flexible **gradebook**, and **tools for monitoring student progress**.

CHECK IT OUT! GO TO www.mynorthstarlab.com FOR A PREVIEW!

TURN THE PAGE TO SEE KEY FEATURES OF **MyNorthStarLab**.

# MyNorthStarLab

**MyNorthStarLab** supports students with **individualized instruction**, **feedback**, and **extra help**. A wide array of resources, including a flexible **gradebook**, helps teachers manage student progress.

The MyNorthStarLab **WELCOME** page **organizes assignments and grades**, and **facilitates communication** between students and teachers.

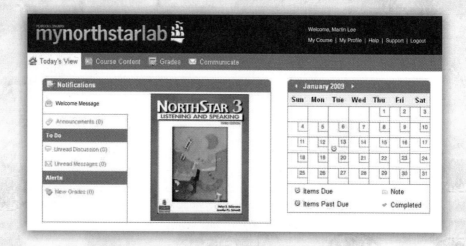

For each unit, MyNorthStarLab provides a **READINESS CHECK**.

➤ Activities **assess** student knowledge **before** beginning the unit and **follow up** with individualized instruction.

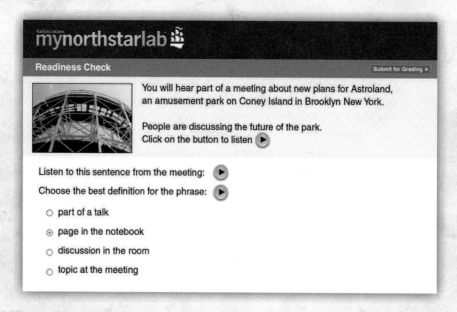

Student book material and **new** practice activities are available to students online.

➤ Students benefit from virtually unlimited **practice anywhere, anytime**.

Interaction with **Internet** and **video** materials will:

➤ Expand students' knowledge of the topic.

➤ Help students practice new vocabulary and grammar.

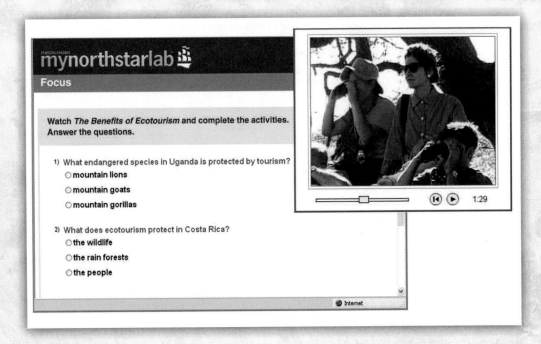

**INTEGRATED SKILL ACTIVITIES** in MyNorthStarLab challenge students to bring together the **language skills** and **critical thinking skills** that they have practiced throughout the unit.

PEARSON LONGMAN
# mynorthstarlab

Integrated Task - Read, Listen, Write        Submit for Grading ▶

## THE ADVENTURE OF A LIFETIME

We at the Antarctic Travel Society encourage you to consider an excited guided tour of Antarctica for your next vacation.

The Antarctic Travel society carefully plans and operates tours of the Antarctic by ship. There are three trips per day leaving from ports in South America and Australia. Each ship carries only about 100 passengers at a time. Tours run from November through March to the ice-free areas along the coast of Antarctica.

In addition to touring the coast, our ships stop for on-land visits, which generally last for about three hours. Activities include guided sightseeing, mountain climbing, camping, kayaking, and scuba diving. For a longer stay, camping trips can also be arranged.

Our tours will give you an opportunity to experience the richness of Antarctica, including its wildlife, history, active research stations, and, most of all, its natural beauty.

Tours are supervised by the ship's staff. The staff generally includes experts in animal and sea life and other Antarctica specialists. There is generally one staff member for every 10 to 20 passengers. Theses trained and responsible individuals will help to make your visit to Antarctica safe, educational, and unforgettable.

### READ, LISTEN AND WRITE ABOUT TOURISM IN ANTARCTICA

**Read.**
**Read the text. Then answer the question.**

According to the text, how can tourism benefit the Antarctic?

▶ **Listen.**
**Click on the Play button and listen to the passage.**
**Use the outline to take notes as you listen.**

Main idea:

Seven things that scientists study:

The effects of tourism:

**Write.**
**Write about the potential and risks in Antarctica.**
**Follow the steps to prepare.**

**Step 1**
- Review the text and your outline from the listening task.
- Write notes about the benefits and risks of tourism.

**Step 2**
Write for 20 minutes. Leave 5 minutes to edit your work.

The MyNorthStarLab **ASSESSMENT** tools allow instructors to customize and deliver achievement tests online.

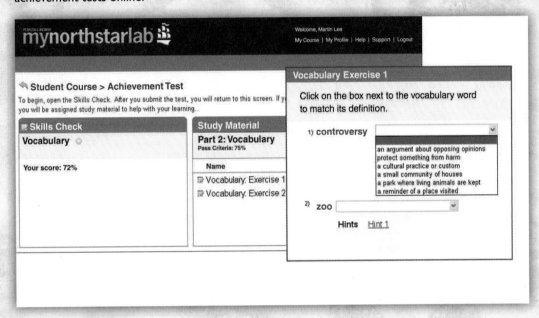

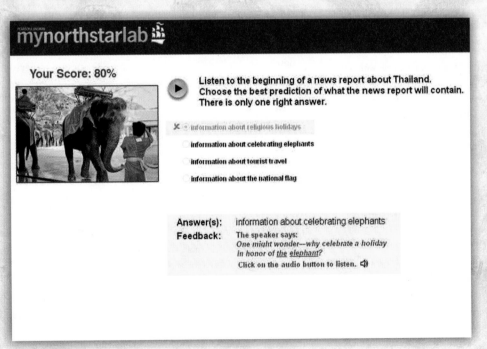

# SCOPE AND SEQUENCE

| UNIT | CRITICAL THINKING | READING |
|---|---|---|
| **1** **The World of Advertising**<br><br>**Theme:** Advertising<br>**Reading One:** *Advertising All over the World*<br>An article<br>**Reading Two:** *Changing World Markets*<br>An excerpt from a speech | Compare personal buying habits<br>Infer word meaning from context<br>Classify information<br>Identify and reevaluate assumptions<br>Connect themes between texts<br>Support opinions with reasons | Predict content<br>Identify main ideas<br>Read for details<br>Make inferences based on details from a text<br>Relate information in the text to life experiences<br>Link main ideas in Reading One to details in Reading Two |
| **2** **Fraud**<br><br>**Theme:** Fraud<br>**Reading One:** *Catch Me if You Can: The Frank Abagnale Story*<br>A magazine article<br>**Reading Two:** *The Michelle Brown Story: Identity Theft*<br>An excerpt from a book | Interpret an illustration<br>Infer word meaning from context<br>Differentiate between main ideas and details<br>Classify information<br>Relate content to prior knowledge<br>Make inferences<br>Support opinions with reasons | Predict content<br>Identify main ideas<br>Read for details<br>Infer information not explicit in the text<br>Express opinions about a text<br>Organize and synthesize information from the readings<br>Use details from both texts to complete an interview |
| **3** **Going to Extremes: Sports and Obsession**<br><br>**Theme:** Extreme sports<br>**Reading One:** *An Interview with Tony Hawk*<br>A magazine interview with a professional skateboarder<br>**Reading Two:** *High School Star Hospitalized for Eating Disorder*<br>A newspaper article | Interpret photographs<br>Identify personal habits and attitudes<br>Infer word meaning from context<br>Differentiate between main ideas and details<br>Interpret character motivation<br>Use a Venn diagram to organize information<br>Brainstorm ideas | Predict content<br>Read for main ideas<br>Identify details<br>Infer information from context<br>Relate text to personal experiences<br>Organize and synthesize information from the readings |
| **4** **Speaking of Gender**<br><br>**Theme:** Language<br>**Reading One:** *Different Ways of Talking*<br>An article<br>**Reading Two:** *Speaking of Gender*<br>An interview with a professor of communication | Interpret a photograph<br>Assess gender-typing<br>Infer word meaning from context<br>Differentiate between main ideas and details<br>Make inferences<br>Analyze gender influence in speech and behavior<br>Support personal opinions with examples from the text | Predict content<br>Read for main ideas<br>Locate details in the text<br>Infer information not explicit in the reading<br>Link readings to personal observations<br>Organize and synthesize information from the readings |

| WRITING | VOCABULARY | GRAMMAR |
| --- | --- | --- |
| Write a TV commercial<br>Freewrite about an ad<br>Write a paragraph with a topic sentence, supporting details, and a concluding sentence<br>Write an opinion paragraph about an ad | Use context clues to find meaning<br>Find and use synonyms and antonyms<br>Use idiomatic expressions | Simple present and present progressive |
| Write a letter<br>Answer questions<br>Organize information<br>Use topic sentences to focus ideas<br>Write a story | Use context clues to find meaning<br>Identify and analyze word forms | Simple past and past progressive |
| Use information from a Venn diagram to complete a paragraph<br>Write a descriptive paragraph<br>Identify components of a factual report<br>Write a factual report | Use context clues to find meaning<br>Identify and use correct word forms | Ability: *can, could, be able to* |
| Complete a paragraph using information from the readings<br>Write interview questions<br>Create a chart<br>Complete an outline<br>Use transitions of contrast<br>Write a contrast paragraph | Use context clues to find meaning<br>Define words<br>Use idiomatic expressions | Comparative adverbs |

# SCOPE AND SEQUENCE

| UNIT | CRITICAL THINKING | READING |
|---|---|---|
| **5 Ecotourism**<br><br>**Theme:** Tourism<br>**Reading One:** *Tourists in a Fragile Land*<br>An opinion essay<br>**Reading Two:** *A Travel Journal*<br>An account of a trip to Antarctica | Use prior knowledge<br>Infer word meaning from context<br>Test assumptions about Antarctica<br>Differentiate between main ideas and details<br>Support opinions with reasons<br>Analyze author's arguments<br>Hypothesize another's point of view | Predict reasons<br>Identify main ideas<br>Identify inaccurate details<br>Make inferences based on details from a text<br>Relate the readings to personal opinions<br>Read a travel journal<br>Organize and synthesize details from the readings |
| **6 The Metamorphosis**<br><br>**Theme:** Storytelling<br>**Reading One:** *The Metamorphosis*<br>An abridged story<br>**Reading Two:** *Ungeziefer*<br>A critique of the story | Recognize personal assumptions<br>Infer word meaning from context<br>Reflect on attitudes towards insects<br>Infer ideas not explicit in a text<br>Examine symbols and imagery in a text<br>Classify information<br>Interpret emotions | Make predictions<br>Recognize main ideas<br>Paraphrase details<br>Interpret a literary text<br>Support answers with information from the text<br>Connect generalizations to specific passages |
| **7 The Choice to Be Amish**<br><br>**Theme:** The simple life<br>**Reading One:** *The Amish*<br>An article<br>**Reading Two:** *A Decision to Leave*<br>An article | Interpret a photograph<br>Read a map<br>Differentiate between main ideas and details<br>Infer word meaning from context<br>Interpret a timeline<br>Classify information<br>Apply information from the readings to new contexts | Make predictions<br>Identify main ideas and details<br>Infer opinions based on content of a text<br>Support main ideas from one text with details from another text<br>Read an essay about a difficult decision |

| WRITING | VOCABULARY | GRAMMAR |
|---|---|---|
| Rewrite inaccurate statements<br>Write an opinion essay<br>Analyze the structure of an essay<br>Evaluate and write effective supporting details<br>Distinguish between facts, examples, and explanations<br>Organize ideas in an outline | Use context clues to find meaning<br>Define words<br>Identify and use correct word forms<br>Find and use synonyms and antonyms | *Because* and *even though* |
| Write an interview<br>Write a descriptive paragraph<br>Answer *wh-* questions<br>Add details to a story<br>Write a story with a moral | Use context clues to find meaning<br>Complete a crossword puzzle<br>Find and use synonyms | Infinitives of purpose |
| Complete a letter<br>Write a summary<br>Write answers to questions<br>Write an outline<br>Use parallel structure in an essay<br>Write an essay about a difficult decision | Use context clues to find meaning<br>Identify synonyms and antonyms<br>Use idiomatic expressions | Noun clauses with *wh-* words |

# SCOPE AND SEQUENCE

| UNIT | CRITICAL THINKING | READING |
|---|---|---|
| **8 Finding a Spouse**<br><br>**Theme:** Marriage<br>**Reading One:** *Finding a Spouse*<br>  An anthropological article<br>**Reading Two:** *What's Wrong with Tradition?*<br>  A letter to the editor | Identify personal assumptions about marriage<br>Differentiate between main ideas and details<br>Evaluate information in the text according to personal beliefs<br>Match traditions to cultures<br>Rank cultural practices on a continuum<br>Classify information | Make predictions<br>Identify main ideas<br>Read for details<br>Make inferences based on information from a text<br>Organize and synthesize information from the readings |
| **9 Is Our Climate Changing?**<br><br>**Theme:** Climate change<br>**Reading One:** *Our Climate Is Changing . . .*<br>  A report on climate change<br>**Reading Two:** *Climate Change: Making Informed Decisions*<br>  A newspaper editorial | Interpret illustrations<br>Infer word meaning from context<br>Differentiate between main ideas and details<br>Classify data<br>Understand and describe a scientific process<br>Understand and complete a causal chain<br>Summarize cause-and-effect relationships | Identify main ideas<br>Read for details<br>Infer author's position<br>Relate the readings to personal opinions<br>Organize ideas from the readings into a causal chain |
| **10 Crime and Punishment**<br><br>**Theme:** Punishment<br>**Reading One:** *Two Points of View*<br>  Two newspaper editorials<br>**Reading Two:** *Charts*<br>  Statistics on the death penalty | Interpret a photograph<br>Distinguish arguments for and against capital punishment<br>Infer word meaning from context<br>Interpret bar graphs and pie charts<br>Classify information<br>Draw conclusions | Make predictions<br>Identify supporting ideas in an argument<br>Relate supporting details to main ideas<br>Express opinions about capital punishment<br>Read graphs and charts<br>Distinguish between fact and opinion |

| WRITING | VOCABULARY | GRAMMAR |
|---|---|---|
| Complete a summary<br>Describe a cultural tradition of courtship<br>Categorize ideas for writing<br>Use related word forms for cohesion<br>Write a point-by-point paragraph<br>Write an essay describing important characteristics in a spouse or partner | Use context clues to find meaning<br>Define words<br>Identify analogies and word forms | Definite and indefinite articles |
| Rewrite inaccurate statements<br>Draw a causal chain<br>Use cause-and-effect transitions<br>Use adverbial conjunctions to show cause<br>Use transitions to show effect<br>Write a cause-and-effect essay | Use context clues to find meaning<br>Identify and use correct word forms<br>Identify collocations | Future possibility: *may, might, could* |
| Write an opinion paragraph<br>Support opinions with facts and data<br>Write an outline for a debate<br>List ideas<br>Use sentence variety<br>Analyze compound sentences<br>Write a persuasive essay | Use context clues to find meaning<br>Define words<br>Identify abstract nouns<br>Practice appropriate word usage | Present perfect and present perfect progressive |

# ACKNOWLEDGMENTS

I would like to thank my husband, Craig Binns, who took care of our children so that I could write. I would also like to thank Carol Numrich for her patience and advice.

*Laurie Barton*

Many people helped in the creative process that resulted in this book. I am grateful to Allen Ascher, who first gave us this opportunity. To John Barnes, Françoise Leffler, and Debbie Sistino, who provided clear direction and guidance, many thanks. Most importantly, I want to express my deep appreciation to our editor, Carol Numrich. Her keen insight, her understanding of what students need, and her grace throughout the process will never be forgotten. Finally, many thanks to Luis Sardinas, Pete Dupaquier, Ellen Buckley, and Carolyn Reno. Their many, many hours of support were invaluable to the success of this project.

*Carolyn Dupaquier Sardinas*

## Reviewers

For the comments and insights they graciously offered to help shape the direction of the Third Edition of *NorthStar*, the publisher would like to thank the following reviewers and institutions.

**Gail August**, Hostos Community College; **Anne Bachmann**, Clackamas Community College; **Aegina Barnes**, York College, CUNY; **Dr. Sabri Bebawi**, San Jose Community College; **Kristina Beckman**, John Jay College; **Jeff Bellucci**, Kaplan Boston; **Nathan Blesse**, Human International Academy; **Alan Brandman**, Queens College; **Laila Cadavona-Dellapasqua**, Kaplan; **Amy Cain**, Kaplan; **Nigel Caplan**, Michigan State University; **Alzira Carvalho**, Human International Academy, San Diego; **Chao-Hsun (Richard) Cheng**, Wenzao Ursuline College of Languages; **Mu-hua (Yolanda) Chi**, Wenzao Ursuline College of Languages; **Liane Cismowski**, Olympic High School; **Shauna Croft**, MESLS; **Misty Crooks**, Kaplan; **Amanda De Loera**, Kaplan English Programs; **Jennifer Dobbins**, New England School of English; **Luis Dominguez**, Angloamericano; **Luydmila Drgaushanskaya**, ASA College; **Dilip Dutt**, Roxbury Community College; **Christie Evenson**, Chung Dahm Institute; **Patricia Frenz-Belkin**, Hostos Community College, CUNY; **Christiane Galvani**, Texas Southern University; **Joanna Ghosh**, University of Pennsylvania; **Cristina Gomes**, Kaplan Test Prep; **Kristen Grinager**, Lincoln High School; **Janet Harclerode**, Santa Monica College; **Carrell Harden**, HCCS, Gulfton Campus; **Connie Harney**, Antelope Valley College; **Ann Hilborn**, ESL Consultant in Houston; **Barbara Hockman**, City College of San Francisco; **Margaret Hodgson**, NorQuest College; **Paul Hong**, Chung Dahm Institute; **Wonki Hong**, Chung Dahm Institute; **John House**, Iowa State University; **Polly Howlett**, Saint Michael's College; **Arthur Hui**, Fullerton College; **Nina Ito**, CSU, Long Beach; **Scott Jenison**, Antelope Valley College; **Hyunsook Jeong**, Keimyung University; **Mandy Kama**, Georgetown University; **Dale Kim**, Chung Dahm Institute; **Taeyoung Kim**, Keimyung University; **Woo-hyung Kim**, Keimyung University; **Young Kim**, Chung Dahm Institute; **Yu-kyung Kim**, Sunchon National University; **John Kostovich**, Miami Dade College; **Albert Kowun**, Fairfax, VA; **David Krise**, Michigan State University; **Cheri (Young Hee) Lee**, ReadingTownUSA English Language Institute; **Eun-Kyung Lee**, Chung Dahm Institute; **Sang Hyock Lee**, Keimyung University; **Debra Levitt**, SMC; **Karen Lewis**, Somerville, MA; **Chia-Hui Liu**, Wenzao Ursuline College of Languages; **Gennell Lockwood**, Seattle, WA; **Javier Lopez Anguiano**, Colegio Anglo Mexicano de Coyoacan; **Mary March**, Shoreline Community College; **Susan Matson**, ELS Language Centers; **Ralph McClain**, Embassy CES Boston; **Veronica McCormack**, Roxbury Community College; **Jennifer McCoy**, Kaplan; **Joseph McHugh**, Kaplan; **Cynthia McKeag Tsukamoto**, Oakton Community College; **Paola Medina**, Texas Southern University; **Christine Kyung-ah Moon**, Seoul, Korea; **Margaret Moore**, North Seattle Community College; **Michelle Moore**, Madison English as a Second Language School; **David Motta**, Miami University; **Suzanne Munro**, Clackamas Community College; **Elena Nehrbecki**, Hudson County CC; **Kim Newcomer**, University of Washington; **Melody Nightingale**, Santa Monica College; **Patrick Northover**, Kaplan Test and Prep; **Sarah Oettle**, Kaplan, Sacramento; **Shirley Ono**, Oakton Community College; **Maria Estela Ortiz Torres**, C. Anglo Mexicano de Coyoac'an; **Suzanne Overstreet**, West Valley College; **Linda Ozarow**, West Orange High School; **Ileana Porges-West**, Miami Dade College, Hialeah Campus; **Megan Power**, ILCSA; **Alison Robertson**, Cypress College; **Ma. Del Carmen Romero**, Universidad del Valle de Mexico; **Nina Rosen**, Santa Rosa Junior College; **Daniellah Salario**, Kaplan; **Joel Samuels**, Kaplan New York City; **Babi Sarapata**, Columbia University ALP; **Donna Schaeffer**, University of Washington; **Lynn Schneider**, City College of San Francisco; **Errol Selkirk**, New School University; **Amity Shook**, Chung Dahm Institute; **Lynn Stafford-Yilmaz**, Bellevue Community College; **Lynne Ruelaine Stokes**, Michigan State University; **Henna Suh**, Chung Dahm Institute; **Sheri Summers**, Kaplan Test Prep; **Martha Sutter**, Kent State University; **Becky Tarver Chase**, MESLS; **Lisa Waite-Trago**, Michigan State University; **Carol Troy**, Da-Yeh University; **Luci Tyrell**, Embassy CES Fort Lauderdale; **Yong-Hee Uhm**, Myongii University; **Debra Un**, New York University; **José Vazquez**, The University of Texas Pan American; **Hollyahna Vettori**, Santa Rosa Junior College; **Susan Vik**, Boston University; **Sandy Wagner**, Fort Lauderdale High School; **Joanne Wan**, ASC English; **Pat Wiggins**, Clackamas Community College; **Heather Williams**, University of Pennsylvania; **Carol Wilson-Duffy**, Michigan State University; **Kailin Yang**, Kaohsing Medical University; **Ellen Yaniv**, Boston University; **Samantha Young**, Kaplan Boston; **Yu-san Yu**, National Sun Yat-sen University; **Ann Zaaijer**, West Orange High School

# UNIT 1

# The World of Advertising

## ①FOCUS ON THE TOPIC

### A PREDICT

*Look at the photograph and discuss the questions with the class.*

1. What kinds of people are most likely to buy this product: teenagers, parents with young children, or senior citizens (age 65 and older)?

2. Imagine that you are writing an advertisement for this product. Which three words best describe the product: *delicious, refreshing, powerful, nutritious, cool?*

I

## B SHARE INFORMATION

**1** Work in groups of four. Complete the chart with the names of products that you usually buy.

| PRODUCT | STUDENT 1 | STUDENT 2 | STUDENT 3 | STUDENT 4 |
|---|---|---|---|---|
| Drinks | | | | |
| Snack foods | | | | |
| Shampoo | | | | |
| Toothpaste | | | | |

**2** Discuss the questions with your group.

1. Do you know any TV commercials or other advertisements for these products? If so, describe the advertisements.

2. Do advertisements sometimes convince you to buy products? Explain.

## C BACKGROUND AND VOCABULARY

How much do you know about the world of advertising? Test your knowledge. Complete the sentences on the next page with the correct word from the dictionary entries. Be sure to use the correct form of the word.

**cam•paign** /kæm'peɪn/ n a series of actions that are intended to achieve a particular result, especially in business or politics

**com•pe•ti•tion** /ˌkɑmpə'tɪʃən/ n [singular] the people or groups that are competing against you, especially in business

**con•vince** /kən'vɪns/ v [T] to persuade someone to do something

**fail** /feɪl/ v [I, T] to be unsuccessful in doing something

**firm** /fɚm/ n a business or small company

**glob•al** /'gloʊbəl/ adj affecting the whole world, or relating to the whole world

**goal** /goʊl/ n something that you hope to achieve in the future

**mar•ket** /'mɑrkɪt/ n a particular country or area where a company sells its goods

**mes•sage** /'mɛsɪdʒ/ n the main idea or the most important idea in a movie, book, speech, etc.

**suc•ceed** /sək'sid/ v [I] to do what you have tried to do

1. To sell a product in a foreign country, a _____ firm _____ often has to write new ads.

2. _____ Global _____ businesses such as McDonald's offer different products in different parts of the world.

3. The _Messages_ ~~Goal~~ of advertisers is to sell their products.

4. Laws about advertising _~~company~~_ ^(Fail) ^(company) are not the same all over the world.

5. Some advertisers _____ Fail _____ because they do not understand the customs of a country.

6. An advertising _~~company~~_ ^(Messegas) may not be easily translated from one language into another.

7. The _Market_ ^(- competition) of Latin America aren't necessarily similar just because most people speak the same language.

8. In Japan, famous movie stars often appear in ads to _convince_ people to buy products.

9. Advertisements that _~~convince~~_ ^(Succed) use different styles of communication in different parts the world.

10. Some advertisements say why their product is better than the _competition_

# 2 FOCUS ON READING

## A READING ONE: Advertising All over the World

*Work with a partner. Discuss problems that you think advertisers might have if they want to sell a product in different countries. List two or three problems in the space below. Share your list with the class.*

**Possible Problems**

_____

_____

_____

_____

*Now read a magazine article on global advertising. How many of the problems that your class discussed are mentioned in the article?*

# Advertising All over the World

**1**   How can a rabbit be stronger than a football hero? How can a rabbit be more powerful than a big, strong man? In the world of advertising, this is quite possible. Consider the example of Jacko. This great Australian football hero appeared on TV and yelled at the audience to buy products. Jacko's angry **campaign** worked well in Australia, so Energizer® batteries invited him north to sell their product in the United States. But Jacko's yelling did not **convince** the American audience to buy batteries. So, good-bye, Jacko. Hello, Energizer Bunny®, the little toy rabbit that has sold far more batteries than Jacko.

**2**   In the world of advertising, selling products is the most important **goal**. As companies are becoming more **global**, they are looking for new ways to sell their products all over the world. It is true that because of global communication, the world is becoming smaller today.

**3**   But it is also true that the problems of global advertising—problems of language and culture—have become larger than ever. For example, Braniff Airlines wanted to advertise its fine leather seats. But when its advertisement was translated from English to Spanish, it told people that they could fly naked! Another example of incorrect translation is how Chevrolet tried to market the Chevy Nova in Latin America. In English, *nova* refers to a star. But in Spanish, *no va* means "doesn't go." Would you buy a car with this name?

**4**   To avoid these problems of translation, most advertising **firms** are now beginning to write completely new ads. In writing new ads, global advertisers consider the different styles of communication in different countries. In some cultures, the meaning of an advertisement is usually found in the exact words that are used to describe the product and to explain why it is better than the **competition**. This is true in such countries as the United States, Britain, and Germany. But in other cultures, such as Japan's, the **message** de pends more on situations and feelings than it does on words. For this reason, the goal of many TV commercials in Japan will be to show how good people feel at a party or other social situation. The commercial will not say that a product is better than others. Instead, its goal will be to create a positive mood or feeling about the product. As a result, movie stars and celebrities often appear in Japanese advertisements.

**5**   Global advertisers must also consider differences in laws and customs. For instance, certain countries will not allow TV commercials on Sunday, and others will not allow TV commercials for children's products on any day of the week. In some parts of the world, it is forbidden to show dogs on television or certain types of clothing, such as jeans. Customs are also related to beliefs. In Asia, it is important for advertisers to understand the local religious and supernatural beliefs. In China and Hong Kong, for example, the number 4 is considered unlucky while the number 8 is associated with earning money, or good luck. The global advertiser who does not understand such laws and customs will not be able to **succeed**.

**6**   Finally, there is the question of what to advertise. People around the world have different customs as well as different likes and dislikes. This is true even in places such as Latin America where most people share a common language. So the best advertisement in the world means nothing if the product is not right for the **market**. Even though some markets around the world are quite similar, companies such as McDonald's have found that it is very important to sell different products in different parts of the world. So when you go to a McDonald's in Hawaii, you'll find Chinese noodles on the menu. If you stop for a hamburger in Germany, you can order a beer with your meal. In Malaysia, you can try a milk shake that is flavored with a fruit that most people in other countries have never tasted.

7    All of these products must be sold with the right kind of message. It has never been an easy job for global advertisers to create this message. But no matter how difficult this job may be, it is very important for global advertisers to do it well. In today's competitive world, most new products quickly **fail**. Knowing how to advertise in the global market can help companies win the competition for success.

## ◀ READ FOR MAIN IDEAS

*Answer the questions. Then compare your answers with the class.*

1. Who is Jacko? What does he show about international advertising?

   _____

2. What problem do advertisers have when they try to translate ads directly from one language to another?

   _____

3. How can a global advertiser avoid problems?

   _____

4. Why should a company offer different products in different countries?

   _____

## ◀ READ FOR DETAILS

*Circle the letter of the best answer to complete the sentences below. Make sure the sentences are correct according to Reading One.*

1. A battery _____ changed its campaign from Jacko to the Energizer Bunny®.
   a. company
   b. goal
   c. market
   d. translator

2. There are many problems with _____, even with languages that are similar, such as English and Spanish.
   a. advertising
   b. marketing
   c. translation
   d. competition

3. Different countries have different styles of _____, which involve different uses of words and feelings.

    **a.** writing
    **b.** communicating
    **c.** advertising
    **d.** competing

4. Some countries do not allow _____ ads for children's products.

    **a.** newspaper
    **b.** TV
    **c.** magazine
    **d.** radio

5. Drinking beer with a meal is an example of a _____.

    **a.** culture
    **b.** message
    **c.** custom
    **d.** law

6. Many new products fail because there is a lot of _____ in the world today.

    **a.** advertising
    **b.** business
    **c.** communication
    **d.** competition

7. The Chevy Nova campaign failed in Latin America because of the _____ of the ads.

    **a.** goal
    **b.** cost
    **c.** style
    **d.** message

8. Ads that show a group of people sharing good feelings are often quite successful in _____.

    **a.** Germany
    **b.** Japan
    **c.** Malaysia
    **d.** Britain

## ◖ MAKE INFERENCES

*Think about what you learned in Reading One, and circle the best answer to complete the sentences. On the left, note which paragraph in the reading the answer comes from. Discuss your answers with a partner.*

   _6_   **1.** A Baskin Robbins ice cream commercial in the Philippines might advertise mango and papaya ice cream as a new flavor because _____.

    **a.** Baskin Robbins is introducing this flavor globally
    **b.** Filipinos love mango and papaya
    **c.** this product was successful in the United States

_____ 2. A shampoo commercial shows a young woman running in slow motion toward her handsome boyfriend. Her long, shiny hair bounces up and down while romantic music plays in the background. As she runs into the arms of her boyfriend, we see her beautiful, smiling face. This picture is replaced by a picture of the shampoo. There is no written or spoken language of any kind. This commercial is probably from _____.

   **a.** Britain
   **b.** Australia
   **c.** Japan

_____ 3. A luxury car commercial shows the car driving on a mountain road through beautiful green hills. Classical music plays in the background as the narrator explains why this car is better than all other cars. This commercial is probably from _____.

   **a.** the United States
   **b.** Latin America
   **c.** Japan

_____ 4. Most likely, _____ caused the Jacko advertising campaign to fail in the United States.

   **a.** differences in product preferences
   **b.** differences in customs
   **c.** problems in translation

_____ 5. A few years ago, the U.S. drugstore chain Sav-on was renamed Osco because that was the name of the company's new owner. This created serious problems, however, because Osco sounds like the Spanish word "hosco", which sometimes has a negative meaning. Spanish-speaking customers didn't like the name, so it was changed back to Sav-on. This is an example of _____.

   **a.** differences in product preferences
   **b.** differences in customs
   **c.** problems in translation

## ◖ EXPRESS OPINIONS

*Discuss the questions with your classmates.*

1. Think of a popular food or drink product from your home country (for example, tamales, green tea, sea cucumbers, or spicy hot sauce). Where else in the world do you think the product would be popular? Can you think of some places where it wouldn't be popular? Give reasons to support your choices.

2. Which kind of advertisement do you think is more convincing: one that uses exact words to describe the product or one that creates a positive feeling or mood? Give examples of advertisements to support your answer.

3. In countries such as China, the United States, and Japan, advertisements often include famous people, or celebrities. Why do you think these ads are successful?

**1** Read a speech by Annalise Müller, president of the Global Advertisers' Association. She spoke at a meeting of advertisers who want to start global campaigns. Part of her speech was published in Adworld magazine. Discuss the questions with the class before you read.

   **1.** Can you think of any countries where commercial advertising was not allowed in the past? Which countries? Why did the governments of these countries forbid commercial advertising?

   **2.** Do you know anyone who has lived in a country where it is difficult for people to buy the products they want? When they want something very badly, what do they do?

# CHANGING WORLD MARKETS

**By Annalise Müller (from *Adworld*)**

1   Good morning. It's good to be here with you all. My goal today is to give you some information about changing world markets. Let's start by looking at the U.S.A. Can you think of a country with more advertising than the United States? Think about watching a movie on TV. You're waiting for the good guy to get the bad guy, and suddenly there's a commercial. A few minutes later, the good guy is in trouble, and you're interrupted by another commercial. Message after message. It's not like that in other countries. In places like France and Spain, you can watch at least a half hour of the program before a commercial interruption. And then the commercials come all at once.

2   China is a different story. For years any kind of commercial advertising was illegal. Government advertising was seen everywhere, but business advertising was nonexistent. Then Sony came along and changed things. The Japanese company led the way for others to come into the country. We can learn something from Sony, too. It's important not to come and start advertising too quickly because that can lead to serious mistakes. Advertisers must take their time and plan their campaigns carefully. They should also consider the type of advertising that is most popular. In China, large public billboards[1] are the cheapest and most common way to advertise. They were used in the past for official government messages and are still used today.

3   Now in Russia, you have to think about your product and whether or not there's a market for it. Fast food, for example, seemed

---

[1] **billboards:** large signs used for advertising, usually outdoors

very strange to Russians at first. In their restaurants, you sit down and the waiter brings you soup, salad, meat, and potatoes—one thing at a time. Russians think of food as something you take your time with, something you enjoy.

4    What happened with pizza in Russia is a very funny story. First, pizza makers had to convince people to try it, and they had to explain that it was similar to Russian *vatrushka*. Then, the Pizzeria restaurant opened up in Moscow. The Russians may have liked it all right, but Pizzeria didn't succeed with foreign visitors because the pizza didn't always have enough tomato sauce and cheese! Another problem was that if you wanted to take the pizza home with you, the chef wouldn't allow it. He didn't want the pizza to get cold.

5    When you're dealing with international markets, you're dealing with different customs, different tastes. Consider Coca-Cola in Brazil. The company sells a drink flavored with *guarana*, an exotic[2] South American fruit. They've been successful in selling it during the February holiday with this message: "the flavor of Carnaval."

6    As you know, things are changing every day. New markets are opening up all the time. We have to consider laws and customs before we start planning a campaign. We also need to think about our product. Will people be able to buy it? Regarding our marketing plan, will people understand it? Remember that for years in China and Russia, people had a hard time buying things. The best advertisement of all was a long line in front of a store. That's how people knew which store was the place to go. So we must think about how things are changing if we expect to be successful. I appreciate your attendance today. It's been a pleasure to be with you.

[2] **exotic:** unusual and exciting because of a connection with a foreign country

**2**  *Discuss the questions with the class.*

1. What are some differences in television advertising around the world?

2. Which type of advertising is popular in China? Why?

3. Why was it difficult to sell pizza in Russia?

## C  INTEGRATE READINGS ONE AND TWO

◀ **STEP 1: Organize**

*Match the main ideas from Reading One with the examples from Reading Two. Write the letter of the example next to the main idea.*

**Examples**

a. For years, commercial advertising was illegal in China.

b. Advertisers had to explain that pizza was similar to Russian *vatrushka*.

c. A Japanese company was the first to start advertising in China.

**d.** Coca-Cola sells a drink in Brazil that is flavored with *guarana*, a South American fruit.

**e.** In Russian restaurants, you sit down and the waiter brings you soup, salad, meat, and potatoes—one thing at a time.

### Main Ideas

_c_  **1.** As companies become more global, they are looking for new ways to sell their products around the world.

_____  **2.** People around the world have different likes and dislikes.

_____  **3.** Global advertisers must consider differences in laws.

_____  **4.** People around the world have different customs.

_____  **5.** All of these products must be sold with the right kind of message.

### ◖ STEP 2: Synthesize

*Complete the paragraph with the appropriate words from the box. Use information from Step 1.*

| | |
|---|---|
| commercial advertiser | global advertising |
| convince | illegal |
| customs | product preferences |
| difficult | *vatrushka* |

China and Russia are good examples of ___global advertisin___. In
**1.**
China, business advertising was ___illegal___. The only type of
**2.**
advertising that existed was government advertising. This changed when Sony
became the first ___product preferences~~ comercial Advtisre~~___ in China. Russia is an example of
**3.**
how different customs and ___customs convince___ affect advertising
**4.**
campaigns. To sell pizza in Russia, advertisers had to ___vatrushka customs convinc___
**5.**
Russians to try it. They compared it to ___vatrushka___, a familiar
**6.**
Russian food. Then they had to deal with Russian food ___vatrushka difco) comercial advt___
**7.**
Take-out pizza, and fast food in general, was not acceptable because of the Russian

preference for slow, sit-down meals. Both China and Russia demonstrate how

global advertising can be ___comercial advertises difficult___
**8.**

# 3 FOCUS ON WRITING

*Explain*

## A VOCABULARY

### ◖ REVIEW

*Read each sentence and the four answer choices. Three of the choices are synonyms (words that have similar meaning) for the boldfaced word. Cross out the word or phrase that is NOT a synonym.*

1. The **goal** of the advertising campaign was to sell more cars to women.
   - **a.** purpose
   - **b.** plan
   - **c.** hope
   - **d.** ~~future~~

2. Women with young children are part of a growing **market**.
   - **a.** ~~group of people~~
   - **b.** group of stores
   - **c.** group of buyers
   - **d.** group of customers

3. The ad's **message** was that the new cars were safe.
   - **a.** idea
   - **b.** information
   - **c.** ~~style~~
   - **d.** main idea

   *Exito*

4. The ads were **successful** because many women believed in the safety of the cars.
   - **a.** effective
   - **b.** ~~safe~~
   - **c.** ~~having a good result~~
   - **d.** convincing

   *sin enbargo*

5. As a result, the ads **convinced** mothers to buy the cars.
   - **a.** encouraged—*Animar*
   - **b.** pushed – *empujar*
   - **c.** persuaded – *convence*
   - **d.** ~~forced~~ —*forzoso*

6. However, the ads **failed to sell** cars to single women without children.
   - **a.** didn't sell
   - **b.** couldn't sell
   - **c.** were unable to sell
   - **d.** ~~tried to sell~~

7. The advertising campaign will become **global** next year.
   - **a.** multinational
   - **b.** worldwide
   - **c.** ~~organized~~
   - **d.** international

8. Ads for the **competition** will not become global.
   - **a.** ~~race~~
   - **b.** other companies
   - **c.** other sellers
   - **d.** different firms

   *Permitido*

9. **Commercial** advertising is now allowed on Chinese billboards.
   - **a.** business
   - **b.** company
   - **c.** product
   - **d.** official

   *vallas*

10. If a product is **exotic**, people in other countries think of it as unusual.
    - **a.** uncommon
    - **b.** ordinary
    - **c.** different
    - **d.** ~~exciting~~

**1** *Read an excerpt from a description of a college course in advertising. Pay special attention to the boldfaced words and phrases. Match the words and phrases on the left with the definitions on the right.*

### Advertising Design

In this class, we will learn how to use color to **catch the eye** and get people to **pay attention**. We will focus on using images to **hold people's attention** and **impress** them with a message. We will also discuss how music can be used to make an impression. Music stays in our heads long after we have heard it, so a **catchy** song is a powerful and impressive way to communicate a message!

| | | | |
|---|---|---|---|
| _c_ | 1. **catch the eye** | a. | something that you hear and remember |
| _b_ | 2. **pay attention** | b. | to keep people interested |
| _d_ | 3. **hold people's attention** | c. | to make people look |
| _a_ | 4. **impress** | d. | to listen and watch carefully |
| _e_ | 5. **catchy** | e. | to affect positively |

**2** *Look at the course description again. How many forms of the word **impress** are there? Underline these forms. Then complete the following sentences with the correct form.*

1. A successful ad creates a good ___Impress___ .
   *(noun)*

2. Ads with famous celebrities are ___interesting___ to many people.
   *(adjective)*

3. The goal of advertising is to ___pay attention___ people and make them
   *(verb)*

   remember a product.

◖ **CREATE**

*In a small group, write a TV commercial using at least five new words from Review and Expand. It can be serious or funny, an announcement or a conversation. It can advertise cars, fashion, diets, or some other product or service. After the teacher checks your grammar, read or act out your commercial for the class.*

*You can begin your commercial with one of these lines:*

"Hello. I'm _____ and I've got good news for you."

"The new _____ is everything you've always wanted!"

"Are you tired? Bored? Do you need a change? Well, . . ."

*You can end your commercial with one of these lines:*

"To find out more, call . . . Get yours today!"

"Call now for more information or log on to . . ."

"Don't miss this great opportunity!"

**GRAMMAR: Simple Present and Present Progressive**

**1** *Compare these sentences from Reading Two. Notice the boldfaced verb forms. How are they different?*

- You're **waiting** for the good guy to get the bad guy, and suddenly there's a commercial.
- The Russians **think** of food as something you take your time with, something you **enjoy.**
- As you know, things **are changing** every day.

| SIMPLE PRESENT AND PRESENT PROGRESSIVE | |
| --- | --- |
| 1. The **simple present** tense is used to describe what sometimes happens, what usually happens, or what always happens. | You **sit** down and the waiter **brings** you soup, salad, meat, potatoes—one thing at a time. |
| 2. We often use the simple present tense with **adverbs of frequency** to express how often something happens: *always, usually, often, sometimes, rarely, seldom, never.* | In some cultures, the meaning of an advertisement **is** *usually* found in the exact words that are used to describe the product and to explain why it is better than the competition. |
| 3. **Non-action verbs** describe emotions, mental states, and situations. We usually use these verbs in the **simple present** tense. | I **appreciate** your attendance today. (emotion)<br><br>The Russians **think** of food as something you take your time with and enjoy. (mental state)<br><br>Fast food, for example, **is** a very strange idea in Russia. (situation) |
| 4. The **present progressive** tense is used to describe actions that are happening at the present time. | As you know, things **are changing** every day.<br><br>New markets **are opening** up all the time. |
| 5. We often use words or phrases such as *today, nowadays, this month, these days, this year* with the present progressive. | Because of global communication, the world **is becoming** smaller **today**. |

**2** *Read the sentences. Complete each one with the correct verb tense.*

1. Many people _____ *believe* _____ that food from different countries is
   (believe / are believing)

   exotic.

2. The number of global advertisers around the world today

   _____ increases is increasing (aumentan) _____
   (increases / is increasing)

3. These advertisers usually __are failing__ if they do not consider
   (fail / are failing)

   differences in culture.

4. Many people __consider__ McDonald's to be an excellent example
   (consider / are considering)

   of a successful international restaurant.

5. Today, more advertising firms __are writing__. different messages for
   (write / are writing)

   different countries to avoid translation problems.

6. Fast food firms always __make__ their food look delicious on TV.
   (make / are making)

7. Many people around the world __like__ ad campaigns that
   (like / are liking)

   are funny.

8. The world market of Internet users __is growing__ nowadays.
   (grows / is growing)

   Hoy en dia

**3** *Complete the sentences with your own ideas. Use the simple present and present
progressive.*

1. These days, famous people who appear in advertisements ~aparecer~ __is breaking__
   __with their parthers__

2. When a TV commercial begins, some people always __boring__
   _____

3. Now, more companies __is making compaigns about the__
   __Global warming__

4. TV ads in my home country usually __Believe it Know everything__
   _____

## C   WRITING

In this unit, you read about advertising and how it works in different
countries around the world.

Now you are going to **write a paragraph describing an advertisement
and explaining whether or not you think it is effective.** Use the
vocabulary and grammar from the unit.*

---

*For Alternative Writing Topics, see page 18. These topics can be used in place of the writing topic for this
unit or as homework. The alternative topics relate to the theme of the unit, but may not target the same
grammar or rhetorical structures taught in the unit.

# PREPARE TO WRITE: Freewriting

When you **freewrite**, you think about a topic and write **whatever comes into your mind.** You don't worry about grammar, spelling, or vocabulary. You just keep your pen moving across the page. Your purpose is simply to get ideas for writing.

**1** *Choose a magazine, TV, or radio ad that catches your attention. What is happening in the ad? Why did it catch your attention? What is your opinion of the ad? Freewrite about the ad for five minutes.*

**2** *Read your freewriting. Did you describe the advertisement? Underline your descriptions. Do you think the ad is effective? Circle any reasons why or why not.*

# WRITE: A Paragraph

**1** *Read the paragraph and answer the questions.*

> The newspaper ad for abuzz.com, a new Internet service, is very effective. First of all, it is a big ad with an interesting photograph. The ad fills two full pages in the newspaper. Because of its size, the ad catches your attention. When you look at the ad, you get the message that abuzz.com is cool and fashionable. The teenage boys in the photograph are wearing the latest teen fashions and carrying skateboards. Finally, the caption on the opposite page makes you want to read the ad more carefully. In big letters the caption reads: "Jonathan knows". When you read this caption, you want to find out what Jonathan knows. This ad for abuzz.com is effective because it makes me want to visit the website to learn more about it.

1. What is the writer's opinion about the ad?

2. How many reasons does the writer give for this opinion?

> A **paragraph** usually presents one **main idea**. The sentence that states the main idea is called a **topic sentence**. The topic sentence is often the first sentence of the paragraph. The following sentences support the topic sentence with **details** like reasons or examples. The **concluding sentence** at the end of the paragraph repeats key words from the topic sentence. Look at the following examples:
>
> - **Topic Sentence:** The newspaper ad for abuzz.com, a new Internet service, is very effective.
> - **Reason 1:** It is a big ad with an interesting photograph.
> - **Reason 2:** When you look at the ad, you get the message that abuzz.com is cool and fashionable.
> - **Reason 3:** The caption under the photograph makes you want to read the ad more carefully.
> - **Concluding Sentence:** This ad for abuzz.com is effective because it makes me want to visit the website to learn more about it.

**2** *The sentences come from one paragraph. Identify each sentence as indicated in the box.*

> **TS** = Topic Sentence      **D1** = Detail 1      **D3** = Detail 3
> **CS** = Concluding Sentence      **D2** = Detail 2

_D3_ **1.** The company's commercials give the same message in different languages: "Time with family is priceless."

_D2_ **2.** It is trying to appeal to a new market: the everyday person who values family.

_D1_ **3.** MasterCard knows that family values have an international appeal because it has done market research and proved it.

_TS_ **4.** MasterCard is changing its advertising campaign for the global market.

_CS_ **5.** As a result, this campaign is working successfully around the world.

**3** *Write the paragraph on a separate piece of paper by putting the sentences in the correct order. Indent the first sentence.*

**4** *Look at your freewriting from Prepare to Write, page 15. In one sentence, write your opinion about the ad. This will be the topic sentence of your paragraph.*

**Example**

The television ad for Target stores is very convincing.

**5** *Write the first draft of your paragraph. Include three details about the ad that support your topic sentence. Write a concluding sentence that restates your opinion about the ad. Don't worry too much about grammar while you write—just concentrate on making your ideas clear.*

◀ **REVISE: Developing Paragraph Unity**

A paragraph has **unity** when **all the supporting details are related to the topic sentence** and none of them is about other topics.

**1** *Read the topic sentence and the supporting detail sentences. Cross out the one supporting detail that does not support the topic sentence.*

**Topic Sentence:** I don't like TV commercials.

**Supporting Details**

  **a.** Commercials interrupt my favorite TV programs.

  **b.** Too many commercials are shown each hour.

  **c.** Some commercials are fun to watch.

  **d.** Most commercials advertise products I don't care about.

**2** *Read the paragraph. Underline the topic sentence. Five sentences do not support the topic sentence. Cross out those sentences.*

I recently saw a very effective advertisement for Pepsi-Cola on television. First, the ad is surprising. You see an elderly woman with gray hair. She looks like someone's grandmother. In fact, she looks just like my friend's grandmother. But the woman is running very quickly down the street. Then she is jumping over a fence. It is amazing to see an elderly person doing these things. Second, the ad is mysterious. During most of the ad, you don't know what product is being advertised. Mysterious ads are not common on TV. The first time I saw the ad, I couldn't understand the product it advertised. However, at the end of the ad, the woman is drinking some Pepsi. Then you understand the message of the ad. Finally, the ad is not respectful of the elderly. Nowadays, some people are making fun of the elderly. I don't like this. In conclusion, the ad is effective because you keep watching it until the end and you remember it later.

**3** Look back at the first draft of your paragraph. Are there any sentences that do not support the topic sentence? If so, cross them out. If necessary, add more supporting details.

◀ **EDIT: Writing the Final Draft**

*Write the final draft of your paragraph. Carefully edit it for grammatical and mechanical errors, such as spelling, capitalization, and punctuation. Make sure you used some of the vocabulary and grammar from the unit. Use the checklist to help you write your final draft. Then neatly write or type your paragraph.*

---

### ✓ FINAL DRAFT CHECKLIST

○ Does the topic sentence state the product's name, the type of advertisement, and the writer's opinion about the topic?

○ Do all the supporting sentences give reasons for the opinion in the topic sentence?

○ Are specific examples from the advertisement used?

○ Does the concluding sentence restate the main idea of the topic sentence?

○ Are the simple present and present progressive verbs used correctly?

○ Does the paragraph use vocabulary from the unit?

○ Is it formatted correctly? Is the first line indented, and are the lines double-spaced? Are there clear margins on both sides of the paragraph?

## ALTERNATIVE WRITING TOPICS

*Write about one of the topics. Use the vocabulary and grammar from the unit.*

1. Some countries have laws that forbid advertising campaigns for tobacco and alcohol. Do you agree or disagree with these laws? Write a paragraph giving your opinion and the reasons for your opinion.

2. Write a paragraph describing a time when an advertisement convinced you to buy something. Were you satisfied with the product? Give details about your experience.

## RESEARCH TOPICS, see page 211.

# Fraud

# ⟨1⟩ FOCUS ON THE TOPIC

## A PREDICT

*Look at the illustration and the title of this unit, and discuss the questions with the class.*

1. What kinds of ads like this are common?

2. Do you know any examples of Internet fraud[1]?

3. What are some other kinds of fraud?

---

[1]**fraud:** the illegal activity of deceiving people in order to gain money or power

## SHARE INFORMATION

*Interview a partner. Ask the questions below. Choose one answer to share with the class.*

1. There are many types of fraud, for example, medical fraud, Internet fraud, and identity theft.

   • Have you, or has anyone you know, ever been a victim of any of these types of fraud?

   • Have you ever read a newspaper or magazine article or seen a TV show about fraud?

2. Do you think frauds are more or less common today than in the past? Give reasons for your answer.

3. Have you ever bought a product that was a fake?

## C BACKGROUND AND VOCABULARY

**1** *Read the article about fraud. Pay attention to the boldfaced words.*

Fraud has been increasing around the world because of computer technology. One example is the Nigerian Bank Fraud. People are contacted by e-mail and asked to help transfer money from Nigeria or other African countries by allowing the money to be placed temporarily in their bank accounts. The real **motive** is not to transfer money, but to obtain personal banking information.

Another type of computer fraud is known as "phishing," or trying to obtain financial information by **impersonating** a bank employee. When this kind of fraud takes place, you receive e-mail messages from someone pretending to represent your bank. You are then asked to provide your account number or other identifying information. This kind of **deception** seems so real that many people respond to it and give away their financial and personal information.

The telephone is also used by **con men and women** who try to **impress** people with amazing prizes and offers. Sometimes they will call and ask for your banking information so that they can put prize money into your account. If you do not trust a person contacting you by phone, ask for his or her name, business phone number, and company address. You can then contact the company yourself to learn whether or not you have reason to be **suspicious**.

Modern communications technology has made it easier for people to trick you with **fake** deals and requests for information. When you go online, you find many websites offering products and services such as medical treatment and legal advice. How can you know if something is real? Fortunately, there are many organizations that can help you make sure that companies and individuals are treating you with **honesty**. If you believe that you are involved in a case of fraud, be sure to report it and ask for help.

**2**  *Circle the correct synonym for each boldfaced word.*

1. A person's **motive** for doing something is his or her _____.

   a. reason

   b. reward

2. If you **impersonate** a bank employee, you _____.

   a. really are one

   b. are pretending to be one

3. When **deception** takes place, people _____.

   a. tell the truth

   b. lie

4. A **con man or woman** is someone who is trying to _____.

   a. trick you

   b. help you

5. If someone **impresses** you with an offer, you believe the offer is _____.

   a. wonderful

   b. false

6. When you are **suspicious** of someone, you _____.

   a. believe them

   b. don't believe them

7. A **fake** deal is one that is _____.

   a. real

   b. not real

8. When people treat you with **honesty**, they are telling you _____.

   a. the truth

   b. lies

# ② FOCUS ON READING

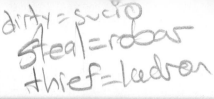

**Ⓐ READING ONE: Catch Me If You Can: The Frank Abagnale Story**

*You are going to read the true story of Frank Abagnale, a former con man. Before you read, look at the list below. Check (✓) three types of fraud that you think you will read about in the story.*

✓ **1.** impersonation        ____ **4.** Internet fraud

____ **2.** telephone fraud        ✓ **5.** offering fake services

____ **3.** selling fake products        ✓ **6.** bank fraud

*Now read Frank Abagnale's story.*

# Catch Me If You Can: The Frank Abagnale Story

1    A doctor . . . a lawyer . . . an airline pilot . . . a college professor . . . former **con man** Frank Abagnale played all these roles as a young man, stealing millions of dollars from banks around the world. His money-making secret? Cashing false checks. His **motive** for playing different roles? Respect and excitement. He enjoyed having other people believe that he was important.

2    He first **impersonated** an airline pilot by wearing a pilot's uniform. Then he created a phony airline ID. The result was very exciting to him. Abagnale never operated a plane, but he used his pilot uniform to fly for free and to date attractive, young flight attendants. Then he discovered a luxury apartment community[1] near Atlanta, Georgia. He paid cash for six months' rent in advance and wrote "medical doctor" on his apartment application. He soon became friends with a doctor in the apartment community. After convincing this man that he, too, was a medical doctor, he was offered a hospital job as a temporary supervisor. Abagnale performed this role by relying on nurses and medical students to do all the work while he simply pretended to be in charge. But finally, when faced with a life-or-death situation involving a newborn baby, Abagnale decided that he could no longer continue the **deception**. He knew that if he kept impersonating a doctor, an innocent child might die. Still, before leaving his hospital job, Abagnale made sure to get his paycheck.

3    Next, he dated another flight attendant, whom he **impressed** by claiming that he had graduated from law school. She introduced him to a real lawyer, who immediately offered him a position as a state attorney. Abagnale accepted the offer, but he needed to create a **fake** transcript from Harvard Law School. He also needed to pass the state law exam. He studied for several weeks but failed the eight-hour exam on his first and second attempts. When he tried a third time, he passed and became a licensed attorney despite the fact that he had never finished high school. He worked as a lawyer for nine months before he met a genuine Harvard graduate who started asking him specific questions about the school and its professors. Because Abagnale could not answer these

---

[1] **luxury apartment community:** area with very expensive and comfortable apartments

**22** UNIT 2

questions, the man became **suspicious** and started questioning Abagnale's **honesty**.

4    The young con man escaped from this uncomfortable situation by heading to the western United States. There he visited college campuses in Utah, where he was impressed with the beauty of female students. He decided to apply for a summer teaching position, which he obtained by making a fake transcript from Columbia University and writing false letters of recommendation. Abagnale was quite happy to work as a "professor." To prepare for class, he simply used the textbook, making sure to stay one chapter ahead of the students. Abagnale also discussed his own personal experiences in class, and the students responded with much interest. But when summer school ended, he could no longer stay in Utah. He knew that the FBI was searching for him because he had been cashing phony checks all over the country. He moved to California and eventually to France, thinking he could live quietly and safely there. However, he was wrong.

5    In France, Abagnale was recognized by a flight attendant and reported to the authorities. Soon, he was in a French prison, where he almost died because of very little food and very dirty surroundings. After six months, he was sent to a prison in Sweden. He learned that police in several European countries were waiting to arrest him for check fraud, and he feared that prison conditions in other places might be even worse than those in France. Eventually, Sweden sent him to the United States, where he spent four years in federal prison.

6    After his release, Abagnale had a problem shared by many other criminals: limited job opportunities. He worked hard in various entry-level positions and showed the ability to become a top manager, but could not get any high positions because of his prison background. He thought about returning to a life of crime, but decided instead to offer his services as a "white-collar crime specialist" teaching banks and other businesses how to avoid becoming the victims of fraud. Soon he was offered a position working with the FBI Financial Crimes Unit. Today, he runs his own company. It specializes in protecting checks and other documents against fraud.

7    His first book, *Catch Me If You Can*, was made into a Steven Spielberg film in 2002. In one interview, he was asked if he had ever thought about becoming an actor, considering his skill at impersonation. The answer was no. The real Frank Abagnale is satisfied with his real life as a company owner and family man.

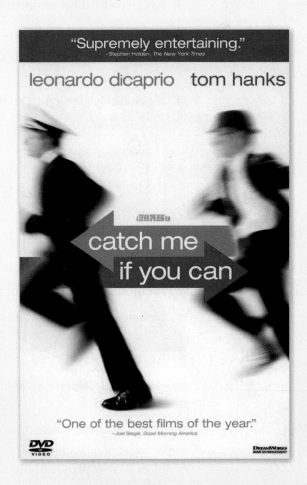

"Supremely entertaining."
–Stephen Holden, *The New York Times*

leonardo dicaprio    tom hanks

A STEVEN SPIELBERG FILM

catch me if you can

"One of the best films of the year."
–Joel Siegel, *Good Morning America*

DVD VIDEO

DREAMWORKS HOME ENTERTAINMENT

*Source:* Based on information in Frank W. Abagnale, *Catch Me If You Can: The Amazing True Story of the Youngest and Most Daring Con Man in the History of Fun and Profit* (Grosset & Dunlap, 1980).

# READ FOR MAIN IDEAS

*Put the events of Frank Abagnale's life in chronological order.*

**3** **a.** He finally succeeds in passing his law exam.

**5** **b.** He moves from France to Sweden.

**6** **c.** He starts his own company.

**1** **d.** He impersonates an airline pilot.

**2** **e.** He quits his hospital job.

**4** **f.** He decides to teach a college class.

# READ FOR DETAILS

*Choose the letter of the best ending on the right to complete each sentence on the left.*

Homework

1. Abagnale used his uniform to gain __j__ .
2. He got his hospital job with the help of __k__ .
3. He quit impersonating a doctor after dealing with __e__ .
4. He passed his law exam after __i__ .
5. He was hired as a college professor because of __c__ .
6. In the United States and Europe, he made money by cheating __a__ .
7. He was afraid of __g__ .
8. When he left prison, he was unable to get __b__ .
9. Today he is employed as __d__ .
10. He thought about continuing his career as __h__ .
11. Despite his talents, he is not interested in __f__ .

**a.** banks
**b.** high-level jobs
**c.** fake recommendations
**d.** a crime expert
**e.** a sick baby
**f.** acting
**g.** bad prison conditions
**h.** a criminal
**i.** several attempts
**j.** free travel
**k.** a neighbor

# MAKE INFERENCES

*Based on your understanding of the text, choose the best way to complete each of these statements.*

1. Frank Abagnale was most successful __a__ .
   **a.** cashing false checks
   **b.** deceiving people in the medical world

2. Frank Abagnale had an easier time impressing _____ .
   **a.** flight attendants
   **b.** lawyers

**3.** Frank Abagnale was most successful at getting a job as a __b__.

    **a.** lawyer

    **b.** professor

**4.** Prison conditions were better for Frank Abagnale in __b__.

    **a.** France

    **b.** the United States

**5.** Frank Abagnale's criminal experience helped him __a__.

    **a.** publish a book

    **b.** start a family

*Now discuss your answers with a partner.*

## ◖ EXPRESS OPINIONS

*Discuss the questions with the class.*

**1.** Which of Abagnale's impersonations do you think was the most dangerous? Why?

**2.** What do you think was more important to Abagnale—money or respect?

**3.** Do you think that Abagnale was punished fairly for his fraud? Explain your answer.

castigados

## B  READING TWO: The Michelle Brown Story: Identity Theft

**1** *Read the story of Michelle Brown, a real woman who experienced identity theft. This is a type of fraud in which a person's banking and other information is used by a criminal, usually to buy things. The story appears in* The Art of the Steal *by Frank Abagnale.*

### The Michelle Brown Story:
# Identity Theft

1    It began on a winter day with a seemingly ordinary message on an answering machine. It was from someone at the bank. Something about her new Dodge Ram pickup and the payment past due on the loan . . .

2    Michelle Brown was a single woman in her late twenties. She lived in southern California and worked as a credit analyst[1]. She was cheerful, and people found her fun to be around. Friends were always telling her how she was too nice. She worked hard and was tidy with her finances. She owned fifteen credit cards but had never been late on a single payment. Ever since she was seventeen, she had perfect credit. She liked everything in her life to be perfect.

*(continued on next page)*

---

[1] **credit analyst:** a bank employee who studies customers' bill-paying records

3     She returned the call. She told the bank officer that there had to be a mistake; she hadn't bought a truck. The officer quickly agreed that he must have the wrong Michelle Brown. The phone numbers on the credit application weren't working . . . To prove beyond a doubt that it was another Michelle Brown he was searching for, she told him her Social Security number. She was stunned—it was the same one that was on the application.

4     Alarmed, she called up the credit reporting agencies[2] and told them that something fishy was going on. They put a fraud alert on her credit and promised to send out a report on her recent purchases. She checked with the Division of Motor Vehicles and learned something astonishing: a duplicate driver's license had recently been issued to a Michelle Brown. Someone else was using her name, her address, her Social Security number, and her driver's license. It was as if someone was slowly erasing her identity . . .

5     When her credit report arrived, there were delinquent[3] bills on it for thousands of dollars, including a sizable phone bill and even a bill for liposuction treatments[4]. What was this? She became afraid to open her own mailbox, for fear of what new debt would be awaiting her. In time, she would learn that there was an arrest warrant[5] out for Michelle Brown in Texas. The charge was conspiracy[6] to sell marijuana. She had never broken a law, any law. How could she be wanted by the police?

6     She began to worry that the other Michelle Brown would break into her apartment in search of her passport or checks, or who knew what else. Whenever she got home after dark she carried a flashlight and searched through the rooms, including every closet. She was weary and angry. When she went to bed at night, she was scared. If she heard the slightest noise, her first thought was that the woman calling herself Michelle Brown was out there in the dark, right beneath her window. Who was this person who was stealing her identity? Why of all the people in the world, did she pick her? And what did she want?

---

[2] **credit reporting agencies:** organizations that keep track of bill-paying records
[3] **delinquent:** late in paying money that is owed
[4] **liposuction treatments:** a type of cosmetic surgery in which body fat is removed
[5] **arrest warrant:** a document giving police the authority to take someone to jail
[6] **conspiracy:** a secret plan by two or more people to do something illegal

*Source:* From *The Art of the Steal: How to Protect Yourself and Your Business from Fraud—America's #1 Crime* by Frank W. Abagnale, Jr., copyright © 2001 by Frank Abagnale. Used by permission of Broadway Books, a division of Random House, Inc.

**2**  *Read the statements and mark them **T** (true) or **F** (false).*

___F___  **1.** Michelle Brown was careless with her finances.

___F___  **2.** One form of identification was stolen from her.

___T___  **3.** The person who stole her identity made a variety of purchases.

___F___  **4.** She began selling drugs as a way of paying her bills.

___T___  **5.** Identity theft affected her emotionally as well as financially.

# C INTEGRATE READINGS ONE AND TWO

## STEP 1: Organize

*Reading One (R1) and Reading Two (R2) contain information about the financial, emotional, and psychological consequences of fraud. Look at the list of consequences below. Place them in the appropriate category by writing the letter of each consequence in the chart.*

| CONSEQUENCES OF FRAUD | IMPERSONATION (R1) | IDENTITY THEFT (R2) |
|---|---|---|
| Financial | a<br>d<br>j | g<br>h<br>k |
| Emotional and psychological | c<br>f<br>i | b<br>e<br>l |

*(handwritten: Frank above Impersonation column; Michael above Identity Theft column)*

a. Banks lost money as many fake checks were cashed.

b. Brown felt weary and angry.

c. Students in Utah believed that Abagnale was a real professor.

d. Legal clients paid for the services of a false lawyer.

e. Brown was unable to sleep at night.

f. Hospital staff respected Abagnale and followed his instructions.

g. Someone had bought a new truck with Brown's credit.

h. Brown faced delinquent bills and new debt.

i. A doctor and a flight attendant both trusted Abagnale and helped him get jobs.

j. A hospital lost money paying Abagnale's paycheck.

k. A fraud alert was put on Brown's credit.

l. Police believed that Brown was trying to sell marijuana.

◀ STEP 2: Synthesize

*Imagine that Frank Abagnale is interviewing Michelle Brown for his book,* The Art of the Steal. *Work with a partner to complete their conversation with information from the chart in Step 1.*

FRANK: There are so many emotional and psychological consequences of fraud.

For example, when I impersonated professionals, I know that I _____

_____

_____

How did you feel when your identity was stolen?

MICHELLE: I _____

_____

But I wasn't just affected emotionally. There were financial

consequences, too. For example, _____

_____

_____

FRANK: That's a very tough situation. In fact, fraud can often have financial

consequences on more than one individual. I know that when I

impersonated people, _____

_____

_____

# ③ FOCUS ON WRITING

## Ⓐ VOCABULARY

◀ REVIEW

*Read the online article about a man in Providence, Rhode Island, who was practicing medicine without a license. Complete the article with words from the box. Use each word only once.*

| | | | |
|---|---|---|---|
| astonishing | fake | honesty | motive |
| con man | fishy | impersonate | suspicious |
| deception | fraud | impressed | weary |

# PHONY[1] DOCTOR GETS 12 YEARS IN PRISON

John E. Curran will spend 12 years in prison because he pretended to be a doctor. In this case of medical _____fraud_____ **1.**, he lied to sick people and said that he could cure them with his "natural" medicine. To __impersonate__ **2.** a doctor, Curran bought ____fake____ **3.** medical degrees on the Internet for $2,650. It was even more __astonishing__ **4.** that he received a "medical degree" from the Asian American Institute in Costa Rica in only two months. This made him seem like a real doctor. He wore a lab coat with *MD*[2] after his name and checked people's blood. He told them they had cancer or other illnesses. Then he sold them "E-Water" and "Green Drink"—two products that would cure them, he said. He also charged people $10,000 for the use of medical machines that he kept in his office. Curran __impressed__ **5.** people with his false medical knowledge. They were __weary__ **6.** of feeling sick and believed his "natural" medicine could help them.

One woman, however, became __suspicious__ **7.** of Curran after paying $1200 a month for his "Green Drink." After three months, Curran refused to check her blood, and she thought this was __Fishy__ **8.**. She went to another doctor and learned that Curran's medicine was not real: it was all a __Deception__ **9.**. In court, Curran asked the judge not to give him a strong punishment. He claimed that he was acting with complete __honesty__ **10.** and that he really wanted to help people with his medicine. He asked the judge to be kind to him. But the judge responded that Curran's __motive__ **11.** was not helping people but wanting to make money. Because the judge believed that money was the reason for Curran's actions, he gave him 12 years in prison. "You are the worst of the worst," said the judge, believing Curran to be a liar, a __Con man__ **12.**.

---

[1] **phony:** fake or false
[2] **MD:** Medical Doctor

**1** Complete the chart with the correct word forms. Use a dictionary if necessary. An **X** indicates that there is no form in that category.

| NOUN | VERB | ADJECTIVE | ADVERB |
|------|------|-----------|--------|
| 1. deception | *deceive* | _____ | _____ |
| 2. _____ | duplicate | _____ | X |
| 3. _____ | _____ | fake | X |
| 4. fraud | X | _____ | _____ |
| 5. honesty | X | _____ | _____ |
| 6. impersonation | _____ | X | X |
| 7. motive | _____ | _____ | X |

**2** Rewrite the sentences by replacing the underlined word with the form in parentheses. Make any necessary grammatical changes.

1. I believe in the <u>honesty</u> of most doctors. (honest)

    I believe that most doctors are honest.

2. I had a bad experience with a man who practiced medicine <u>fraudulently</u>. (fraudulent)

    _____

3. His <u>motive</u> was making money. (motivate)

    _____

4. Not many people understood his <u>fakery</u>. (fake)

    _____

5. I wasn't the only person involved in his <u>deception</u>. (deceive)

    _____

6. He wasn't a real doctor, but he <u>impersonated</u> one well. (impersonation)

    _____

7. He had <u>duplicated</u> someone else's medical license. (duplicate)

    _____

◖ CREATE

*Imagine that you spent a lot of money on a fraudulent product or service. Write a letter to other customers, warning them about your bad experience. Use five new words.*

**1** *Read these sentences based on Frank Abagnale's story. Look at the boldfaced verbs. What is the difference between the verb forms? Notice the words in italics. How are the meanings of* **when** *and* **while** *different?*

- Frank Abagnale **was hiding** in France *when* a flight attendant **reported** him to the authorities.
- *When* he **met** the doctor who helped him, they **were** both **renting** apartments in the same community.
- *While* the FBI **was searching** for him, he **was enjoying** himself in California.

| SIMPLE PAST AND PAST PROGRESSIVE | |
|---|---|
| I. Use the **simple past** tense to talk about actions, states, and situations in the past that take place at one point in time. The simple past tense of regular verbs is formed by adding **-d** or **-ed** to the base form of the verb. | He finally **passed** the law exam. |
| 2. Use the **past progressive**, also called **past continuous,** to describe a continuous nonstop action that was in progress at a specific time in the past. Examples of specific time expressions include: *yesterday, last night, at that time.* The past progressive is formed like this: **be (past) + verb + -ing**. | *At that time,* he **was working** at a law firm. |
| 3. Use the **past progressive** with the **simple past** tense to talk about an action that was interrupted by another action. Use the simple past tense for the interrupting action. Use **when** to introduce the simple past tense action. | He **was living** in France *when* a flight attendant **saw** him. |
| 4. If you put the **when** clause first, you must put a **comma** at the end of the clause. | *When* the flight attendant **saw** him, he **was living** in France. |
| 5. Use the **past progressive** with *while* to describe two actions in progress at the same time in the past. The **simple past** can also be used in the *while* clause without changing the meaning. | He **was enjoying** himself in California *while* the FBI **was searching** for him. <br><br> He **was enjoying** himself in California *while* the FBI **searched** for him. |

**2** *Complete the sentences with the correct form of the words in parentheses. Use the* ***simple past*** *or* ***past progressive***. *Add a comma when necessary.*

1.  I was living in a new town when _I learned about a case of check fraud._
    (I / learn about a case of check fraud)

2.  First, two men knocked on all the doors in my neighborhood while _____

    _____
    (my neighbors / relax at home on Sunday)

3.  The men offered to do gardening work when _____

    _____
    (my neighbors / answer their door)

4.  Next, the men asked my neighbors to write checks for $50 to their company,

    CAS. The men added an "H" to the checks when _____

    _____
    (they / take the checks to the bank)

**Note:** In the United States, it is legal to get cash in exchange for checks that have *cash* written on them instead of a person's name.

**5.** The men added another zero to $50 while _____

(they / add the "H")

**6.** The two men were stealing a lot of money when _____

_____

(a bank clerk / finally become suspicious of what they / do)

**7.** When the clerk called the police _____

_____

(the police / arrest the two men)

**8.** I learned about this fraud while _____

(I / watch the news on TV)

**3** *Think about the last time you became suspicious of something a person was doing. What were you doing? What was the other person doing? On a separate piece of paper, write two sentences with **while** and two sentences with **when**. Use simple past and past progressive. Use commas when necessary.*

## C WRITING

In this unit, you read about different kinds of fraud: impersonation, check fraud, and identity theft.

Now you are going to **write a paragraph describing an experience with fraud, yours or that of someone you know.** Use the vocabulary and grammar from the unit.*

### ◀ PREPARE TO WRITE: Answering Questions

*Think about an experience that you or a friend had with fraud. Answer the questions.*

**1.** What happened in this experience?

_____

**2.** Why was this experience a fraud?

_____

**3.** What were the consequences?

_____

**4.** How did you or the other person feel after this experience? Why?

_____

---

*For Alternative Writing Topics, see page 37. These topics can be used in place of the writing topic for this unit or as homework. The alternative topics relate to the theme of the unit, but may not target the same grammar or rhetorical structures taught in the unit.

# WRITE: A Story

When you **describe an experience,** you are **telling a story** about **something that happened** to you or someone else.

**1**  *Read the paragraph and answer the questions.*

> When my friend went to a car repair service, it was the worst experience of his life. He went there for a simple oil change. He was getting ready to go on a 200-mile trip to Boston, and he wanted to be sure his car was in good shape. The mechanic checked his engine and said the car needed much more than an oil change. He told him that it needed $1,000 worth of other repairs. My friend decided to let him do all the repairs because he was concerned about his trip. The mechanic charged him a total of $1200 when he was finished with everything. A few hours later, my friend's car suddenly broke down while he was driving to Boston. He went to another car repair service, and they told him that his engine was now broken because of the other mechanic. He had to pay $1500 for more repair. Now he had no more money left for his trip to Boston. He was very angry, so he decided to return to the first mechanic and ask for his money back. When he arrived at the car shop, it was closed. The mechanic had moved to another town, and my friend never saw him again.

1. What is the topic sentence of this paragraph?

2. How does the writer support the topic sentence?

---

When **describing an experience,** it is important to begin with a clear topic sentence that tells **what kind of experience** it was. The following sentences tell **what happened**. They include details that support the idea of the topic sentence. The concluding sentence tells **what happened at the end**. Look at the following examples:

- **Topic Sentence:** When my friend went to a car repair service, it was the worst experience of his life.
- **What happened first:** He wanted to get ready for a trip and paid $1200 for car repair.
- **What happened next:** His car broke down and he had to pay another $1500 for more repair.
- **What happened next:** He stopped his trip and decided to get some of his money back.
- **Concluding Sentence:** The mechanic had moved to another town, and my friend never saw him again.

**2** *Discuss the questions.*

1. What kind of experience was this? What idea is expressed in the topic sentence?

2. How do the following sentences support this idea? Do they include positive or negative details?

3. What happened at the end? How is the concluding sentence related to the topic sentence?

**3** *Look at your answers from Prepare to Write, page 33. In one sentence, explain what kind of experience you had. This will be the topic sentence of your paragraph.*

Example

My brother had a very embarrassing experience with a con man.

**4** *Write the first draft of your paragraph. Tell what happened, and include only details that support your topic sentence. Write a concluding sentence that tells what happened at the end. Don't worry too much about grammar while you write—just concentrate on describing the experience clearly.*

◀ **REVISE: Using a Topic Sentence to Focus Ideas**

A paragraph telling a story needs to have one main idea. This main idea is expressed in the topic sentence. **A good topic sentence is clear.** It helps the reader to **focus on the main idea.**

**1** *Read the paragraphs. Underline the topic sentences.*

1.

> My sister wasted a lot of money on a fraudulent weight loss product. She saw an ad on TV for a special kind of tea. The ad promised that people who drink the tea lose weight very quickly. When she ordered the tea, she learned that she had to buy a six-month supply of the tea. This cost her $200. Unfortunately, the tea tasted terrible and it made her sick. She wasted $200 on a product that didn't work at all.

2.

> I had a bad experience with a dentist who promised to make my teeth look white. First, he charged me $800 for the tooth-whitening service. After I paid for the service, he told me that I couldn't drink coffee any more. I stopped drinking coffee for two days, and then I wanted to start drinking it again. As soon as I drank coffee, my teeth lost their new, white look. This was a very bad experience for me, and I'm still angry about it.

**2** Choose the best topic sentence for these paragraphs. Circle the letter of your choice. Compare your answers with a partner's.

1. _____. She was looking for a job, and she found a website for people who work at home. The website said she could make $8000 a month running a home business. She sent an e-mail to the man in charge of the website. He told her to send him a check for $100 for special training software. She sent him the check but never heard from him again. When she looked for the website again, it was gone.

   **a.** My friend wanted to make $8000 a month.
   **b.** My friend was cheated by an Internet con man.
   **c.** My friend was angry because she was cheated.

2. _____. It started when I left a magazine at the gym. It had my name and address on it. Somebody found the magazine and used my name and address to open a credit card. Soon, I started receiving bills for new clothes, furniture, and a trip to Hawaii. My bank didn't help me. My credit was ruined. I couldn't sleep or eat, and I started having problems at work because of the stress.

   **a.** I had a terrible experience because of a magazine.
   **b.** I experienced identity theft at the gym.
   **c.** My experience with identity theft almost destroyed my life.

3. _____. She had terrible back pain, and he told her that she needed to change her bed. He offered her a special deal on a new bed, and she bought it. When her back pain continued, he told her that she didn't need the bed at all. She needed to buy some vitamins from him. He told her to take two vitamins a day during the week and three vitamins a day on weekends. She didn't understand his advice at all.

   **a.** My sister was confused by the advice of a fraudulent doctor.
   **b.** My sister was angry because of the advice of a fraudulent doctor.
   **c.** My sister still had back pain after seeing a fraudulent doctor.

**3** The topic sentences in these paragraphs are not clear. They do not help the reader to focus on the main idea. Read the paragraphs. Then rewrite the topic sentences so that they are clear and focused.

1. Once, I bought some new face cream. I wanted to look younger, and I thought the face cream would help me. But I couldn't find it anywhere. I tried four different stores in my city. Finally, I drove to another city. I got stuck in traffic for almost two hours. When I finally arrived at the store, it was closed. I went back the next week and bought the face cream. But it didn't work at all!

   **New topic sentence:** _____

2. We are all human, and we all make mistakes. Last year, I used a credit card to buy some language learning CDs. The salesman promised that I could learn three different languages while I slept. Unfortunately, I learned nothing. I tried to return the CDs, but I couldn't get my money back. It took me several months to pay for them, and I really regret buying the CDs.

   **New topic sentence:** _____

3. My uncle bought a fraudulent hair product. He has been bald for a long time. Last year, he saw an ad for a new hair product on TV. My uncle bought the product and used it right away. Then he went to a party and noticed that people were laughing at him. He looked in a mirror and saw that his bald head was turning blue. He tried washing off the color, but nothing worked.

**New topic sentence:** _____

**4** *Look back at the first draft of your paragraph. Is the topic sentence clear and focused? Does the rest of the information in your paragraph support the topic sentence?*

◀ **EDIT: Writing the Final Draft**

*Write the final draft of your paragraph. Carefully edit it for grammatical and mechanical errors, such as spelling, capitalization, and punctuation. Make sure you used some of the vocabulary and grammar from the unit. Use the checklist to help you write your final draft. Then neatly write or type your paragraph.*

---

### ✓ FINAL DRAFT CHECKLIST

○ Is the topic sentence clear and focused?
○ Are all the supporting details related to the topic sentence?
○ Does the paragraph clearly describe what happened in the experience?
○ Does the concluding sentence explain what happened at the end?
○ Are the simple past and past progressive verbs used correctly?
○ Does the paragraph use vocabulary from the unit?
○ Is it formatted correctly?

---

## ALTERNATIVE WRITING TOPICS

*Write about one of the topics. Use the vocabulary and grammar from the unit.*

1. Write a paragraph describing the main characteristics of a con man or woman. What are some things that most con men or women have in common?

2. How can you protect yourself against identity theft or Internet fraud? What can you do? What can banks and other organizations do? Write a paragraph or two explaining your ideas.

3. In this unit you read about different types of fraud. Now write a paragraph or two giving some new examples of how technology has increased the dangers of fraud in our world today.

---

**RESEARCH TOPICS,** see page 211.

when DO ador last pump house last time?

# Going to Extremes: Sports and Obsession

*skate*

*↓ snowboarding*

*mountain*

*snowboard*

*→ track*

## ① FOCUS ON THE TOPIC

### Ⓐ PREDICT

*Look at the photographs and discuss the questions with the class.*

1. Can you name the sports these people are doing? How do you think they feel about their sports?

2. What kind of person participates in these sports?

3. How are *extreme sports* different from *non-extreme sports*?

**SHARE INFORMATION**

*Mark the statements **A** (agree) or **D** (disagree), according to whether you agree or disagree.*

_D_  1. Watching sports on TV is a great way to relax.

_A_  2. It's more fun to watch professional sports in person.

_A_  3. Children are positively influenced by famous athletes.

_D_  4. For some athletes, their desire to be the best is bad.

_A_  5. I would like to be good enough at my favorite sport to go to the Olympics.

_D_  6. I would be willing to work out eight hours a day to be one of the best athletes in the world.

_A_  7. I was inspired by an athlete to work harder in my life.

*Now discuss your answers with a classmate.*

C **BACKGROUND AND VOCABULARY**

An **obsession** is a very strong desire to do or be something. For example, many famous athletes have obsessions. They might practice for very long hours, which could have a positive result when they win an Olympic gold medal. Their obsessions could also mean that they do something dangerous.

*Do you think skateboarders ever do anything dangerous?  Look at these skateboarders.  Discuss your answer with a classmate.*

*Read the information about skateboarding. Then circle the definition that best matches the meaning of each boldfaced word or phrase.*

**Some Skateboarding Facts and History**

1. 1950s—The first skateboard was made by surfers. They used it like a surfboard on the sidewalk. Skateboarding had the same **style** as surfing.
   **a.** the way something is done
   **b.** the way something is made

2. 1970s—Skateboarders started skating in empty swimming pools so they could go up and go faster because they wanted a more **intense** experience.
   - (a.) successful
   - b. stronger

3. 1980s—Skateboard companies **focused** on selling more skateboards and street skateboarding became popular again.
   - (a.) to give all your attention to something
   - b. to try to avoid something

4. 1990s—Skateboarders started jumping and riding on stairs, rails, and poles. Tony Hawk **got hooked on** skateboarding.
   - (a.) to get hurt while playing
   - (b.) to become unable to stop doing something

5. For him, it was an **escape** from pain.
   - (a.) a way to forget about problems
   - b. an exciting adventure

6. Tony Hawk became the only skateboarder to ever **achieve** a 900 in a competition. (A 900 is 2½ turns in the air.)
   - (a.) to make an effort
   - b. to succeed in doing something

7. He says, "I'm never happy if I can't **perfect** something."
   - a. to make something as good as it can be
   - b. to be able to do something

8. Barbara Odanaka has founded The International Society of Skateboarding Moms. She says that, when she was a kid, skateboarding helped her learn how to focus her **energy** and work toward a goal.
   - (a.) the physical and mental strength that makes you able to be active
   - b. the mental strength that makes you very smart

9. In 1977, she **made it** as a sponsored skateboarder.
   - (a.) to be successful in a particular activity
   - b. to create something

10. There is a **controversy** about skateboarding because of its danger.
    - a. a public law
    - (b.) a strong disagreement

11. There are more than 12.5 million skateboarders in the world today. They think their sport is totally **awesome.**
    - (a.) interesting
    - (b.) terrific

12. For kids, one **benefit** of getting involved in a sport like this is that they have something positive to do, so they don't get into trouble.
    - a. an advantage
    - (b.) a reason

## A  READING ONE: An Interview with Tony Hawk

*You are going to read an interview with Tony Hawk, a professional skateboarder. Before you read, write down three questions that you think the interviewer will ask Mr. Hawk about his sport and his life.*

1. _why, Do you want to very much it spo_   like very much this sports?
2. _Did you when did you think jump for_
3. _last time?_

# Interview with Tony Hawk from *Wheels on Fire* Magazine

**Tony Hawk,
1999 Summer X Games, San Francisco**

*Wheels on Fire* (**WOF**): Let's start with the high point of your career. Can you pick one out to share with us?

**Tony Hawk (TH):** Oh yes, definitely. For me, the high point came when I was traveling to France and I had to fill out a tourist information card. You know, the thing you fill out when you're entering a new country? Well, I got to write down "skateboarder" as my occupation. How cool!

**WOF:** You mean that was better than what you **achieved** at the 1999 Summer X Games?

**TH:** You mean landing the 900? That was **awesome**, too. But that was pure obsession—story of my life. Nothing new for me there.

**WOF:** How was landing that trick an obsession for you?

**TH:** Well, like everything I do on a skateboard, I have to get it right. It took me 13 years of practice to **perfect** the 900, and on that day, I think it took me something like 12 times before I **made it**.

**WOF:** Did you really work on one trick for 13 years? That does seem like an obsession!

**TH:** Yeah, but you know, it's a good obsession—if you can say that obsession is good. It's like this—I was this weird, skinny kid at school. Once I got into skateboarding and started wearing baggy skater clothes, it got worse. I was a freak. All the jocks[1] picked on me. And I didn't have a chance with the girls—forget it. But skating—that was my **escape**. Every day after school I escaped to the skate park, and the focus on skating—this really **intense** focus that took all my concentration—I guess that was one way I could block out all the pain of growing up.

[1] **jocks:** slang term meaning "athletes"

**WOF:** Did your parents support your obsession with skating?

**TH:** Yeah, they were great. Mom took me and some friends down to the Oasis Skate Park when we were about 10 years old. They had this flat beginners' area where you could practice before you were ready to skate in the empty swimming pools. I was so skinny that the skate equipment didn't even fit me right. But once I **got hooked**, nothing else mattered. I drew pictures of skating all day, and I even skated in the house.

**WOF:** Your parents let you skate in the house?

**TH:** Yeah. They were pretty cool. Mom and Dad were older when they had me, so I guess you can say they were relaxed enough to let me do what I needed to do.

**WOF:** How about your schoolwork? Were you able to get by in school?

**TH:** Yeah, that was fine. I don't mean to brag or anything, but I was a gifted student. So I was able to get my schoolwork done with decent grades. My only problem was being able to sit still in class. I had so much physical **energy**. But school was basically OK for me until some of the teachers started taking my skateboard away. They started lecturing me about the dangers of the sport.

**WOF:** That couldn't stop you from skating!

**TH:** No way. The cool thing was that my parents worked it out for me to go to a different high school. The principal there was awesome. He let us design our own PE [physical education] classes, so take a wild guess. What class did I create?

**WOF:** Skateboarding.

**TH:** You got it. That was my PE class. By that time, I was turning professional and starting to win prize money at competitions. During summer vacation, I was able to travel around to cool places like Australia, Europe, and Canada. I was able to show off some techniques.

**WOF:** Is that when your new **style** became famous?

**TH:** Yeah. You know, a lot of other skaters had this smooth, flowing style. Compared to them, I was kind of like a robot. And I was always coming up with new tricks, new surprises.

**WOF:** When did they first call you the Michael Jordan of skateboarding?

**TH:** I guess that was back in '95 at the Extreme Games. You remember—that event they had on the sports channel? That was a combination of skateboarding, BMX cycling, and rollerblading. There were a lot of good skaters there. I was just the one who got the attention. That's how TV is—I guess they can only **focus** on one thing at a time. But there were a lot of outstanding people there, believe me.

**WOF:** Let's go back to the high point. Now that you've looked back on your career a bit, was it still being able to write "skateboarder" as your occupation?

**TH:** Yeah. I love that. You know, there's so much **controversy** about skateboarding—some people think it's a crime and they don't want us to skate in public places, but I just love being able to say it's my occupation. My occupation and my obsession!

**WOF:** As an occupation, it has rewarded you pretty well, wouldn't you say?

**TH:** Yeah, there were some great **benefits** along the way—like being able to buy my own home when I was still in high school. And later, being able to buy another home out in the desert—and build my own skate park. But now that I think about it, you know what I'm really proud of achieving?

**WOF:** Making skateboard history when you landed the 900?

**TH:** Nope. It was having Disney animators use some of my tricks in the Tarzan movie. When my son watched Tarzan swinging through the trees, he realized that it had something to do with me. And he thought I was awesome! Now that's the greatest feeling you can get, believe me.

---

*Source:* Based on information in *Hawk Occupation: Skateboarder* by Tony Hawk with Sean Mortimer (Regan Books, 2001).

# ◖ READ FOR MAIN IDEAS

*Write **T** (true) or **F** (false) for each statement.*

_F___ **1.** Tony Hawk is ashamed of his occupation.

_F___ **2.** He wants all his skateboard tricks to be perfect.

_F___ **3.** His classmates liked him because of his skateboarding ability.

_F___ **4.** His parents thought that skateboarding was a waste of time.

_F___ **5.** He had a smooth and flowing style.

_T___ **6.** He earned a lot of money before the age of 25.

# ◖ READ FOR DETAILS

*Write one-sentence answers to the questions. Then compare answers with a partner.*

**1.** What did Tony Hawk achieve at the 1999 Summer X Games?

_900    when he was 900_

**2.** How much time did he spend practicing his most famous trick?

_13 years_

**3.** When did he begin skateboarding?

_10 years_

**4.** Where did he learn to ride a skateboard?

_He was training in Europe Skate park_

**5.** What kind of problems did he have in school?

_w Everybody saw like a freak._

**6.** Who saw Tony's tricks in a Tarzan movie?

_his son saw him_

# ◖ MAKE INFERENCES

*Decide which of the statements can be inferred from Reading One. Check (✓) the correct answers. Refer to the reading to find support for your answers. Compare your answers with a partner.*

_✓___ **1.** Baggy skater clothes weren't popular at Tony's first school.

_✗___ **2.** Tony didn't try difficult tricks at first.

_✗___ **3.** Tony's parents married late in life.

_✓___ **4.** The principal at Tony's first school didn't support his skateboarding.

_✓___ **5.** Tony got excellent grades at his second school.

_✓___ **6.** At Tony's second school, he was popular with the other students.

_____ 7. Tony probably hadn't traveled abroad much before he changed schools.

_____ 8. Tony had appeared in competition on TV before he landed the 900.

_____ 9. Tony seems embarrassed by his fame.

_____ 10. Tony has appeared in movies.

◖ **EXPRESS OPINIONS**

*Discuss the questions with a partner.*

1. Tony used his obsession with skateboarding to block out the pain of growing up. What kind of pain do you think Tony had? Was his pain unique, or is this type of pain typical for teenagers?

2. Is having an obsession a good or bad thing?

**B** **READING TWO: High School Star Hospitalized for Eating Disorder**

**1** *Read the newspaper article about a high school gymnast.*

# High School Star Hospitalized for Eating Disorder

1    Sierra High School gymnast Ashley Lindermann was hospitalized Tuesday for complications related to anorexia nervosa. Her coach, Dianne Coyle, says that she will not be returning to the gymnastics team this season.

2    "It's really a loss—not only to the team but also to Ashley personally," says Coyle. "She had hopes of qualifying for the Olympics. But her health comes first, of course. Once she is better, I'm sure she can get back into the sport and go for the gold."

3    Dr. Paula Kim, director of the Eating Disorders Clinic at Baldwin Hospital, explains that it is not unusual for athletes, especially gymnasts, to become obsessed with their weight. One reason for this is that in gymnastics, the lighter the body, the more skillfully it can perform. She explains that an obsession with weight can lead to extreme dieting, which affects not only the body but also the mind.

4    "For the anorexic, the mental focus becomes very small: food and weight. In a way, it's easy to see how this helps the anorexic manage the fear of living in the big, uncontrollable world out there. You may not be able to control how other people feel about you, but you can control what you put in your mouth. You can also control how many hours you spend at the gym. Soon you get hooked on controlling your weight."

5    High school counselor Lisa Rodriguez has expressed concern that Lindermann's illness is related to pressure.

6    "There's an enormous amount of pressure that goes along with training for the Olympics," she says. "I know that she comes from an athletic family—I think that's why she felt she had to achieve so much in sports. Also, when you talk about the Olympics, you're talking about being the best of the best. I think that added to Ashley's feeling of pressure."

7    Since joining the Sierra High gymnastics team as a sophomore two years ago, Ashley has broken all school records and led the team to three regional championships.

*(continued on next page)*

8    Coach Coyle says, "As soon as I met Ashley, I could tell right away that she was obsessed with the sport. And that's not the kind of athlete that you have to push. My goal with Ashley was to try and help her have more of a balanced life. I talked to her about how she was doing in her classes, what she might want to study in college. I also told her and all the members on the team to take at least one or two days a week just to let their bodies rest. I know there's some controversy about her situation, but all I can say is that I'm very, very sorry that Ashley got sick."

9    Coyle's concern for Lindermann's health is shared by her teammates and friends. Some of them recall how the tiny gymnastics star worked out at the health club in addition to hours of regular practice with the team. They describe how the walls of her bedroom are covered with photos of Olympic winners—

Mary Lou Retton and Nadia Comaneci to name a few.

10    Lindermann, who currently weighs only 72 pounds (32.6 kgs.), is expected to remain in the hospital for at least a few months.

**2**  *Circle the best answer to complete the statements.*

1. Ashley's coach hopes that she will leave the hospital and ___a___ .
   **a.** focus on her health
   **b.** join the Olympic team

2. Anorexia nervosa is an obsession with ___b___ .
   **a.** exercise
   **b.** weight

3. One reason for becoming anorexic is that it gives you a feeling of ___a___ .
   **a.** more control
   **b.** mental focus

4. Some of the pressure in Ashley's life was because she wanted to be the best gymnast in _____ .
   **a.** her country
   **b.** the world

5. Before she went to the hospital, her coach had been pushing her to focus on gymnastics _____ .
   **a.** less
   **b.** more

### STEP 1: Organize

*Below is a list of characteristics and a Venn Diagram. Put characteristics that describe Tony Hawk in the left circle, characteristics that describe Ashley Lindermann in the right circle, and those that describe both athletes in the middle part where the two circles overlap.*

**Characteristics**

Competitive

Dedicated

Desire to be the best

Need to feel in control

Life of pressure

World seems scary

Family is supportive  *Tony*

Family adds pressure

Obsession leads to success

Obsession leads to anorexia  *Ashey*

Obsession helps to escape pain  *Tony*

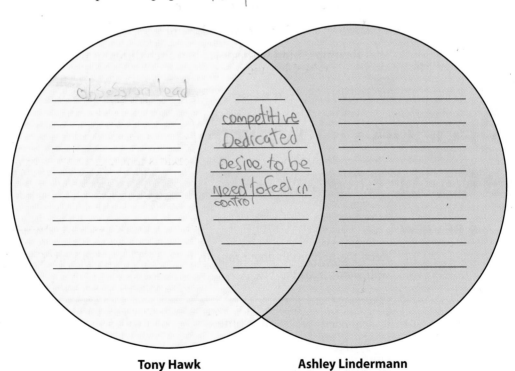

**Tony Hawk**          **Ashley Lindermann**

*Handwritten in left circle:* obsession lead

*Handwritten in overlap:* competitive / Dedicated / Desire to be / Need to feel in control

*How are Tony Hawk and Ashley Lindermann similar and different? Use your Venn diagram from Step 1. Work with a classmate to complete the comparison / contrast paragraph below.*

Tony Hawk and Ashley Lindermann were athletes who had both similarities and differences. They were both _in the sport, the both need to feel in control and they have a lot of dedicated to their Activity._

_____ However, there were some differences, too. Tony Hawk's obsession _helps to escape pain in the skateboarder, in change Ashey's obsession_

_____ It is interesting that their obsession with sports had such different results for both of them.

# ③ FOCUS ON WRITING

## Ⓐ VOCABULARY

◀ **REVIEW**

*Read the paragraph about famous ballerina Gelsey Kirkland. Complete the paragraph with words from the box.*

| | | | | |
|---|---|---|---|---|
| achieved | awesome | control | focus | intense |
| athlete | benefit | escape | hooked on | obsessed |

# DANGEROUS OBSESSION

Gelsey Kirkland was a professional ballerina with the New York City Ballet and the American Ballet Theater in the 1970s. She _Archived_ ¹. legendary fame in her dancing partnership with Mikhail Baryshnikov. She was an absolutely outstanding _athlete_ ². and performer. However, she became totally _obsessed_ ³. with having a thin body. As a result of her obsession, she ate a very small amount of food. For example, she sometimes ate only one apple a day while following a very

_intense_ ⁴. dance practice schedule. Perhaps this was a way for her to feel more _controll_ ⁵. in her life. She could _focus_ ⁶. on just eating and weight. Her feelings toward Mikhail Baryshnikov, who was considered one of the most " _awesome_ ⁷. " male dancers in the world, also became obsessive. Sadly, her love for Baryshnikov caused her much personal pain, and to _scape_ ⁸. from her unhappiness, she began using drugs and got _hooked on_ ⁹. them. Finally, she wrote a book about her life and career entitled *Dancing on My Grave*. Perhaps readers of this book will _benefit_ ¹⁰. from learning about the experience of this talented, yet unhappy, dancer.

Complete the chart with the correct word forms. Use a dictionary if necessary. An **X** indicates there is no form in that category.

| NOUN | VERB | ADJECTIVE | ADVERB |
|---|---|---|---|
| 1. achievement | achieve | achieved | X |
| 2. athleter | X | athletic | athletically |
| 3. benefit | Benefit | beneficial | beneficially |
| 4. concentration | concentrate | concentrared | X |
| 5. controversy | X | controversial | X |
| 6. energy | energize | energetic | energetically |
| 7. focus | focus | focused | X |
| 8. intensity | intensify | intense | intensely |
| 9. mentality | X | mental | Mentally |
| 10. obsession | obsess | obssive obsessed | obsessively |
| 11. Perfection | perfect | Perfect | perfectly |
| 12. Performance | perform | performed | X |
| 13. physicality | X | physical | phisically |
| 14. pressure | Pressure | press | X |
| 15. calification | Quali | qualifying | X |

achieve

HomeWORK

◀ CREATE

Write a paragraph describing one of your achievements, hobbies, or relationships. Use at least five of the words from the box in your paragraph. You may change the form of the word.

| | | | | | |
|---|---|---|---|---|---|
| achieve | beneficial | escape | hooked on | perfected | pressure |
| awesome | concentration | focus | obsessed | physical | |

## B GRAMMAR: Ability: *Can, Could, Be able to*

**1** *Look at the following examples from Reading One. Think about the meaning of the boldfaced words.*

- I guess that was one way I **could** block out all the pain of growing up.
- They had this flat beginners' area where you **could** practice before you were ready to skate in the empty swimming pools.
- Mom and Dad were older when they had me, so I guess you **can** say they were relaxed enough to let me do what I needed to do.
- **Were** you **able to** get by in school?

| ABILITY: *CAN, COULD, BE ABLE TO* ||
|---|---|
| I. **Can** describes ability in the present. | He **can** do skateboard tricks. |
| 2. **Be able to** describes ability in the present. | She **is able to** swim fast. *(present)* <br><br> He**'s not able to** ride a horse. *(negative present)* |
| 3. **Could** or **was / were able to** describes general ability in the past. | When he was a boy, he **could** ride his bike all day. <br><br> Last winter, they **were able to** ski four times. <br><br> He **wasn't able to** join the Olympic team. *(negative past)* |
| 4. Use **be able to** to describe ability in forms other than present tense (**can**) or past tense (**could**). | They **will be able to** win the race. *(future)* <br><br> They **have been able to** win two championships. *(present perfect)* |

**2** *A young skateboarder wrote a letter to Tony Hawk. Complete the sentences with* **can,** **can't, could, couldn't,** *or* **be able to** *to express ability.*

Dear Mr. Hawk,

My name is Michael Craig, and I live in Florida. I am nine years old, and I

guess you _____can_____ say that I'm obsessed with skateboarding. My

1.

dream is to _____able to_____ ride a skateboard like you do. I really

2.

_____could_____ believe your tricks! Last week I started practicing the 900,

3.

but I _____couldn't_____ make it. My mom came outside and started yelling

4.

at me. She thought I _____could_____ kill myself doing that trick, but I told

5.

her not to worry.

I'm a pretty decent skateboarder for my age. How old were you when you

_____w-b_____ finally land a 900? I want to _____be able to_____ do that

6.                                                              7.

by my tenth birthday. I'm going to practice a lot.

Mr. Hawk, I know that you're a busy professional skateboarder, but I really

hope that you will _____ write me back very soon.

8.

_____ you please find time for a skateboarding star of the

9.

future?

Thanks for reading my letter. Keep up the intense skateboarding. You're

the best!

Yours truly,

Michael Craig

**3** On a separate piece of paper, write down five statements about yourself, each using a different verb expressing ability from the list below. Write some statements that are true and some statements that are false. Exchange papers with a classmate. Guess which statements are true and which are false.

| be able to | not be able to | can | can't | could | couldn't |

In this unit, you read about Tony Hawk and other athletes who go to extremes.

Now imagine that you are a newspaper reporter. You are going to **write a factual paragraph about how Tony Hawk landed the 900.** Use the vocabulary and grammar from the unit.*

**◀ PREPARE TO WRITE: Group Brainstorming**

**1** Work in a small group. On a piece of paper, brainstorm questions you would want to ask Tony Hawk about how he landed the 900. Think of as many questions as you can and write them down. Do not worry about spelling and grammar.

**2** Share your list with the class. The teacher will write the questions on the board.

**◀ WRITE: A Factual Report**

Look back at the newspaper article in Reading Two. How is it different from the style of Reading One? What do you think is the purpose of the newspaper article?

A news article is an example of a **factual report**. Good newspaper articles **answer five basic questions**—called the 5Ws. Important information includes:

- **Who** is the story about?
- **What** is the story about?
- **When** did the story take place?
- **Where** did the story take place?
- **Why** or **How** did the story happen?

In a factual report, **quotations** (people's exact words) may also be used to give more facts or opinions.

---

*For Alternative Writing Topics, see page 57. These topics can be used in place of the writing topic for this unit or as homework. The alternative topics relate to the theme of the unit, but may not target the same grammar or rhetorical structures taught in the unit.

**1** *Refer to "An Interview with Tony Hawk" on pages 42–43 to complete the following tasks.*

A. Look at Reading One. Think like a newspaper reporter. Write five questions you would want to ask Tony Hawk about the 900, using the 5Ws.

1. _____

2. _____

3. _____

4. _____

5. _____

B. Look at the facts below about the 900. Match them with the correct categories. Write the correct letter in the blank before each fact.

**Categories**

a. Who landed the 900?

b. What is a 900?

c. When did Tony Hawk land the 900?

d. Where did he do it?

e. How did he perfect the 900?

**Facts**

___a___ 1. Tony Hawk was the first skateboarder to ever land the 900.

_____ 2. To understand what a 900 is in skateboarding, you first have to understand where the number comes from.

_____ 3. It means how many turns you do in the air.

_____ 4. If you are skating in a half-pipe (like an empty swimming pool), and you ride up the side of the pool into the air, then do a half-turn and come down, that is a 180, or a half turn.

_____ 5. A 900 is 2½ turns in the air.

_____ 6. In the 1980s, Tony could easily do a 540, or 1½ turns in the air.

_____ 7. The first time he tried to do a 900 was in 1986.

_____ 8. Ten years later, in 1996, he tried to do the 900 again at a skate show, but he crashed into the top rim of the half-pipe, hitting it with his shins.

_____ 9. Because he got injured every time he tried the 900, he could only try to do it once a month.

_____ 10. As he analyzed the turn, he realized that he needed to shift his weight from his front leg to his back leg after the first turn.

_____ 11. During the 1999 Summer X Games in San Francisco, he felt really good. He tried the 900 one more time and landed it.

**2** *Plan the first draft of your paragraph by completing the outline below. Use the 5Ws information to explain how Tony Hawk landed the 900.*

1. Write a topic sentence that tells the topic of your paragraph.

   _____

2. Give at least five to seven supporting details.

   _____

   _____

   _____

   _____

   _____

   _____

3. Write a concluding statement which restates the controlling idea in the topic sentence.

   _____

**3** *Use your outline and your notes from Prepare to Write, page 53, and Step 1, page 47, to write the first draft of your paragraph.*

◀ **REVISE: Considering Your Audience**

> When you write, think about your **audience**, the people who will read what you write. Remember that they may know less about the topic than you do. Make sure you **clearly explain new words or expressions.**
>
> - **Sentence:** Sierra High School gymnast Ashley Lindermann was hospitalized Tuesday for complications related to anorexia nervosa.
> - **Problem:** Some people may not know what anorexia nervosa is.
> - **Revised sentence:** Sierra High School gymnast Ashley Lindermann was hospitalized Tuesday for complications related to anorexia nervosa, *an illness in which the person is obsessed with dieting.*

There are several **ways to add more information to a sentence:**

1. Add more information **in the middle** of the sentence.

   Example

   - Dr. Paula Kim explains that it is not unusual for athletes to become obsessed with their weight.
   - Dr. Paula Kim, *director of the Eating Disorders Clinic at Baldwin Hospital,* explains that it is not unusual for athletes to become obsessed with their weight.

**2.** Add more information after a comma **at the end** of the sentence.

Example

- She explains that an obsession with weight can lead to extreme dieting.

- She explains that an obsession with weight can lead to extreme dieting, *which affects not only the body but also the mind.*

**1** *Read the paragraph. The underlined words need more explanation. Use the explanations that follow to rewrite the sentences on a separate piece of paper. Compare your answers with a classmate's.*

According to ANRED, eating disorders continue to be on the rise among athletes, especially in sports that emphasize being thin. Sports such as gymnastics, figure skating, dancing, and synchronized swimming have a higher percentage of athletes with eating disorders. According to an American College of Sports Medicine study, eating disorders affected 62% of the females in these sports. Cathy Rigby has admitted she struggled with anorexia for 12 years. Anorexia nervosa affects about 1% of female adolescents in the United States. Bulimia nervosa affects about 4% of college-aged women. If you want more information, contact the NEDIC.

**a.** ANRED = Anorexia Nervosa and Related Eating Disorders, an organization that provides information about eating disorders

**b.** Cathy Rigby = a 1972 Olympic gymnast

**c.** anorexia nervosa = an eating disorder in which the person diets so much that they become too thin

**d.** bulimia nervosa = an eating disorder in which the person diets, becomes hungry, overeats, and then vomits to get rid of the food

**e.** NEDIC = National Eating Disorder Information Center

**2** *Look back at the first draft of your paragraph. Are there any words or expressions that another reader may not understand? Underline anything that needs to be explained, and find out the explanations.*

# ◀ EDIT: Writing the Final Draft

*Write the final draft of your paragraph. Carefully edit it for grammatical and mechanical errors, such as spelling, capitalization, and punctuation. Make sure you used some of the vocabulary and grammar from the unit. Use the checklist to help you write your final draft. Then neatly write or type your paragraph.*

## ✓ FINAL DRAFT CHECKLIST

- ○ Does your topic sentence state the main idea of the paragraph?
- ○ Are there three or more supporting details?
- ○ Are the supporting details in order?
- ○ Are there reasons, facts, examples, or explanations to support the details?
- ○ Does the conclusion restate the main idea of the topic sentence in a new way?
- ○ Did you add information to explain ideas that were unclear?
- ○ Did you use *can, could,* or *be able to* to express ability?
- ○ Did you use vocabulary from the unit?

## ALTERNATIVE WRITING TOPICS

*Write about one of the topics. Use the vocabulary and grammar from the unit.*

1. Write a factual report about a famous athlete that you admire. Why do you admire him or her? What has this athlete accomplished?

2. There are other activities that can lead to a dangerous obsession. Some people enjoy watching their favorite movie stars so much that they begin stalking, or obsessively following, the stars. Other examples include shopping and using the Internet. Write a report explaining how obsession with an activity can become dangerous. Give some examples about obsessions of people you know or people in the news.

## RESEARCH TOPICS, see page 212.

# UNIT 4 Speaking of Gender

## 1 FOCUS ON THE TOPIC

### A PREDICT

*Look at the photograph and discuss the questions with the class.*

1. Do you think the baby is a boy or a girl? Why?
2. Read the title of the unit. What do you think it means?

*Work in a small group. Discuss the questions.*

1. Males and females are born with physical differences. In what other ways are they different? Do you believe these other differences start at birth?

2. How are male and female babies treated differently in your home culture? Do they wear different colors at birth? Are there any other differences?

3. How do boys and girls play differently in your home culture? What toys do boys and girls play with? What kinds of games do they play?

4. What are some differences that make it difficult for males and females to understand each other as they grow up?

5. Do you think there are any differences in the ways that men and women use language to communicate? Can you think of any differences in the ways that men and women speak?

**C** **BACKGROUND AND VOCABULARY**

**1** *Read this description of a college course in linguistics, the scientific study of language and the use of language in societies. Pay attention to the boldfaced words.*

**LINGUISTICS 120**

### GENDER DIFFERENCES IN LANGUAGE

In this course, we will study how men and women use language differently. We will answer the following questions:

1. Gender is a basic part of our **identity**. When we think about who we are, we begin by thinking of ourselves as male or female. How do we use language to communicate who we are?

2. There are differences in the way that boys and girls play. Which gender is more interested in giving every member a turn? Which gender is more concerned with following the rules of a game? Is it true that one gender is more interested in playing **fairly**?

3. Our home culture strongly affects our behavior. In our home culture, we learn how to act as males and females. How does our culture affect our communication style as males and females? How is our use of language **influenced** by our gender?

4. Is it possible to know the gender of a speaker just by listening to his or her speech? Does language **reflect** our gender? If so, what are the signs? Do men use a **masculine** speaking style? Are there ways of speaking that are directly related to being a male? Do women use a **feminine** speaking style? Are there ways of speaking that are directly related to being a female?

5. Do people of different genders have different ideas of what is important or valuable? If so, how do they express these ideas in their speech? How do men and women use language to **emphasize** different things? Which gender uses language more often to **compete** with each other—male or female? Which gender uses language more often to get along with each other—male or female?

6. All human beings want to be respected by others. They want others to admire them, and they want to feel important. This is **status**. How do males and females use language to gain status? Are there any differences?

**2**  *Match the words on the left with the definitions on the right.*

_____ 1. **identity**        **a.** level or position

_____ 2. **fairly**          **b.** to show something clearly

_____ 3. **influenced**      **c.** sense of self

_____ 4. **reflect**         **d.** male; manly

_____ 5. **masculine**       **e.** to try to be better than others

_____ 6. **feminine**        **f.** to show that something is special or important

_____ 7. **emphasize**       **g.** guided or changed

_____ 8. **compete**         **h.** female; womanly

_____ 9. **status**          **i.** equally

## Ⓐ READING ONE: Different Ways of Talking

*Read the first paragraph of the reading. Write your answers to the questions.*

1. How did Joy's parents respond to the news that they were having a girl? What did they do?

   _____

   _____

   _____

2. What did their friends and relatives do when they heard the news?

   _____

   _____

   _____

3. Look at the reading's title. Look back at your answers to questions 1 and 2. Predict what the reading will be about. Write your ideas here.

   _____

   _____

   _____

*Discuss your ideas with the class. Then continue reading "Different Ways of Talking."*

# Different Ways of Talking

1    A few hours after Joy Fisher's birth, her parents took pictures of her. Joy's mother dressed her in a cute little pink dress so that everyone who saw the pictures would know that the new baby was a girl. Even before she was born, Joy's parents knew that she was going to be female. When Joy's mother was six months pregnant, she got a sonogram, or picture of the baby. When the doctor said, "I'm sure you have a little lady in there," Joy's parents told all their relatives and friends that their baby was a girl. Gifts soon arrived, including pink dresses and dolls. Joy's parents decorated her room in pink and white.

2    A few years later, Joy's brother, Tommy, was born. His room was painted blue, and he received books and a football as gifts. Joy enjoyed helping her mother take care of the new baby. She also enjoyed playing with other girls at school. Now, Tommy has also entered school, where he plays with other boys. The games Joy and Tommy play

are quite different. Joy loves jumping rope with her two best friends. Tommy likes to play ball with a large group of boys. Sometimes when they play a game, he is the captain. He enjoys telling the other boys what to do. Joy, on the other hand, doesn't like it when new girls join her friends and try to change the way they jump rope. She thinks that some of these girls are too bossy.

3    Both Joy and Tommy are growing up in the culture of the United States. They are learning what it means to be a girl and a boy in this culture. Their sex at birth, female and male, is now becoming a gender—a way of thinking, speaking, and acting that is considered **feminine** or **masculine**. Each culture has its own way of defining gender, and very early in life gender becomes a basic part of a person's **identity**. According to Deborah Tannen, a professor at Georgetown University, gender differences are even **reflected** in the ways that men and women use language. Tannen and others who study communication believe that these differences begin early in life.

4    For example, in the United States and Canada, boys and girls usually play in same-sex groups. Boys might play in large groups in which every boy knows his place. Some are leaders; others are followers. Boys **compete** with one another for leadership. Many boys like to get attention by boasting, or talking about how well they can do things. The games that they play often have complicated rules, and each boy tries hard to win.

5    Girls, in contrast, usually play in smaller groups. Sometimes they play with only one or two "best friends." Most girls want other girls to like them, and this is more important to them than winning. Girls may be interested in playing **fairly** and taking turns. For example, when girls jump rope together, two girls hold the rope while others jump. Then the rope-holders take their turn jumping.

6    Tannen has found that these differences are reflected in the ways that children use language while they play. Boys often use commands when they talk to each other. For instance, when Tommy is captain, he might say, "You go first. Don't wait for me." As the leader of the other boys, he tells them exactly what to do. But when Joy wants to **influence** her friends, she uses different forms of language. Instead of using commands, she will say, "Let's try it this way. Let's do this." This is how she tries to direct the other girls without sounding bossy. By using the form "let's," she also **emphasizes** the fact that the girls all belong to the same group.

7    As Joy and Tommy grow up, they will continue to speak differently. In junior high school, Joy's **status** will depend on her circle of friends. If her friends are popular, then Joy may enjoy high status at school. For this reason, Joy and many other girls are interested in gossip. If Joy has some information to share about a popular girl at school, this proves that she has a friendship with this girl. In this way Joy can use gossip to gain more status in her school.

8    Tommy, on the other hand, may be less interested in gossip. His status does not depend on who his friends are at school. Tommy gains status through his own ability to play sports well or earn high grades. Later in life, Joy may continue to be interested in talking about other people and their lives. Tommy will be less interested in personal talk and more concerned with discussions of sports

*(continued on next page)*

and news. These give him a chance to gain status by showing others his knowledge.

9 Different ways of speaking are part of gender. As adults, men and women sometimes face difficulties in their communication with each other. Studies of communication show that if a woman tells her husband about a problem, she will expect him to listen and offer sympathy. She may be annoyed when he simply tells her how to solve the problem. Similarly, a husband may be annoyed when his wife wants to stop and ask a stranger for directions to a park or restaurant. Unlike his wife, he would rather use a map and find his way by himself.

10 Language is also part of the different ways that men and women think about friendship. Most North American men believe that friendship means doing things together such as camping or playing tennis. Talking is not an important part of friendship for most of them. American women, on the other hand, usually identify their best friend as someone with whom they talk frequently. Tannen believes that for women, talking with friends and agreeing with them is very important. Tannen has found that women, in contrast to men, often use tag questions. For example, a woman might say, "This is a great restaurant, isn't it?" By adding a tag question to her speech ("isn't it?"), she is giving other people a chance to agree with her. Likewise, many women use more polite forms—"Can you close the door?" "Could you help me?" "Would you come here?" Men, however, often speak more directly, giving direct commands—"Close the door." "Help me." "Come here."

11 These differences seem to be part of growing up in the culture of the United States and following its rules of gender. If men and women can understand that many of their differences are cultural, not personal, they may be able to improve their relationships. They may begin to understand that because of gender differences in language, there is more than one way to communicate.

*Source:* Based on information in Deborah Tannen, *You Just Don't Understand: Women and Men in Conversation.* (William Morrow and Company, Inc. 1990)

*Did the reading include the information you expected? Look at your ideas on page 62.*

## ◖ READ FOR MAIN IDEAS

*Based on the reading, mark each statement **T** (true) or **F** (false). Rewrite the false statements to make them true.*

                     Gender

__F__ 1. A child's sex at birth determines how the child will think, act, and speak later in life.

_____ 2. People learn masculine and feminine behavior.

_____ 3. Men and women learn to use language differently.

_____ 4. Gender differences can be seen in the ways that children use language when they fight.

_____ 5. Differences in communication between males and females are the same in all cultures.

_____ 6. Girls gain status by showing their knowledge about sports and news.

_____ 7. Girls get much of their identity from being part of a group.

_____ 8. Men usually talk more about other people than women do.

*Circle the best answer for each question. Write the number of the paragraph where you found the answer.*

**Paragraph**

1. In what kind of group does Tommy like to play?     2
    a. He likes to play in groups of both boys and girls.
    b. He likes to play in large groups.
    c. He likes to play in small groups.

2. How did Joy's mother first show that Joy was a girl?     _____
    a. She put a pink hairband around her head.
    b. She put a pink dress on her.
    c. She painted her room blue.

3. What does Tommy like about being captain?     _____
    a. He likes boasting.
    b. He likes telling other boys what to do.
    c. He likes having the other boys like him.

4. How do boys get attention?     _____
    a. They argue with others.
    b. They talk about their abilities.
    c. They change the rules.

5. Who do girls usually play with?     _____
    a. They play with small groups of girls.
    b. They play with large groups of girls.
    c. They play with groups of both boys and girls.

6. What is one reason why girls are interested in gossip?     _____
    a. Gossip teaches them how to act.
    b. Gossip allows them to use commands.
    c. Gossip can bring them status.

7. Why might a woman get angry with her husband?     _____
    a. She feels that he doesn't listen.
    b. She feels that his advice is wrong.
    c. She feels that he doesn't care.

8. How do American men show friendship?     _____
    a. They talk together often.
    b. They agree with each other.
    c. They do things together.

9. How can men and women improve their relationships?     _____
    a. learn more about each other personally
    b. understand their communication differences
    c. pay attention to gender rules

*Circle the answers to these questions about Reading One. Write the number of the paragraph where you found the information to support your answer. Discuss your answers with a partner.*

**Paragraph**

1. Which statement would Deborah Tannen most likely agree with?  ＿＿＿
   a. Gender differences begin when children begin school.
   b. Some cultures have very few gender differences.
   c. Gender differences begin shortly after birth.

2. What might Joy's mother do if the sonogram were wrong and Joy were born male?  ＿＿＿
   a. complain to the doctor
   b. redecorate Joy's room
   c. feel glad to have a son

3. What might Tommy do if he played with Joy and her friends?  ＿＿＿
   a. invite other boys to join the group
   b. argue with them
   c. tell them what to do

4. Compared to Tommy's friendships, Joy's friendships are probably ＿＿＿.  ＿＿＿
   a. more boring
   b. longer lasting
   c. less competitive

5. Which pair might be the most interested in having a long dinner together?  ＿＿＿
   a. two female friends
   b. two male friends
   c. a brother and a sister

◖ EXPRESS OPINIONS

*Discuss the following questions in a small group.*

1. Husbands and wives sometimes disagree about asking for directions. What do you think are the most serious communication problems that men and women have?

2. What do you think is the biggest difference between male and female speech?

3. In English, girls often use the word "let's" to create the feeling of belonging to a group. Does your native language have any words that create this feeling? Do you feel more comfortable using these words or using commands?

**1** *Read an interview with Dr. Anne Rockwell, a professor of communication at a well-known university. She is being interviewed by Keena Jones, a reporter for* Lingo *magazine.*

# Speaking of Gender

By Keena Jones (from *Lingo* magazine)

**KEENA JONES:** I know you've written a lot about gender and language, Dr. Rockwell.

**DR. ROCKWELL:** Yes, I have. I find it very interesting. For example, you just called me "Doctor." That used to always suggest a man, not a woman.

**KJ:** Maybe I should call you "Doctorette."

**DR:** Actually, I prefer to be called "Doctor."

**KJ:** Why is that?

**DR:** Well, you know, English has several feminine words that people sometimes use when they're referring to women. You probably know them, right? *Poetess, songstress, bachelorette*? Now these words aren't used too often, but they exist in the language. However, some women don't like such words because they feel as if these words make women less important than men.

**KJ:** What do you mean by that?

**DR:** For instance, if you say the word *actress*, people don't always think of a serious artist. They might think of some silly, beautiful female who's more worried about her makeup than she is about Shakespeare. But when you say *actor*—that's not silly at all. That's a serious word, a respectable word.

**KJ:** I see.

**DR:** That's why I would never call myself a doctorette. Or a professoress—never!

**KJ:** Fine. I'll call you doctor.

**DR:** And I'll call you Ms. Jones. That's a very good example of how the language has changed in recent years, partly as a result of the women's movement.

**KJ:** You mean the title of *Ms.*?

**DR:** Not just that. We've changed dozens of words related to occupations. Think of all the words that used to end in *-man. Policeman, fireman, mailman, . . .*

**KJ:** I guess they've all changed. Now we say *police officer, firefighter, . . .* but what about *mailman*?

**DR:** *Mail carrier.* And do you know why? We've removed gender from these words because, after all, both men and women can do these jobs.

**KJ:** I suppose. But not everyone would agree with you.

**DR:** Maybe not. But you know, even though I believe men and women are equal in their abilities, I do think there are differences in the way they speak.

**KJ:** Do you really think so?

**DR:** Absolutely. Look at all the color words that women know! If a man and woman go shopping together, the man will look at a shirt and say, *I like the purple one.* But a woman will look at the same shirt and call it *lavender . . .* or *periwinkle. . . .*

**KJ:** Or *mauve*?

**DR:** Right! Women use more words for color. They also use some adjectives that men don't use . . . such as *lovely, cute, adorable.*

*(continued on next page)*

**KJ:** I guess you're right. Most men don't seem to use those words.

**DR:** Most of them don't. But you know, language and gender are both so closely related to culture. In fact, I've studied seventeen countries, and I found out that in Japan, for example, men and women use different word endings. So if a man doesn't want to sound bossy, he'll use the feminine word ending, *-no*, instead of *-ka*. *Ka* sounds more masculine, more direct.

**KJ:** So a man will talk like a woman in certain situations. That's fascinating. Thank you.

**DR:** My pleasure.

**2** *Write short answers to the questions. Share your answers with the class.*

1. Why do some women dislike feminine word forms such as "poetess" or "bachelorette"?

_____

_____

2. What are some occupation words that no longer reflect gender?

_____

_____

3. Why have these words changed?

_____

_____

4. What are two differences in the way that women use words?

_____

_____

## C INTEGRATE READINGS ONE AND TWO

**◀ STEP 1: Organize**

*The readings give examples of gender differences in language use. Complete the chart with information from both readings.*

## GENDER DIFFERENCES IN LANGUAGE USE

**Males**

1. Boys often boss each other when they speak.
2. Boys use _____.
3. Boys use playing sports to gain status.
4. Husbands usually tell wives how _____ problems.
5. Men often use maps to find directions.
6. Male friendship means _____ together.
7. Men speak directly and use commands.
8. Men use basic words for color such as "_____."
9. Men avoid using some adjectives.
10. Men use "_____" as a Japanese word ending.

**Females**

1. Girls don't like to sound __bossy__.
2. Girls use "let's."
3. Girls use _____ to gain status.
4. Wives want their to husbands to listen to problems.
5. Women often ask _____ for directions.
6. Female friendship means talking.
7. Women use polite forms and _____.
8. Women use extra words for color such as "lavender" or "periwinkle."
9. Women often use such adjectives as "_____," "_____," or "_____."
10. Women use "_____" as a Japanese word ending.

◀ **STEP 2: Synthesize**

*Use the chart in Step 1 to complete a paragraph that includes information from both readings. In your paragraph, describe two differences:*

- different words and expressions used by males and females
- different attitudes expressed through language by males and females

**Topic Sentence:** There are many differences in the ways that males and females use language.

One difference is that males and females use different words and expressions. For example, _____.

Also, _____

_____.

Another example is that _____

_____.

A second difference is that males and females express different attitudes through language. For instance, _____

_____ .

In addition, _____ .

It is also true that _____ .

**Concluding Sentence:** These differences begin early in life and continue through adulthood.

# ③ FOCUS ON WRITING

## Ⓐ VOCABULARY

### ◖ REVIEW

*Read a letter from a man to his brother. The writer describes a visit to his wife's family. Complete the letter with words from the box. Use each word only once.*

| | | | |
|---|---|---|---|
| compete | feminine | occupation | status |
| emphasize | influence | reflect | women's movement |
| fairly | masculine | | |

Dear Jack,

     I finally have a few free minutes to write you a letter. Let me

_____ one thing: Ashley's family is so different from ours.
   **1.**

Imagine a family with five sisters! Ashley's dad was away this weekend, so I had

the only _____ role in the family. There wasn't much to do; we
       **2.**

mostly sat around and talked. I couldn't _____ them to do
            **3.**

anything else! It made me miss the old days when you and I used to

_____ with each other at family parties. Remember our
  **4.**

volleyball games?

Parties at this house are a lot more _____ than our parties
5.
were. When I played cards with her sisters, they talked and talked about the

rules. It was all about playing _____.
6.

But still, I have to say these are incredible women. Each sister has an

interesting _____. There are two doctors, two writers, and a
7.
lawyer in this family. It's hard to keep track of which sister has the highest

_____. Their lives all _____ how the
8.                                          9.
_____ has changed things. It's amazing.
10.

Anyway, I hope you had a good holiday. I'll be back next week, and I hope

we can play some volleyball soon.

Your big brother,

Jonathan

## ◖ EXPAND

*Read the paragraph. Pay special attention to the boldfaced expressions.*

When I was a girl, my parents taught me to speak politely. They wanted
me to be **lady-like**. They didn't want me to sound **rough and tough**. I
learned how to ask questions like, "Could you help me, please?" or "Would
you mind giving me a little help with this?" I was also trained to make sure
that other people agreed with me. Instead of saying, "It sure is hot today!" I
would say something like this: "It's really hot, isn't it?" I was polite and
indirect, never **blunt**. But I loved to **gossip** with my friends. We would get
together and share **the dirt** on everyone. The more secret the information,
the more we loved it. We would talk about how other girls dressed or who
they were dating. We enjoyed this kind of **juicy** talk—it was a lot more
interesting than sports or whatever the boys talked about. Looking back on
all this, I guess I learned how to speak like a typical girl.

*Now match each expression on the left with its opposite on the right. Use a dictionary if necessary.*

_____ **1. lady-like**　　　　**a.** not talk about other people

_____ **2. blunt**　　　　　　**b.** flattery[1]

_____ **3. the dirt**　　　　　**c.** feminine

_____ **4. juicy**　　　　　　 **d.** masculine

_____ **5. rough and tough**　**e.** boring

_____ **6. gossip**　　　　　　**f.** indirect

_____

[1]**flattery**: nice things that you say about someone, but which you do not really mean

◖ **CREATE**

*Use five words from the box to write five questions about language use. Then use the questions to interview a partner about the way that he or she used language while growing up. Share information from the interview with the class.*

| | | |
|---|---|---|
| blunt | influence | masculine |
| feminine | juicy | rough and tough |
| gossip | lady-like | the dirt |

Example  How did your parents influence your speech?

1. _____

2. _____

3. _____

4. _____

5. _____

**B** **GRAMMAR: Comparative Adverbs**

**1** *Read the conversation between two male friends. How are the boldfaced phrases similar in meaning? How are they different?*

BILL:　Where's your wife today?

BOB:　She's out shopping with her sister.

BILL:　That's good. You don't have to go with her.

BOB:　Right. I hate shopping for clothes. I can**'t** shop **as patiently as** she can. She can shop for hours!

BILL:　My wife can, too. I'd rather find what I need and go home.

BOB:　Me, too. I hate to shop **as slowly as** my wife does.

BILL:　Yeah. I think most guys shop **more quickly than** women do.

## COMPARATIVE ADVERBS

**Comparative adverbs** are used to compare the actions expressed by verbs.

Actions can be compared by using *as . . . as, not as . . . as, more . . . than,* and *less . . . than.*

My mother speaks **as quickly as** my father. *(equal)*

My sister **doesn't** speak **as quickly as** my brother. *(not equal)*

Most boys play **more competitively than** girls. *(different)*

Most men speak **less politely than** women. *(different)*

**2** *Complete the paragraph with the comparative form of the adverbs in parentheses.*

My sister went to Mexico to learn Spanish. At first, she couldn't speak

_____ native speakers. Native speakers spoke much
    **1. (fluently)**

_____ she did, so it was difficult for her to understand them.
    **2. (rapidly)**

She spoke a lot _____ they did, and sometimes she had to
    **3. (slowly)**

repeat herself. Her goal was to speak Spanish _____ native
    **4. (skillfully)**

speakers, so she decided to go to language school. There she studied Spanish

_____ any other student. Her teacher was proud of her. After
    **5. (carefully)**

two years studying Spanish and living in Mexico, she spoke just a little

_____ a native speaker.
    **6. (perfectly)**

## C WRITING

*Discuss the questions with a partner.*

- How do males and females speak differently in your home culture?
- Do males and females use different kinds of polite language?
- What topics do males like to discuss? What topics do females like to discuss?

> Now you are going to **write a contrast paragraph focusing on two or three important differences between male and female speech in your home culture.** Use the vocabulary and grammar from the unit.*

_____

*For Alternative Writing Topics, see page 77. These topics can be used in place of the writing topic for this unit or as homework. The alternative topics relate to the theme of the unit, but may not target the same grammar or rhetorical structures taught in the unit.

*Use the chart to list some of the ways that males and females use language differently in your home culture. One difference has been listed as an example.*

| DIFFERENCE 1 | DIFFERENCE 2 | DIFFERENCE 3 | DIFFERENCE 4 | DIFFERENCE 5 |
|---|---|---|---|---|
| **Males:** Use more general words for color ("blue") | **Males:** | **Males:** | **Males:** | **Males:** |
| **Females:** Use more specific words for color ("baby blue" or "navy blue") | **Females:** | **Females:** | **Females:** | **Females:** |

## ◀ WRITE: A Contrast Paragraph

When **contrasting**, you explain how two or more ideas are **different**. You can use **point-by-point organization.** When you use point-by-point organization, the points (ideas) in a paragraph are discussed one-by-one.

**1** *Read the paragraph and look at the point-by-point outline on the next page. Complete the outline with details and examples from the paragraph.*

> When I speak English, the way I speak is different depending on the situation. One important difference is the formality of language. In class, I can use more informal language because we are all friends. On the other hand, outside of class I don't want to be impolite by speaking too informally. For example, when I'm talking to a clerk in the supermarket, I say, "Would you mind putting that in a bag?" This is more polite than saying, "Put that in a bag." Another difference is asking for help. If I know a person well, I feel comfortable asking what a word means or whether I am saying something correctly. However, if I am speaking to a stranger, I don't like asking for help with my English. Sometimes I pretend to understand something that I don't really understand at all! Finally, I notice that my ability to speak English well depends on the topic. If we discuss a topic in class, I learn a lot of new vocabulary words, and I can express my ideas more easily. On the other hand, sometimes I have trouble with new topics because I don't know enough words in English. These are some of the differences in the ways that I use English, my second language.

**Outline**

I. Formality of language

    **A:** In English class: _____

    **B:** In the supermarket: _____

II. Asking for help

    **A:** Speaking to people the writer knows well: _____

    _____

    **B:** Speaking to strangers: _____

    _____

III. Topics

    **A:** Topics discussed in class: _____

    _____

    **B:** Other topics: _____

    _____

**2** *Use your notes from Prepare to Write, page 74, and Step 1, page 69, to write the first draft of your paragraph.*

◀ **REVISE: Using Transitions of Contrast**

**1** *Read a paragraph about the differences in the male and female use of language. Look at the boldfaced words. What do they mean? Discuss with a partner.*

> Men and women sometimes have difficulties in their communication with each other. According to linguistic research, a man might get angry when his wife wants to ask a stranger for directions to a park or a restaurant. **Unlike** his wife, he would rather use a map and find his way by himself. Another language difference is reflected in friendship. For most North American men, talking is not an important part of spending time with a friend. American women, **on the other hand**, usually identify their friends as people with whom they talk frequently. These differences sometimes make it difficult for men and women to communicate. **However,** they can learn to understand their differences and have better relationships.

Writers use **transitions** to help readers move from one idea to another. They help readers understand the relationship between ideas. A variety of transitions are used to show **contrast** (differences) between ideas.

Some **transitions of contrast** appear at the beginning of a sentence followed by a comma. They can also be placed between the subject and the verb of a sentence. These include *however* and *on the other hand.*

- Men rarely use tag questions in English. **However,** women use them frequently.
- American women, **on the other hand,** usually identify their friends as people with whom they talk frequently.

Other transitions that begin a sentence are followed by a noun or noun phrase. These include *unlike* and *in contrast to.*

- **Unlike** his wife, he would rather use a map and find his way by himself.
- **In contrast to** boys, most girls play with one or two best friends.

**2** Look at the paragraph on page 74. Underline the transitions of contrast.

**3** Rewrite the sentences. Use the transition words in parentheses. You may need to change or omit some parts of the sentences.

1. Tommy enjoys playing with a large group of boys. Joy doesn't like it when new girls join her friends. (on the other hand)

   _____

2. Boys often compete with one another for leadership. Girls are not usually interested in competing with each other. (unlike)

   _____

3. Boys often gain status through playing sports. Girls often gain status through gossip. (in contrast to)

   _____

4. Men usually want to use a map to find directions. Women usually want to ask strangers for directions. (on the other hand)

   _____

5. My English class is very informal. The office where I work is very formal. (however)

   _____

6. Speaking English to people I know well is easy. Speaking English to strangers is sometimes difficult. (in contrast to)

   _____

**4** Look back at the first draft of your paragraph. Where can you add transitions to show the contrast between ideas?

**◀ EDIT: Writing the Final Draft**

*Write the final draft of your paragraph. Carefully edit it for grammatical and mechanical errors, such as spelling, capitalization, and punctuation. Make sure you used some of the vocabulary and grammar from the unit. Use the checklist to help you write your final draft. Then neatly write or type your paragraph.*

## ✓ FINAL DRAFT CHECKLIST

- ○ Does your paragraph contain a clear topic sentence stating the main idea?
- ○ Does it contain two or three important differences?
- ○ Are the differences supported by examples and / or details?
- ○ Are transitions of contrast used correctly?
- ○ Are commas used to punctuate transitions?
- ○ Does your paragraph end with a clear concluding sentence?
- ○ Does your paragraph include comparative adverbs?
- ○ Does it include vocabulary from the unit?

## ALTERNATIVE WRITING TOPICS

*Write about one of the topics. Use the vocabulary and grammar from the unit.*

1. In this unit you learned about gender differences in language. Now think more generally about the ways that boys and girls are treated as they grow up. How are they treated the same? How are they treated differently? Write a paragraph or two comparing and contrasting the ways that boys and girls are treated in your home culture.

2. Write a report comparing the status of men and women in your home culture. How do men and women gain status? Consider their use of language as well as other ways that status can be gained.

3. Imagine a culture in which there are very few gender differences. Do you think life would be more or less interesting? Would life be easier or more difficult? Write a paragraph or two explaining your opinion. Give specific reasons to support your opinion.

## RESEARCH TOPICS, see page 212.

# UNIT 5 Ecotourism

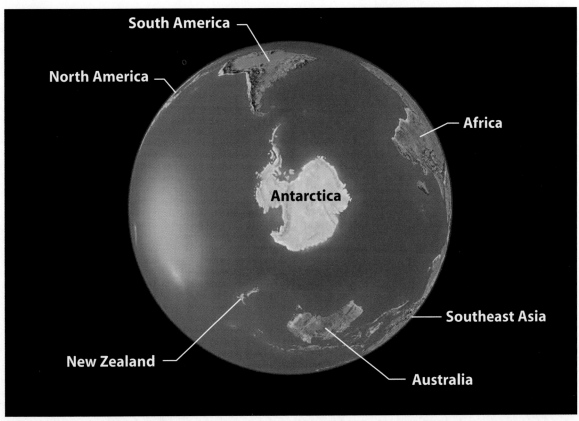

South America

North America

Africa

Antarctica

Southeast Asia

New Zealand

Australia

# ① FOCUS ON THE TOPIC

## A PREDICT

*Look at the map and discuss the questions with the class.*

1. Where is Antarctica?

2. More and more people are traveling to Antarctica. Why do you think they want to go there?

3. What is *ecotourism*? What do ecology[1] and tourism have in common?

---

[1] **ecology:** the way in which plants, animals, and people are related to each other and to their environment, or the study of this

Work in a small group. Discuss your past travel experiences. Share your group's answers with the class.

Describe a place that you have visited that had lots of natural beauty (trees, mountains, an ocean, and so on). Have visitors damaged or harmed this place in any way?

**C  BACKGROUND AND VOCABULARY**

**1** Study the words and definitions. You will see these words in the activity that follows. You will also see them in Reading One on page 82.

1. **coastal:** in the ocean or on the land near the coast (the area where the land meets the water)

2. **consequences:** things that happen as a result of a particular action or situation

3. **fragile:** easily broken, damaged, or ruined

4. **harsh:** difficult to live in and very uncomfortable

5. **inhabit:** to live in an area or a place

6. **landscape:** the way an area of land looks

7. **preserve:** to save something or someone from being harmed or destroyed

8. **remote:** far away from towns and cities

9. **research:** to study a subject in detail, especially in order to discover new facts or test new ideas

10. **tourist:** someone who is traveling or visiting a place for pleasure

11. **vast:** extremely large

**2** How much do you know about Antarctica? Take this quiz—just for fun. Circle the answer you think best. Then discuss your answers with the class.

1. About _____ of Antarctica's **vast** land is covered with ice.
   a. 25%          c. 75%
   b. 50%          d. 98%

2. While Antarctica's **landscape** appears cold and snowy, the land of Antarctica is actually a _____.
   a. desert          c. jungle
   b. forest          d. plain

3. The coldest temperature of the **harsh** Antarctic winter is approximately ____.

    **a.** −35°C          **c.** −90°C

    **b.** −50°C          **d.** −120°C

4. Antarctica is **inhabited** by penguins and other animals, including ____.

    **a.** bears          **c.** eagles

    **b.** seals          **d.** snow leopards

5. In ____, a group of explorers led by Roald Amundsen became the first people to reach the **remote** South Pole.

    **a.** 1890          **c.** 1920

    **b.** 1911          **d.** 1952

6. The number of **tourists** visiting Antarctica increased from 4,698 in 1991 to approximately ____ in 2007.

    **a.** 8,000          **c.** 18,000

    **b.** 10,000          **d.** 30,000    30. thirty thousand

7. In ____, 12 countries signed the Antarctic Treaty to **preserve** the continent for scientific **research**.

    **a.** 1959   fiftynine       **c.** 1990

    **b.** 1978   nineteen      **d.** 2002

8. In ____, Emilio Palma was the first person born in Antarctica; his parents were living in the **coastal** area of Hope Bay.

    **a.** 1878          **c.** 1978

    **b.** 1950          **d.** 2006

9. Antarctica is colder than the Arctic as a **consequence** of its elevation; most of the continent is more than ____ above sea level.

    **a.** ½ kilometer          **c.** 10 kilometers

    **b.** 2 kilometers          **d.** 50 kilometers

10. In 1999, Tim Jarvis and Peter Treseder walked across the **fragile** Antarctic environment to the South Pole in ____ days.

    **a.** 25          **c.** 46

    **b.** 36          **d.** 99

*Averiguar = find out*

# ② FOCUS ON READING

## A | READING ONE: Tourists in a Fragile Land

*Read the first paragraph of an opinion essay about tourism in Antarctica, written by a scientist who works there. Predict reasons why the scientist says, "I feel Antarctica should be closed to tourists." Share your ideas with the class. Read the rest of the essay and compare your ideas with the scientist's.*

# TOURISTS IN A FRAGILE LAND

**1** AS A SCIENTIST WORKING IN ANTARCTICA, I spend most of my time in the lab studying ice. I am trying to find out the age of Antarctic ice. All we know for certain is that it is the oldest ice in the world. The more we understand it, the more we will understand the changing weather of the Earth. Today, as with an increasing number of days, I had to leave my work to greet a group of **tourists** who were taking a vacation in this continent of ice. And even though I can appreciate their desire to experience this **vast** and beautiful **landscape**, I feel Antarctica should be closed to tourists.

**2** Because Antarctica is the center of important scientific **research**, it must be **preserved** for this purpose. Meteorologists are now looking at the effects of the ozone hole[1] that was discovered above Antarctica in 1984. They are also trying to understand global warming[2]. If the Earth's temperature continues to increase, the health and safety of every living thing on the planet will be affected. Astronomers have a unique view of space and are able to see it very clearly from Antarctica. Biologists have a chance to learn more about the animals that **inhabit** the **coastal** areas of this frozen land. Botanists study the plant life to understand how it can live in such a **harsh** environment, and geologists study the Earth to learn more about how it was formed. There are even psychologists who study how people behave when they live and work together in such a **remote** location.

**3** When tourist groups come here, they take us away from our research. Our work is difficult,

---
[1] **ozone hole:** a hole in the layer of gases that protect the Earth from the bad effects of the sun
[2] **global warming:** a general increase in world temperatures caused by increased amounts of carbon dioxide around the Earth

and some of our projects can be damaged by such simple mistakes as opening the wrong door or bumping into a small piece of equipment. In addition, tourists in Antarctica can also hurt the environment. Members of Greenpeace, one of the world's leading environmental organizations, complain that tourists leave trash on beaches and disturb the plants and animals. In a place as frozen as Antarctica, it can take 100 years for a plant to grow back, and tourists can easily damage penguin eggs. Oil spills are another problem caused by tourism. Oil spills not only kill penguins but can also destroy scientific projects.

4 The need to protect Antarctica from tourists becomes even greater when we consider the fact that there is no government here. Antarctica belongs to no country. Who is making sure that the penguins, plants, and sea are safe? No one is responsible. In fact, we scientists are only temporary visitors ourselves. It is true that the number of tourists who visit Antarctica each year is small compared to the number of those who visit other places. However, these other places are inhabited by local residents and controlled by local governments. They have an interest in protecting their natural environments. Who is concerned about the environment of Antarctica? The scientists, to be sure, but not necessarily the tour companies that make money from sending people south.

5 If we don't protect Antarctica from tourism, there may be serious **consequences** for us all. We might lose the results of scientific research projects. It's possible that these results could teach us something important about the causes and effects of climate change. Some **fragile** plants and animals might die and disappear forever. This could damage the balance of animal and plant life in Antarctica. We know from past experience that when things get unbalanced, harmful changes can occur. Clearly, Antarctica should remain a place for careful and controlled scientific research. We cannot allow tourism to bring possible danger to the planet. The only way to protect this fragile and important part of the planet is to stop tourists from traveling to Antarctica.

## ◀ READ FOR MAIN IDEAS

*In the body of his essay (paragraphs 2, 3, 4), the scientist gives three main reasons why Antarctica should be closed to tourists. Number the reasons in the order they appear in Reading One.*

___4___ There is no government to protect Antarctica.

___2___ Many different scientists learn new things by studying Antarctica.

___3___ Tourists can damage Antarctica's environment.

# ◀ READ FOR DETAILS   ~~Homework~~

**(1)** *Complete the outline with details from Reading One.*

> **I.** Scientists learn new things in Antarctica because it is different from other places.
>
> **A.** *it's the oldest* ice in the world
>
> **B.** unique ___*view*___ of space
>
> **C.** very ___*harsh*___ environment
> *uncomfortable*
>
> **II.** Problems in Antarctica may cause negative effects.
>
> **A.** loss of scientific *result research project.*
>
> **B.** disappearance of *(fragile) plants and animal, forever*
>
> **C.** damage to the balance of *animal and plant life in the anbrtica*

**2** *These statements are false or incomplete. Rewrite them according to Reading One so that they are true and complete.*

1. The author of the essay knows the age of Antarctic ice.

   **The writer of the essay is trying to find out the age of Antarctic ice.**

2. The writer wants Antarctica to be closed.

   *the writer wants Antarctica to be closed for tourism*

3. Psychologists study how people behave when they get lost in Antarctica.

   *psychologist study Behave how people behave whether they live and work together*

4. Oil spills in Antarctica have killed scientists.

   *oil spill in Antarctica have killed not only kill penguins but can also destroy scientic project*

5. Tour companies may be concerned about the environment of Antarctica.

   *tour companies may not be*

6. If we stop tourism in Antarctica, there may be consequences for tour companies.

   _____

7. We know from past experience that when things get balanced, harmful changes can occur.

   _____

**84** UNIT 5

◖ **MAKE INFERENCES**

*Homework* · *Probably* · *no-thank*

Read the statements and mark them **L** (likely) or **U** (unlikely). Refer to Reading One to find support for your answers. Compare your answers with a partner's.

_LIKE_ **1.** We will find out how old the ice in Antarctica is. *likely How doing*
*sabremos* *if scientif follow*
*Research about it*

_LIKE_ **2.** Living in Antarctica can be stressful.

_LIKE_ **3.** For Greenpeace, Antarctica is one of the most important areas in the world.

_unlike_ **4.** Antarctica will form a government.

*Because in Antartic only you look at the ice or and iceberg and the bito*

_____ **5.** Scientists enjoy tourists. *unlike*

◖**EXPRESS OPINIONS**

Discuss the questions with a partner.

**1.** If you were a scientist in Antarctica, how would you feel about tourists? Explain. *I would be Angry*

**2.** Can you find any weaknesses in the writer's opinion? Do you agree with everything he says? How much do you agree with him? *— all*
*yes*

**3.** Would you be interested in visiting Antarctica as a tourist? Why or why not?
*no, I prefer to leave work to the scientif.*

**1** *Read these entries from the journal of a tourist who traveled to Antarctica.*

# A TRAVEL JOURNAL

Read

## Chile, South America
February 16

The sunlight was shining so brightly as our plane flew over the snow-covered Andes mountains, which seemed to go on forever.

## Cape Horn
February 18

We spent the morning at a small church named Star of the Sea. This is a quiet place where visitors are invited to remember the sailors from all over the world who died here. They were all trying to sail around the southern point of South America, and many of them lost their lives at sea.

## Drake Passage—aboard the tour ship Explorer
February 19

We were welcomed today by the captain and crew. They gave us warm Antarctic jackets and introduced themselves to us. Sea birds followed the ship closely, sailing in the cold wind. As we headed south, we saw a pink ship in the distance. Our captain explained that it was not a ship but an iceberg[1]—the first one of our trip.

## Deception Island, Antarctica
February 21

We landed on Bailey Head, where thousands and thousands of penguins greeted us. The crew gave us a set of rules to follow to protect the environment. Mark, one of the scientists on our ship, asked us to bring him any trash that we find. He is studying the amount of trash created by tourists in Antarctica each year.

Tonight we'll listen to Christina, another scientist. She will explain the plant and animal life to us. Then she will show us a DVD on Antarctica.

The more I see, the more I want to learn.

---

[1] **iceberg:** an extremely large piece of ice floating in the sea

laughed like children because it was so much fun to be up there. Later, we explored a glacier[3] in motorized rubber boats. The ice was as thick as the crushed ice in a soft drink, but we pushed through it.

*Barcos* *Grena*

### Detaille Island, Antarctica
February 28

Because we wanted to celebrate crossing the Antarctic Circle, we drank some champagne today. Not many visitors come this far south! Mark explained that the ice is blue down here because it catches all the colors of the rainbow except for blue. I have always thought of Antarctica as nothing but white. But now I see a clear blue light shining through the mountains of ice all around us, and I have no words to describe the beauty.

*Barco* *enorme Grande*

Our ship passed a huge field of frozen sea. Mark invited us to come out and play. We weren't sure at first, but when we felt how solid it was, we jumped and ran. All around us were mountains and glaciers that no one has ever explored. It amazed me to think that no human hand or foot has ever touched them; only a few human eyes have seen them.

Even though it will be hard to describe, I will try to explain this amazing experience to my friends at home.

We all felt sad today when we realized that our ship was heading north. We really don't want to leave Antarctica, a unique world.

### Cuverville Island, Antarctica
February 23

*Despierto*

We awakened this morning to the noisy sound of penguins. They're loud! We met a team of biologists living in tents. They are studying the effect of tourists on baby penguins. When our captain invited the biologists to come on board for a hot shower, they joined us immediately. Then we cruised through the icebergs, which appeared in unbelievable shapes and sizes, as the sun was sinking in the sky. They seemed to be works of art by an ice sculptor.[2]

### Paradise Bay, Antarctica
February 25

*Tierra firme*

Today, we reached the mainland of the continent. Our guide today was Stephanie, who helped us walk through snow to a point about 500 feet above sea level. When we reached the top, we

---

[2] **sculptor:** an artist who makes objects from clay, wood, metal, etc.
[3] **glacier:** a large area of ice that moves slowly over an area of land

**2** *Discuss the questions with the class.*

1. How did the writer feel about her trip? What adjectives describe her emotions?

2. What opinion does the writer have about tourism in Antarctica? How do you know?

**STEP 1: Organize** *Homework*

*This chart compares the views of the scientist with the views of the tourist. Look back at Readings One and Two, and fill in the missing information.*

| OPINIONS OF THE SCIENTIST | OPINIONS OF THE TOURIST |
|---|---|
| 1. The Antarctic environment must be preserved for research. | As tourists learn about Antarctica and return home to tell their friends and families about its importance, they may want to help preserve the environment of Antarctica. |
| 2. We cannot control the behavior of tourists. | the tourists can be careful with the Enviroment if the scientists Explain plant and animal life to us. |
| 3. Some our projects can be damaged by such simple mistakes of the tourists. | Tourists can actually help scientists with their experiments. |
| 4. Tourists don't care about Antarctica. | the scientific can teach us about the of the Antartic. |

**STEP 2: Synthesize**

*Imagine that the tourist in Reading Two meets the scientist in Reading One. Work with a partner to complete their dialogue. Use information from the chart in Step 1, but do not copy—try to use your own words. Act out your dialogue.*

TOURIST: [*excited*] I understand that you've done some research in Antarctica. I love that place!

SCIENTIST: [*worried*] Have you been there? As a tourist?

TOURIST: Yes. It was the trip of a lifetime.

SCIENTIST: Well, to be honest with you, the tourists can damaged scientific projects

| | |
|---|---|
| TOURIST: | Right the scientific can teach us about |
| SCIENTIST: | but the tourist have to know How take care |
| | the enviroment. |
| TOURIST: | yeah, but we need some Help in this new world. |
| SCIENTIST: | but we need make research first. |

# ③ FOCUS ON WRITING

## Ⓐ VOCABULARY

### ◖ REVIEW

*Work in a small group. Match the adjectives in the box with the nouns from Readings One and Two surrounding them. List as many possible combinations as you can think of on the lines below.*

icebergs          environment ✗

effect                              beauty

      **Adjectives**

      coastal ✗      landscape ✗

sunlight      fragile

      frozen

      harsh      consequences

      natural

      remote

temperature      scientific      continent

      vast

research          glaciers

coastal environment, coastal landscape, _____

_____

_____

_____

_____

_____

_____

_____

*Work in pairs. Read the chart. Then analyze the relationships between the vocabulary words given below. First, circle the word that best completes each comparison. Be sure that the second pair of words has a similar relationship to the first pair. Second, label each comparison with the letter of the correct category.*

| CATEGORY | DEFINITION | EXAMPLE |
|---|---|---|
| Synonym (**S**) | The words have a similar meaning. | work : job |
| Antonym (**A**) | The words have opposite meanings. | harsh : gentle |
| Cause / effect (**C / E**) | One word or phrase is the result of another word or phrase. | oil spill : death of penguins |
| Degree (**D**) | One word has a stronger meaning than the other. | damaged : destroyed |

**S** 1. unique : rare = huge : _____
    **a.** fragile      **b.** remote      **c.** vast

2. heavy rain : flood = vast ice fields : _____
    **a.** cooler temperature      **b.** ozone layer      **c.** global warming

3. protected : preserved = surprising : _____
    **a.** temporary      **b.** amazing      **c.** fragile

4. harsh : comfortable = inland : _____
    **a.** coastal      **b.** global      **c.** ocean

5. ice fields : natural air conditioning = government : _____
    **a.** global warming      **b.** protection      **c.** environment

6. consequence : effect = traveler : _____
    **a.** climate      **b.** tourist      **c.** researcher

7. project : work = far : _____
    **a.** harsh      **b.** remote      **c.** coastal

8. careful : controlled : = delicate : _____
    **a.** quiet      **b.** fragile      **c.** unbelievable

9. tourists : trash = scientists : _____
    **a.** research      **b.** environment      **c.** continents

10. inhabit : live = beautiful : _____
    **a.** scenic      **b.** uncrowded      **c.** pleasant

*Think of a place of natural beauty that you have visited. Write sentences using the words in parentheses to describe this place.*

**1.** (harsh) _____

_____

**2.** (scenic) _____

_____

**3.** (temperatures) _____

_____

**4.** (inhabit) _____

_____

**5.** (tourists) _____

_____

**B** **GRAMMAR:** *Because and Even though*

**1** *Look at the sentences. What do they mean?*

- **Because** Antarctica is the center of important scientific research, it must be preserved.
- **Even though** I can appreciate tourists' desire to experience this beautiful landscape, I feel Antarctica should be closed to them.

| BECAUSE AND EVEN THOUGH ||
|---|---|
| **1.** *Because* gives a **reason.** | Antarctica must be preserved **because** it is the center of important scientific research.<br><br>**Because** Antarctica is beautiful, tourists enjoy it. |
| **2.** *Even though* explains an **unexpected result.** It can also express a **contrast,** or difference. (**Although** can be used in a similar way.) | Some researchers in Antarctica do not find answers to their scientific questions **even though** they work very hard. (*unexpected result*)<br><br>**Even though** some people want to visit Antarctica, others do not. (*contrast*). |

**3.** Notice that the sentences above each have a **main clause** and a **dependent clause.** (A main clause can stand alone. A dependent clause cannot.)

The **dependent clauses** begin with *because* or *even though.* Always use a **comma** after the dependent clause when it begins the sentence.

*Homework* (handwritten)

**2** *Join each pair of sentences using* **because** *or* **even though**. *Add a comma when the dependent clause comes before the main clause.*

1. I had to interrupt my research and greet tourists. I was very busy.

   I had to interrupt my research and greet tourists even though I was very busy.

2. I understand why tourists want to see Antarctica. They shouldn't be allowed to visit.

   even thro

3. The earth's temperature is rising. Meteorologists are worried.

   Meteorologists are worried because the earth's temperature is rising

4. Antarctica's unique environment is in danger. There is no government in Antarctica to help preserve it.

   Because

5. Tourists enjoy the beauty of Antarctica. They sometimes damage the environment.

   even though

6. Scientists are interested in protecting Antarctica's natural environment. Tour companies are not.

   even th

7. We had an amazing time on this remote continent. It was difficult to travel in such a harsh environment.

8. Antarctica is unbelievably scenic. Tourists recommend it to their friends.

   Because

**3** *Use your own ideas to complete the sentences using* **because** *or* **even though**. *Circle the appropriate verb form.*

1. I would / wouldn't like to visit Antarctica because I want to help to preserve it.

2. the scientists are _____,

   tourism in Antarctica is a problem.

3. Antarctica should / shouldn't be closed to tourists _____

   _____.

4. I would / wouldn't like to be a scientific researcher in Antarctica _____

   _____.

(handwritten margin notes: aún cuando / a pesar de que)

**92** UNIT 5

In this unit, you read an opinion essay written by a scientist and a travel journal written by a tourist. Now imagine that you are a tourist in Antarctica. What is your opinion about tourism there?

You are going to **write an opinion essay from a tourist's point of view.** You will give reasons why Antarctica should be open to tourism. Use the vocabulary and grammar from the unit.*

### ◀ PREPARE TO WRITE: Listing

**1** *Look back at* "Opinions of the Tourist" *in Step 1, page 88. Copy these opinions here. Add two more of your own opinions to the list.*

1. _____
2. _____
3. _____
4. _____
5. _____
6. _____

**2** *Share your list with a partner. Do you have different opinions? Discuss them.*

### ◀ WRITE: An Opinion Essay

An **essay** is a piece of writing that has more than one or two paragraphs and is organized in a specific way. An **opinion essay** expresses an opinion about something. There are three important parts of a good opinion essay:

**Introductory Paragraph**

- Introduces your topic.
- Includes a thesis statement that states the main idea of the essay (your opinion).

**Body (at least 1 paragraph)**

- Each paragraph of the body has a topic sentence and supporting details. The details can be reasons, facts, examples, and explanations.

**Concluding Paragraph**

- Restates the main idea expressed in your thesis statement.

---

*For Alternative Writing Topics, see page 97. These topics can be used in place of the writing topic for this unit or as homework. The alternative topics relate to the theme of the unit, but may not target the same grammar or rhetorical structures taught in the unit.

**1** *Refer to Reading One to complete the tasks.*

1. Look at the introductory paragraph. Find the thesis statement. Copy it here.

_____

2. Underline the topic sentence of each of the body paragraphs.

3. In paragraphs 2, 3, and 4 what types of supporting details are used (reason, fact, example, or explanation)?

Paragraph 2

_____

Paragraph 3

_____

Paragraph 4

_____

4. Find the concluding sentence that restates the main idea. Write it here.

_____

**2** *You are going to write an opinion essay from a tourist's point of view. Your essay will have four paragraphs: an introductory paragraph, two body paragraphs, and a concluding paragraph. In the body, you will give details to support your opinion. Plan your first draft by completing the outline below.*

**I. Introductory Paragraph**

Thesis statement (your opinion about tourism):

_____

_____

**II. Body Paragraph**

Topic sentence:

_____

Supporting details:

_____

_____

_____

**III. Body Paragraph**

Topic sentence:

_____

Supporting details:

_____

_____

_____

**IV. Concluding Paragraph**

Restatement of thesis (restate your opinion about tourism):

_____

**3** *Use your outline and your notes to write the first draft of your essay.*

◀ **REVISE: Choosing Effective Supporting Details**

The **supporting details** in your body paragraph should help the reader understand your opinion. Effective supporting details may include **reasons, facts, examples,** and **explanations.**

**1** *Read an essay about tourism on Cape Cod. The underlined supporting details in the body are weak because they do not provide reasons, facts, examples, or explanations to support the writer's opinion.*

My family lives on Cape Cod in Massachusetts. Cape Cod is a long piece of land that goes out into the Atlantic Ocean. There are beaches on two sides. It is a beautiful place, but there is too much tourism. I think Cape Cod should be closed to tourists.

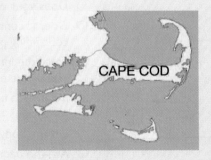

Tourism is hurting Cape Cod in several ways. First, there are not many good jobs for people on Cape Cod. (**a**) <u>The jobs don't pay well</u>. In addition, living on Cape Cod during the summer is very expensive. (**b**) <u>Everything is expensive</u>. Finally, tourists hurt the environment. (**c**) <u>There are too many people</u>.

I would like to live on Cape Cod for the rest of my life. However, I will have to leave if so many tourists visit each summer. That's why I believe that tourism is not good for Cape Cod.

**2** *The supporting details below are stronger because they include more specific information. Work with a partner. Read the details. Decide which details should replace the underlined weak details in the paragraph in Exercise 1. Write the appropriate letter next to each detail.*

_____ 1. About 5.3 million people visit Cape Cod each year. These people bring their cars, so there is a lot of traffic. They walk on the beaches and pollute the ocean.

_____ 2. Most jobs are in hotels, restaurants, or souvenir shops. These jobs have low pay and require very hard work.

_____ 3. The cost of renting or buying a house is very high. Summer houses rent for $800 and up per week, which is too expensive for the average person.

**3** *What kind of supporting details do the new sections contain: reasons, facts, examples, or explanations? Do you think the details are effective? Why or why not?*

**4** *Look back at the first draft of your essay. Are the supporting details effective? Do they include reasons, facts, examples, and explanations that make the ideas clear? If not, make the appropriate revisions.*

◀ **EDIT: Writing the Final Draft**

*Write the final draft of your essay. Carefully edit it for grammatical and mechanical errors, such as spelling, capitalization, and punctuation. Make sure you used some of the vocabulary and grammar from the unit. Use the checklist to help you write your final draft. Then neatly write or type your essay.*

---

### ✓ FINAL DRAFT CHECKLIST

- ○ Does your essay express your opinion about how tourism can help Antarctica?
- ○ Does it contain an introductory paragraph, two body paragraphs, and a concluding paragraph?
- ○ Does the introductory paragraph contain a thesis statement stating the main idea of the essay?
- ○ Does each body paragraph contain a topic sentence stating the main idea of the paragraph?
- ○ Do the body paragraphs contain at least two details supporting your opinion?
- ○ Are the details supported with effective reasons, facts, examples, or explanations?
- ○ Does the concluding paragraph restate the main idea expressed in the thesis statement?
- ○ Are the *because* and *even though* clauses used correctly?
- ○ Do these clauses have the correct punctuation?
- ○ Did you use vocabulary from the unit?

# ALTERNATIVE WRITING TOPICS

*Write about one of the topics. Use the vocabulary and grammar from the unit.*

1. What are the advantages and disadvantages of living in a remote area? Would you like to live in a remote area? Why or why not? Write an essay explaining your opinion.

2. With all the human suffering in the world, is it still important to protect plants and animals? Why? Write an essay giving your opinion about this topic.

## RESEARCH TOPICS, see page 213.

# The Metamorphosis

# ①FOCUS ON THE TOPIC

## A PREDICT

1. Look at the photograph of the cockroach. Work in a small group. Write as many adjectives as you can to describe the cockroach and your feelings about it.

2. Read the title of the unit. *Metamorphosis* means a process in which something changes completely into something else. What do you think this unit will be about?

99

*Work in a small group. Discuss the questions.*

1. What kinds of insects are you afraid of? What kinds of insects do you like?

2. Have you ever had a bad dream about an insect? Explain.

3. Do you know of any insects that people like to eat? Which ones?

4. Movies about insects have been successful. Why do you think people like this type of movie?

**1** *Read about Franz Kafka, the author of the story in Reading One. Pay special attention to the boldfaced vocabulary.*

**F**RANZ KAFKA was born in 1883 in the Czech city of Prague (then belonging to Austria) to a German-speaking Jewish family. He was the only son, and he had three younger sisters. His father was a large, strong, **brave** man with a powerful personality. His mother was quieter. She was a thinker. Franz was like his mother. He was also a thinker.

Franz was very small, skinny, and had a weak personality. When the family cook walked him to school each day (other children walked to school by themselves), the other boys teased him. After school, he liked to run with the older boys to show that he was strong. When the older boys got into fights with other boys, he got **beat up** and went home crying.

Franz was **terrified** of his father. Once, when he was three or four years old, he had gone to bed and could hear his mother and father talking in the next room. He called out for a glass of water. His father yelled at him to be quiet. When Franz yelled for water again and again, his father became angry. He ran into Franz's room, **grabbed** him out of bed, and locked him outside in the dark. Franz never forgot how very afraid he was alone in the dark.

Franz Kafka studied law in Prague, and, in 1908, started to support himself as a clerk in an insurance company. Later he found an even better job and was well-liked. He wrote "The Metamorphosis" in 1912. Even though he was constantly getting promoted in his company and **managed to** get two novels published in his lifetime, he always felt that he was a disappointment to his father.

In 1917, he became sick with tuberculosis, a **disgusting** disease. He often coughed up a bloody, **smelly substance**. Because of this, Kafka had to often live in hospitals throughout Europe in order to **soothe** his lungs. In 1921, he saw a man dying from tuberculosis and was very frightened. He started to **faint** and ran out of the room. Although he was engaged many times, he never got married because he thought he would be a **useless** husband. In 1924, at the age of 40, he finally died of tuberculosis. We now **realize** that Kafka is one of the greatest German writers.

**2** *Match the words on the left with the definitions on the right.*

\_\_\_\_\_ 1. **brave**        **a.** to take something quickly and roughly

\_\_\_\_\_ 2. **beat up**      **b.** not afraid of danger

\_\_\_\_\_ 3. **terrified**    **c.** to relieve

\_\_\_\_\_ 4. **grab**         **d.** to succeed in doing something difficult

\_\_\_\_\_ 5. **manage to**    **e.** anything one can touch

\_\_\_\_\_ 6. **disgusting**   **f.** to hit repeatedly

\_\_\_\_\_ 7. **smelly**       **g.** to lose consciousness, as if you were asleep

\_\_\_\_\_ 8. **substance**    **h.** very afraid

\_\_\_\_\_ 9. **soothe**       **i.** not working well or of no use

\_\_\_\_\_ 10. **faint**       **j.** strongly disliked

\_\_\_\_\_ 11. **useless**     **k.** to start to know something you had not noticed before

\_\_\_\_\_ 12. **realize**     **l.** having a bad odor

# ②FOCUS ON READING

## A READING ONE: The Metamorphosis

*This paragraph is from the story you are going to read. Read it. Then answer the questions on the next page.*

Well, it was time to get up. Surely, as soon as he got out of bed, he would realize this had all been a bad dream. He tried to move his back part out first, but it moved so slowly, and he had a hard time. His thin little legs seemed useless, just moving and moving in the air, not helping him at all. Then he tried the front part. This worked better, but he still couldn't move enough to get out of bed. He began rocking back and forth, stronger and more intensely, and finally threw himself onto the floor, hitting his head as he fell.

1. Something has happened to this man. Why is it so hard for him to get out of bed?

_____

_____

_____

2. What does this sentence mean: "Surely, as soon as he got out of bed, he would realize this had all been a bad dream"?

_____

_____

_____

3. What do you think the rest of the story will be about?

_____

_____

_____

*Now read the story.*

# THE METAMORPHOSIS

## FRANZ KAFKA

1    One morning, Gregor Samsa woke up from a bad dream and **realized** he was some kind of terrible insect. He was a cockroach, and he was as large as a man! Lying on his back, he could see his large brown belly and thin legs. He tried to turn over onto his side, but every time he tried, he would roll onto his back again.

2    He began to think about his job as a traveling salesman. He hated his job, but he had to do it to support his father, mother, and sister because his father no longer worked. He looked at the clock and realized he had overslept—it was 6:30! He was late. The next train left at 7:00. He would have to hurry to make it. A few minutes later his mother yelled to him: "It's 6:45. You're late. Get up!" When he answered her, he was surprised to hear his voice; it sounded so high. "Yes, mother. I'm getting up now." His sister now whispered through the door, "Gregor, are you all right? Do you need anything?"

3    Well, it was time to get up. Surely, as soon as he got out of bed, he would realize this had all been a bad dream. He tried to move his back part out first, but it moved so slowly, and he had a hard time. His thin little legs seemed **useless**, just moving and moving in the air, not helping him at all. Then he tried the front part. This worked

better, but he still couldn't move enough to get out of bed. He began rocking back and forth, stronger and more intensely, and finally threw himself onto the floor, hitting his head as he fell.

4    All of a sudden, he heard a knock at the door. It was his manager, who had come to see why he was late. "Oh," thought Gregor, "I hate my job." Then the manager spoke. "Mr. Samsa, I must warn you that you could lose your job because of this. Lately, your work has not been very good, and now I find you in bed when you should be at work!" Gregor panicked and said, "No, no, I will come out immediately. I was sick, but now I feel much better." The manager and Gregor's family did not understand a single word he said, for his speech was now the hiss of an insect. As he talked, he managed to move himself to the chest of drawers, tried to stand up, then slipped and fell, holding tightly to a chair with his thin legs. He finally **managed to** open the door to talk to his manager.

5    At the sight of him, the manager screamed, his mother **fainted**, and his father wept. The manager was **terrified**. He began to back out of the room to leave, and Gregor realized he couldn't let him go. He let go of the door and dropped into the living room on his tiny little legs. His mother, who had just opened her eyes, screamed, while the manager disappeared out the door. His father quickly **grabbed** a walking stick and a newspaper and began to **beat up** Gregor so he would go back into his room. Once Gregor was inside, the door was locked from the outside.

6    Gregor awoke as it was getting dark. He smelled food and saw that his sister, Grete, had left him one of his favorite meals, a bowl of milk with bread in it. But, when he tasted it, it was **disgusting**, and he turned away. He slid under the couch and slept there until morning.

7    The next morning, Gregor's sister looked in and was surprised to see that he hadn't eaten a thing. She picked up the bowl and soon returned with some old vegetables, bones, and **smelly** cheese, which she offered to him. After she left, Gregor hungrily ate them all up. And so the days passed, for she was the only one **brave** enough to come into the room.

8    Gregor grew tired of being in the bedroom day and night, and soon took to walking back and forth across the walls and ceiling. It felt much better than walking on the floor. His sister noticed this because of the brown sticky **substance** left from his feet wherever he walked. She decided to move most of the furniture out of the room to make more walking space for Gregor. But Gregor wanted to keep a picture on the wall—a picture of a beautiful woman dressed in pretty clothes. While Grete and her mother were in the other room, he quickly climbed the wall and pressed himself against the picture to stop them from taking it. When his mother saw him, she screamed and fainted. His sister then became very angry with him. He followed her into the dining room to help her, but this frightened her. When his father returned home and learned what had happened, he became very angry. Gregor tried to return to his bedroom to get away from his father, but was unsuccessful. He couldn't fit through the doorway. Suddenly, his father started throwing apples at him. The first few didn't hurt him, but then one pierced his body, and he felt terrible pain. His mother rushed over to his father to beg him not to kill Gregor, as Gregor slowly crawled back to his room.

9    The apple remained in Gregor's back and stopped him from being able to walk easily. This gave him great pain. His sister also began to care less and less about feeding him

*(continued on next page)*

and cleaning his room. Well, he wasn't very hungry anyway. He was just weary. The dust and dirt gradually became thick on the floor and stuck to him whenever he moved.

10    The family now left his door to the dining room open for two hours every night after dinner, and he could listen to their conversation. He really loved this. When he listened to them, he could escape from his pain. One night, they forgot to lock Gregor's door. When his sister began to play the violin, which she had not done for a long time, he felt so good. The music was beautiful and **soothed** him. He had begun to walk toward her to tell her how wonderful it was, when his family saw him. The music suddenly stopped. Grete became very upset. "Momma, Poppa," she said, "This cannot go on. We must find a way to get rid of this thing. It is destroying our lives."

11    Gregor slowly crawled back to his room. He lay there in the dark and couldn't move. Even the place in his back where the apple was no longer hurt. He thought of his family tenderly as he lay there, and, when the light began to come through the window, he died.

12    When Gregor was found dead the next morning, the whole family seemed to feel relieved. For the first time in a long, long time, they went out and took a train ride to the country, making plans for the future.

_____

*Source:* Abridged from "The Metamorphosis," by Franz Kafka (1883–1924).

## ◖ READ FOR MAIN IDEAS

*Read the main ideas listed below. They are all false. Rewrite each main idea so that it correctly describes the story.*

1. Gregor dreams he has become an insect.

   _____

2. His family thinks it's funny when they see Gregor.

   _____

3. Only his mother takes care of him, and she eventually stops.

   _____

4. He dies in the living room as he thinks of his job.

   _____

5. His family feels helpless when he dies.

   _____

*To **paraphrase** a sentence means to say it in a different way, using your own words. The sentences below are paraphrases of sentences in the story. Write the exact sentence from the story that has the same meaning as each paraphrase.*

1. His sister wanted to know if he was OK.

   His sister now whispered through the door, "Gregor, are you all right?
   Do you need anything?"

2. Because he was very afraid, he promised to come out of his room quickly.

3. The manager felt afraid and tried to leave carefully, and Gregor knew he must stop him.

4. He moved easily and quietly under the sofa and stayed there until the next day.

5. His sister was amazed early the next day when she noticed he had not touched his food.

6. At first they didn't hurt him, but then one cut into him and hurt him badly.

7. Gradually, his sister lost interest in taking care of him.

8. It was time to think of how to remove him.

# ◖ MAKE INFERENCES

*Write **T** (true) or **F** (false) for each statement. If you write **T**, find an example in the text to support the statement, and write it on the line. Discuss your answers with a partner.*

_____ 1. In the beginning of the story, Grete loved her brother and cared about him.

_____

_____ 2. Gregor wanted to be an insect so that he wouldn't have to go to work.

_____

_____ 3. Gregor's family was afraid of him.

_____

_____ 4. Gregor was very lonely.

_____

_____ 5. Grete stopped thinking of Gregor as a person and thought of him only as a disgusting cockroach.

_____

# ◖ EXPRESS OPINIONS

*Write answers to the questions below on a separate piece of paper. Then discuss your answers with the class.*

1. Why do you think Kafka chose to have Gregor turn into a cockroach? Why not an animal?

2. What kind of relationship does Gregor have with his family? How does that affect Gregor's feelings about himself?

3. What is your opinion of Gregor at the end of the story? Do you see him the same way his family does?

4. What is your opinion of Gregor's family at the end of the story?

## Ⓑ READING TWO: Ungeziefer

**1** *Many critics[1] have studied Kafka's stories. Read what one critic wrote about "The Metamorphosis." Think about what Kafka was trying to say in his story.*

---

[1] **critics:** people who give opinions about the quality of things, especially the arts, such as paintings, literature, and music

# UNGEZIEFER

1    "The Metamorphosis" is a short story which is both funny and sad at the same time. It is funny because of how Gregor must learn to move his new "cockroach" legs and body. On the other hand, it is sad because he loses the love of his family as a result of his becoming so disgusting.

2    Why did Kafka choose to tell a story about a man who turns into a cockroach? Certainly many people are afraid—even terrified—of cockroaches and other insects. They think cockroaches are ugly and disgusting. Why would Kafka choose something that most of us hate? What was his purpose?

3    One explanation comes from a word that Kafka used in his story. Kafka wrote his story in German, and he used the German word *ungeziefer*, or vermin,[1] which can be used to mean a person who is rough and disgusting. In English, we do the same thing. If we call a person a "cockroach," we mean that the person is weak and cowardly.[2] Gregor, the man, is like a cockroach. He is weak and disgusting. Why? Because he doesn't want to be the supporter of his family. He hates his job and wishes he didn't have to do it in order to pay off the family debt. In addition, his family has been like a parasite[3] to him.

Gregor's family members have all enjoyed relaxing, not working, while he alone has had to work. When he becomes a cockroach, he becomes the parasite to the family. So Gregor's true self is metamorphosed into an insect because his true self wants to be like a child again, helpless and having no responsibility.

4    Another explanation comes from Kafka's relationship with his father. Kafka was a small, quiet man. He saw himself as weak and spineless[4] compared to his father, who was physically large and had a powerful personality. It is the same with Gregor. He also sees himself as a failure. By turning himself into an insect, Gregor is able to rebel against his father and, at the same time, punish himself for rebelling. This punishment results in his being physically and emotionally separated from his family with no hope of joining them again, and finally he dies.

5    Kafka's choice of an insect makes this story work because many people feel insects are disgusting. Gregor becomes the vermin, the disgusting son that nobody cares about. His family rejects him because of his appearance, yet he continues to love them to the end.

---

[1] **vermin:** small, wild animals, like rats, that can carry diseases and are difficult to control
[2] **cowardly:** afraid, easily frightened
[3] **parasite:** an animal or plant that lives in or on another animal or plant and gets its food from it
[4] **spineless:** not brave at all

**2**  *Answer the questions. Then share your answers with a partner.*

1. Does the critic think this is a funny story, a sad story, or a happy story? Explain.

_____

_____

2. What does *ungeziefer* mean?

_____

◀ **STEP 1: Organize**

*Look at the key points made by the critic. Find examples of those points in Reading One and complete the chart with one or two examples from the story.*

| R2: CRITIC'S INTERPRETATION OF "THE METAMORPHOSIS" | R1: DETAILS FROM "THE METAMORPHOSIS" |
|---|---|
| **1.** The story is funny. | At the sight of him, the manager screamed, his mother fainted, and his father wept. |
| **2.** The story is sad. | |
| **3.** Gregor wants to be a child again. | |
| **4.** Gregor is weak and disgusting. | |
| **5.** Gregor's family has been like a parasite to him. | |
| **6.** Gregor wants to punish his family. | |
| **7.** Gregor loves his family. | |

# ◖ STEP 2: Synthesize

*Write an interview with the critic. Find out why he interprets "The Metamorphosis" the way he does. Fill in the questions and answers. Use your work from Step 1.*

INTERVIEWER: Why do you think that "The Metamorphosis" is funny?

CRITIC: _Well, for example, when Gregor opened his bedroom door, the manager screamed, his mother fainted, and his father wept._

INTERVIEWER: Do you think "The Metamorphosis" is also sad?

CRITIC: _____

_____

INTERVIEWER: Can you tell me what you think of Gregor?

CRITIC: _____

_____

INTERVIEWER: _____?

CRITIC: _____

_____

INTERVIEWER: _____?

CRITIC: _____

_____

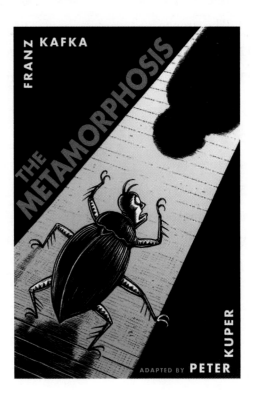

# 3 FOCUS ON WRITING

## A VOCABULARY

### ◖ REVIEW

**1** Complete the crossword puzzle on the next page. Read the clues below and choose words from the box.

| | | |
|---|---|---|
| beat | grab | soothed |
| ~~brave~~ | managed to | substance |
| cockroach | realize | terrified |
| disgusting | smelly | useless |
| faint | | |

**Across**

1. I think that people who are not afraid of snakes are very _____.

3. The insect _____ crawl up the wall.

7. The man was _____ by the soft music.

8. She's sick and she looks like she's going to _____.

10. The strange _____ was green and sticky, and it smelled sweet.

12. His father _____ Gregor back into his bedroom.

13. His feet were _____ after being in shoes all day.

**Down**

2. It was a shock to _____ that he was a cockroach.

4. Hurry up! _____ your coat and let's go.

5. The food he was eating was _____.

6. The most disgusting insect is a _____.

9. She was _____ when she saw the cockroach.

11. Gregor's legs were _____; he couldn't stand up.

## ◖ EXPAND

**1** *Look at the pairs of sentences from "The Metamorphosis." What do you notice about the relationship between the boldfaced words in each pair?*

1. **a.** He **began** to think about his job as a traveling salesman.
   **b.** He **started** to think about his job as a traveling salesman.

2. **a.** He hated his **job**, but he had to do it to support his father, mother, and sister because his father no longer worked.
   **b.** He hated his **work**, but he had to do it to support his father, mother, and sister because his father no longer worked.

> The pairs of boldfaced words above are called **synonyms** because they have a similar meaning. A synonym might also give a more specific or precise meaning of a word. For example, *knocking on the door* is more specific than *hitting the door*.

**2** *Compare sentence **b** with sentence **a** in each pair of sentences. How does the meaning change when you replace the boldfaced word in **a** with a synonym? Circle your opinion about the new meaning for each pair of sentences. Then discuss the variation in meanings with the class.*

1. **a.** One morning, Gregor Samsa woke up from a bad dream and **realized** he was some kind of terrible insect.
   **b.** One morning, Gregor Samsa woke up from a bad dream and **understood** he was some kind of terrible insect.

   **New meaning:** Similar / (More General) / More Specific

2. **a.** **Surely**, as soon as he got out of bed, he would realize this had all been a bad dream.
   **b.** **Certainly**, as soon as he got out of bed, he would realize this had all been a bad dream.

   **New meaning:** Similar / More General / More Specific

3. **a.** All of a sudden, he heard a **knock** at the door.
   **b.** All of a sudden, he heard a **tap** at the door.

   **New meaning:** Similar / More General / More Specific

4. **a.** The manager and Gregor's family did not **understand** a single word he said, for his speech was now the hiss of an insect.
   **b.** The manager and Gregor's family did not **comprehend** a single word he said, for his speech was now the hiss of an insect.

   **New meaning:** Similar / More General / More Specific

5. **a.** At the sight of him, the manager screamed, his mother fainted, and his father **wept**.
   **b.** At the sight of him, the manager screamed, his mother fainted, and his father **cried**.

   **New meaning:** Similar / More General / More Specific

6. **a.** But, when he tasted it, it tasted **terrible**, and he turned away in disgust.
   **b.** But, when he tasted it, it tasted **awful**, and he turned away in disgust.

   **New meaning:** Similar / More General / More Specific

7. **a.** She picked up the bowl and soon returned with some old vegetables, bones, and **smelly** cheese, which she offered to him.
   **b.** She picked up the bowl and soon returned with some old vegetables, bones, and **stinky** cheese, which she offered to him.

   **New meaning:** Similar / More General / More Specific

8. **a.** The first few didn't hurt him, but then one **pierced** his body, and he felt terrible pain.
   **b.** The first few didn't hurt him, but then one **entered** his body, and he felt terrible pain.

   **New meaning:** Similar / More General / More Specific

Write a paragraph about an insect you have seen. Use at least five of these words in your paragraph. You may change the form of the word.

| | | | | |
|---|---|---|---|---|
| awful | certainly | disgusting | manage to | stinky |
| beat | cockroach | faint | realize | substance |
| brave | cried | grab | soothe | useless |

_____

_____

_____

_____

_____

_____

## B GRAMMAR: Infinitives of Purpose

**1** Read the sentences. Underline the verbs that have the form **to + verb**. What questions do these verbs answer?

- Gregor worked to support his family.
- His sister whispered to him to ask if he was all right.
- He rocked back and forth to get out of bed.

### INFINITIVES OF PURPOSE

| Questions | Answers |
|---|---|
| **Why** did Gregor work? | He had **to support** his family. |
| **Why** did his sister whisper to him? | She wanted **to ask** if he was all right. |
| **Why** did he rock back and forth? | He rocked back and forth **to get out** of bed. |
| I. Infinitives (**to + verb**) that are used to explain the purpose of an action are called **infinitives of purpose**. They answer the question **"Why?"** | Gregor worked **to support** his family.<br><br>His sister whispered to him **to ask** if he was all right. |
| 2. You can also use the longer form *in order to + verb*. | Gregor worked **in order to support** his family.<br><br>His sister whispered to him **in order to ask** if he was all right. |

**2** *Match the questions on the left with the answers on the right.*

**Questions**

_d_ **1.** Why did Gregor's manager come to his house?

____ **2.** Why was Gregor locked in his room?

____ **3.** Why did his father grab a walking stick and a newspaper?

____ **4.** Why did Grete go into Gregor's room every day?

____ **5.** Why did Gregor follow Grete into the dining room?

____ **6.** Why did Gregor come out of his room?

____ **7.** Why did his family take a train ride?

**Answers**

**a.** She needed to feed him.

**b.** He wanted to listen to the music.

**c.** He wanted to help her.

**d.** He wanted to see why Gregor was late.

**e.** They wanted to celebrate his death.

**f.** His family wanted to keep him there.

**g.** He wanted to beat Gregor.

**3** *Combine the questions and answers (from the previous activity) to make sentences that answer the question "Why"?*

**1.** Gregor's manager came to his house to see why he was late.

**2.** _____

**3.** _____

**4.** _____

**5.** _____

**6.** _____

**7.** _____

## C WRITING

In this unit, you have read a story with a moral and a critical essay about the story.

Now you are going to **write a story about insects or animals.** Use a story from your home country, or use your imagination and make up your own story. Use the vocabulary and grammar from the unit.*

---

*For Alternative Writing Topics, see page 119. These topics can be used in place of the writing topic for this unit or as homework. The alternative topics relate to the theme of the unit, but may not target the same grammar or rhetorical structures taught in the unit.

# ◖ PREPARE TO WRITE: Answering *Wh-* Questions

**1** *Think of a story from your home country about insects or animals, or make up your own story. You learned in Unit 3 about the 5Ws:* **who, what, when, where,** *and* **why** *or* **how**. *Now answer each of those questions about your story.*

1. **Who** is the story about? _____

2. **What** is the story about? _____

3. **When** did the story take place? _____

4. **Where** did the story take place? _____

5. **Why** or **How** did the story happen? _____

**2** *Share your answers with a partner.*

# ◖ WRITE: A Story with a Moral

Most folktales have a **moral**, or a **practical lesson**, that can be learned from them. All the characters and events lead the reader to one main point—the moral at the end of the story.

**1** *Read "The Ant and the Chrysalis," a story from Aesop's Fables.*

> ### *The Ant and the Chrysalis*
>
> One day, an Ant was walking in the forest, looking for food. He found a Chrysalis on the ground. The Ant didn't know what it was. Then the Chrysalis moved slightly, and the Ant realized the Chrysalis was alive. "Poor animal!" said the Ant. "I can run across the ground and climb the highest tree," he boasted, "I am free to do what I want, but you cannot move!" The Ant continued, "Poor, poor animal. I feel so sorry for you." The Chrysalis could hear what the Ant was saying, but he did not answer.
>
> A few days later, the Ant returned to see the Chrysalis again. However, he found only the shell of the Chrysalis. The Ant wondered what had happened. Suddenly, he felt something above him. He looked up and saw a beautiful Butterfly. "Look at me," said the Butterfly, "I'm not a Chrysalis anymore! Now tell me about your freedom—if you can catch me!" The Butterfly flew high into the air. The Ant never saw the Butterfly again.

*Now, in a small group, discuss the meaning of the story. Put a check (✓) next to the moral that you think best explains the practical lesson of the story.*

_____ 1. Don't judge people by how they look.

_____ 2. Don't boast about how great you are.

_____ 3. Don't feel sorry for other people.

**2** Read the beginning of "The Ant and the Dove," another story from Aesop's Fables. Then read the moral of the story. With a partner, write a few sentences to complete the story. Make sure the ending leads to the moral. When you have finished, compare endings with the class.

---

### The Ant and the Dove

Once upon a time, an Ant went to the river to get a drink. When he leaned over the water, he fell in. The Ant couldn't swim and was about to drown. A Dove was sitting in a tree over the river. He saw the Ant in trouble and wanted to help. He picked off a leaf and dropped it in the water near the Ant. The Ant climbed onto the leaf and floated safely to land again. The Ant said, "Thank you, Dove. I am just a small ant. What can I ever do to repay you?" The Dove replied, "Don't worry, little friend. Your thanks is enough."

A short time later, the Ant saw a Hunter. The Hunter stopped under the tree and pointed his gun at the Dove. The Ant realized that the Hunter was going to kill the Dove. So the Ant _____

_____

_____

_____

_____

---

**Moral:** If you help someone, that person will help you in return.

**3** An ant is the main character in both stories. Write the answers to these questions, then share your answers with a classmate.

   1. How is the ant's character different in the two stories?

   2. Why did the writer choose an ant as a character for the stories? Could a different insect or animal be used? Why or why not?

**4** You are going to write your story using information from the five Wh- questions. Begin your story with one of the phrases commonly used to start a folktale: Once upon a time, One day, or A long time ago. Write the moral at the end of the story. Plan your first draft by completing this outline.

   1. Write the opening sentence of your story.

   _____

   _____

**2.** In one to three paragraphs, answer the five *Wh-* questions and tell the story.

_____

_____

_____

_____

_____

_____

_____

**3.** End your story with a moral.

_____

_____

**5** Use your outline and your notes from Prepare to Write, page 115, to write the first draft of your story.

◀ **REVISE: Adding Detail**

> When you write, think about how to **make the writing more interesting** and alive by **adding adjectives and adverbs**. Remember that adding adjectives and adverbs can grab the reader's attention and make them want to read the rest of the story.
>
> - **Sentence:** One morning, Gregor Samsa woke up from a dream and realized he was some kind of insect.
> - **Problem:** This could be more interesting.
> - **Revised Sentence:** One morning, Gregor Samsa woke up from a *bad* dream and realized he was some kind of *terrible* insect.

In the following sentences, **adjectives and adverbs are added** to make the story more real and interesting.

**1.** Add **adjectives** to describe the nouns.

Example

- Lying on his back, he could see his belly and legs.
- Lying on his back, he could see his *large brown* belly and *thin* legs.

**2.** Add **adverbs** to describe the verbs.

Example

- After she left, Gregor ate them all up.
- After she left, Gregor *hungrily* ate them all up.

**1** Read the paragraph and notice the underlined words. Use the adjectives from the box to make the underlined words more interesting.

| | | | |
|---|---|---|---|
| breathtaking | delicate | ~~fine~~ | small |
| clear | fantastic | little | ugly |
| curious | | | |

## The Ant and the Chrysalis

One ___fine___ day, a _____ Ant was walking in the forest, looking
for food. He found a _____ Chrysalis on the ground. The _____
Ant didn't know what it was. Then the Chrysalis moved slightly, and the
Ant realized the Chrysalis was alive. "Poor _____ animal!" said the
Ant. "I can run across the ground and climb the highest tree," he boasted,
"I am free to do what I want, but you cannot move!" The Ant continued,
"Poor, poor animal. I feel so sorry for you." The Chrysalis could hear what
the Ant was saying, but he did not answer.

A few days later, the Ant returned to see the Chrysalis again. However,
he found only the _____ shell of the Chrysalis. The Ant wondered what
had happened. Suddenly, he felt something above him. He looked up and
saw a beautiful Butterfly. "Look at me," said the _____ Butterfly, "I'm
not a Chrysalis anymore! Now tell me about your _____ freedom—if
you can catch me!" The Butterfly flew high into the _____ air. The Ant
never saw the Butterfly again.

**2** Look back at the first draft of your story. Are there any words that might be made more interesting by adding an adjective or an adverb? Underline anything that could be made more interesting and add some adjectives or adverbs.

# ◀ EDIT: Writing the Final Draft

*Write the final draft of your story. Carefully edit it for grammatical and mechanical errors, such as spelling, capitalization, and punctuation. Make sure you used some of the vocabulary and grammar from the unit. Use the checklist to help you write your final draft. Then neatly write or type your story.*

## ✓ FINAL DRAFT CHECKLIST

- ○ Did you begin your story with one of the phrases commonly used to start a folktale?
- ○ Did you answer the 5Ws?
- ○ Are there supporting details?
- ○ Are there examples or explanations to support the details?
- ○ Does your story have a moral at the end?
- ○ Did you add adjectives and adverbs to make the story more interesting?
- ○ Did you use examples of infinitives of purpose?
- ○ Did you use vocabulary from the unit?

## ALTERNATIVE WRITING TOPICS

*Write about one of the topics. Use the vocabulary and grammar from the unit.*

1. Write an e-mail to a friend explaining your reaction to "The Metamorphosis." Did you like the story or not? Why? Which character in the story was the most interesting to you? Why?

2. Horror movies are very popular. Write a report explaining why you think people like to watch them. Include some examples of popular horror movies.

## RESEARCH TOPICS, see page 214.

# The Choice to Be Amish

## 1 FOCUS ON THE TOPIC

### A PREDICT

**1** Work in a small group. Look at the photograph. When do you think this photograph was taken? Check (✓) the correct answer.

_____ **a.** 2008        _____ **c.** 1907

__✓__ **b.** 1970        _____ **d.** 1870

Discuss the reasons for your choice.

**2** Why do you think the driver is using a horse and buggy instead of a car? Check (✓) your answer.

_____ **a.** He enjoys using a horse and buggy.

✗ **b.** This is part of his religion.

_____ **c.** He can't afford to drive a car.

_____ **d.** He is in the tourist business.

*Discuss the reasons for your choice.*

## B SHARE INFORMATION

*Work in a small group. Look at the items that are part of life in the modern world. Which items are most important to you? Rank each item from 1 to 10 (1 = really don't need it; 10 = definitely need it every day).*

**9** **a.** car
**7** **d.** television
**3** **g.** dryer

**8** **b.** phone
**5** **e.** microwave oven
**1** **h.** dishwasher

**10** **c.** computer
**4** **f.** washing machine
**6** **i.** electric lights

*Compare your rankings. Discuss your reasons for each ranking.*

## C BACKGROUND AND VOCABULARY

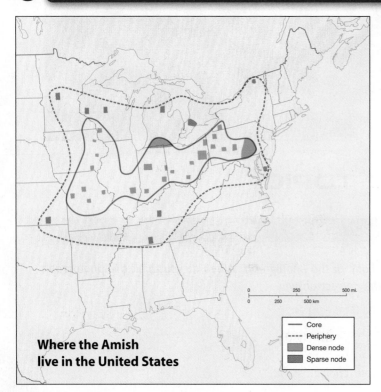

**Where the Amish live in the United States**

Core
Periphery
Dense node
Sparse node

**The Amish** people are Christians who live in the United States and Canada. They came from Europe in the early eighteenth century because they were looking for religious freedom. They still believe in a simple life focused on family, work, and religion. Today, most Amish avoid using modern technology such as cars.

*Source:* From *Homelands: A Geography of Culture and Place Across America* by Richard L. Nostrand and Lawrence E. Estaville. Copyright © 2002 by The Johns Hopkins University Press. Reprinted by permission of The Johns Hopkins University Press.

**1** *Look at the map showing the area of the United States where the Amish live today. Read the timeline. Pay attention to the boldfaced words.*

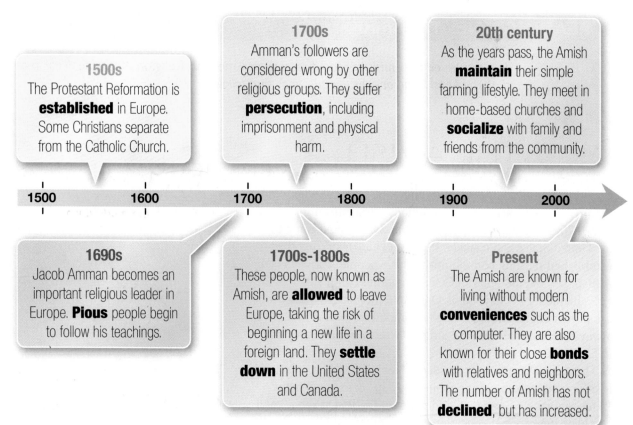

**1500s**
The Protestant Reformation is **established** in Europe. Some Christians separate from the Catholic Church.

**1700s**
Amman's followers are considered wrong by other religious groups. They suffer **persecution**, including imprisonment and physical harm.

**20th century**
As the years pass, the Amish **maintain** their simple farming lifestyle. They meet in home-based churches and **socialize** with family and friends from the community.

1500   1600   1700   1800   1900   2000

**1690s**
Jacob Amman becomes an important religious leader in Europe. **Pious** people begin to follow his teachings.

**1700s-1800s**
These people, now known as Amish, are **allowed** to leave Europe, taking the risk of beginning a new life in a foreign land. They **settle down** in the United States and Canada.

**Present**
The Amish are known for living without modern **conveniences** such as the computer. They are also known for their close **bonds** with relatives and neighbors. The number of Amish has not **declined**, but has increased.

**2** *Match the words on the left with the definitions on the right.*

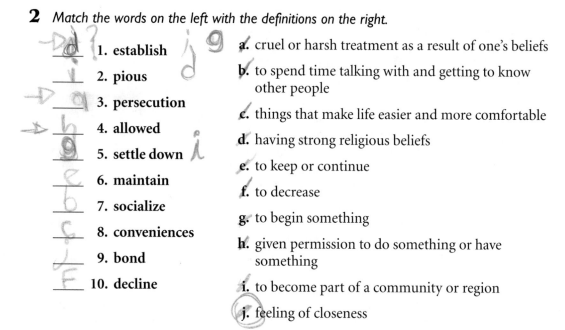

_____ 1. establish
_____ 2. pious
_____ 3. persecution
_____ 4. allowed
_____ 5. settle down
_____ 6. maintain
_____ 7. socialize
_____ 8. conveniences
_____ 9. bond
_____ 10. decline

a. cruel or harsh treatment as a result of one's beliefs
b. to spend time talking with and getting to know other people
c. things that make life easier and more comfortable
d. having strong religious beliefs
e. to keep or continue
f. to decrease
g. to begin something
h. given permission to do something or have something
i. to become part of a community or region
j. feeling of closeness

The Choice to Be Amish   **123**

# ② FOCUS ON READING

## Ⓐ READING ONE: The Amish

*Two articles on the Amish appeared recently in* American Religion *magazine. First, read the "The Amish" and answer the questions that follow.*

# THE AMISH

1   North America is a land of immigrants, many of whom left their home countries to escape religious **persecution**. In the early 1700s, a group of Christians from Switzerland came to the United States and Canada. **Pious** and hard-working, they **established** farming communities. These people, known as the Amish, still live in Ontario, Canada, and in several states in the U.S., including Pennsylvania, Ohio, and Indiana. Avoiding the use of modern technology such as computers, their goal has always been to **maintain** the simple farming life that they had in Europe.

2   The Amish people are considered "reclusives" because they live separately from other people. They speak Pennsylvania Dutch, a form of German. Children learn English at school and complete their formal education by the end of the 8th grade. Because the Amish have traditionally worked on family farms, they see no need for higher learning. Working on farms and small family-owned businesses allows fathers, mothers, and children to remain together all day. Men dress in dark suits and wear full beards, while women wear plain long dresses and head coverings. The Amish work hard on their farms without using modern farm equipment or electricity. They normally do not drive cars or keep telephones in their homes. While the Amish pay taxes, they neither vote nor serve in the military.

3   As farming has **declined** in the United States, more Amish have recently entered the outside world as factory and restaurant workers. This means that more young people are spending time away from the Amish community and becoming familiar with the "English" way of life. While Amish people still use the horse and buggy in their daily lives, many learn about the outside world through contact with car and taxi drivers who are hired to provide them with transportation. One Amish woman, Ruth Irene Garrett, left her community to

## A DECISION TO LEAVE

1   It is estimated that 80–90% of Amish youth in *rumspringa* decide to stay in their Amish communities. Isaac Schlabach is a young man who represents the 10–20% of Amish youth who decide to join the outside world. As a boy growing up on an Amish farm, Isaac became determined not to live as his parents did, struggling all day with labor and chores for very little financial reward. Two weeks before his baptism, which would mark his commitment to the Amish way of life, he decided to leave his family and friends for an uncertain life in the outside world. His older brother had already left, and Isaac knew that he would face a lifetime of regret if he did not try, at least once, to see what life was like in the world of television, cars, and computers. In the back of his mind, Isaac was secure in the knowledge that if he wanted to return to the farm, there would always be a place for him.

2   He left a simple note for his parents, wishing to avoid their shock and tears. His parents soon followed him to Ohio, where they

marry her family's driver. In her book *Crossing Over* she describes how difficult it was to leave her family and friends. After Garrett left her community, family and friends stayed away from her. Because the Amish have a custom of *shunning*, or staying away from, people who leave the Amish way of life, the choice to leave means losing the opportunity to stay in touch with family and friends.

4  One very important Amish custom is adult baptism. Through baptism, a person becomes a full member of the Amish church and is expected to follow all church rules. The period before baptism is known as *rumspringa*, which can be translated as "running around." At age 16, young people are **allowed** to leave their parents' homes and meet together in youth groups for singing and playing games. In some communities, young people are allowed to attend parties, drive cars, and **socialize** in the outside world. Most Amish youth in rumspringa decide to join the Amish church, **settle down**, marry and raise families. However, some choose to live in the outside world, a decision which usually leads to a permanent separation from their Amish family and friends. It is estimated that 80–90% of Amish youth decide to remain within their communities. The **bonds** of family and religion are very strong. According to Dr. Donald Kraybill, author of *The Riddle of Amish Culture*, the Amish way of life meets important social and psychological needs, providing its members with "identity, meaning, and belonging."

5  Those who consider leaving the Amish community face a very difficult decision: leaving their family and friends to join the modern world with all its **conveniences** and opportunities. Joe Keim, the oldest of 14 children, left the Amish as a young man. Since leaving, he and his wife have helped hundreds of other Amish people in their decision to join the outside world. Still, after more than 20 years, he and other former Amish sit together at their "English" church on Sundays. "After all this time, we still need community," he explains. "We feel most comfortable when we're together."

6  Joe Keim's comment shows how the closeness shared by Amish people continues even after individuals have left their Amish communities. Despite all the changes of technology and society, the Amish way of life has survived and continues to grow.

told him that he would soon be forced to serve in the military if he remained in the outside world. Isaac simply didn't care. He had gotten a modern-style haircut and exchanged his Amish clothing for jeans. As a 17-year-old, he was eager to test his skill in a world of opportunity. Looking ahead, he decided to invest in real estate with his brother, hoping to achieve financial security for the rest of his life. The two moved to Texas and managed to buy a house. They gradually acquired more and more houses, which brought them rental income and allowed them to continue investing.

3  Today Isaac works full-time, attends college, and manages his properties. He has found a busy and satisfying life in a world that he had been taught to believe was dangerous and evil. Looking back on his Amish childhood, he recognizes the value of his upbringing, which included hard physical work and neighborly concern for others. He also appreciates the fact that his parents never argued in front of their 14 children, despite all the stresses of raising a large family on a limited budget. His only regret is the loss of contact with his Amish relatives, especially his mother, whom he contacts once or twice a year. At the same time, he enjoys all the rewards that have come as a result of his success in the modern world of business.

◀ **READ FOR MAIN IDEAS**

*Read the statements and mark them **T** (true) or **F** (false). Change the false statements to make them true.*

*F* 1. The Amish came to the United States and Canada with the goal of ~~making more money.~~ avoid the persecution

*T* 2. Even though Amish are born in North America, they still have to learn English as a second language in school.

*F* 3. Amish contact with the outside world has recently increased.

*F* 4. Amish who choose to leave usually stay ~~in touch~~ with their family and friends. Don't *lost lose touch*

*F* 5. Most Amish youth decide to leave the outside world as a result of their experiences in *rumspringa*. Don't *amish church*

*T* 6. Former Amish living in the outside world tend to stay in touch with each other.

Homework ½ ?

◀ **READ FOR DETAILS**

*Read each sentence, and cross out the one detail that is not included in the reading.*

1. The Amish came to North America as _____.
   a. immigrants
   b. small business owners — NO
   c. a persecuted group
   d. religious believers

   escoger cual no es verdad

2. The Amish are considered "reclusives" because of their _____.
   a. language
   b. clothing
   c. refusal to pay taxes
   d. avoidance of technology

3. The Amish learn about life in the outside world as a result of contact with _____.
   a. teachers in school
   b. hired drivers
   c. co-workers at factories
   d. customers at restaurants

4. During the *rumspringa* period, Amish youth get together to _____.
   a. sing
   b. use the Internet
   c. play games
   d. have parties

5. Most Amish youth choose to stay in their communities because of their _____.

   a. simple life
   b. sense of identity
   c. closeness to family
   d. religious beliefs

6. Some Amish who join the outside world _____.

   a. still attend church
   b. are helped by others who have left
   c. feel most comfortable with former Amish
   d. do so quickly and easily

   *no*

## ◖ MAKE INFERENCES

*Read the quotations from Amish youth. Which ones would most likely be said by a young person who has left the Amish community? Mark those statements **L** (left). Which ones would most likely be said by a young person who has stayed with the Amish community? Mark those statements **S** (stayed). Discuss your answers with a partner.*

S 1. "Nothing is more important to me than my religion."

L 2. "I appreciate the conveniences of the modern world."

L 3. "You need education to be a successful person."

S 4. "The group is more important than the individual."

S 5. "Modern technology makes people lazy."

L 6. "Change is usually for the better."

S 7. "It's good to belong to a large family."

## ◖ EXPRESS OPINIONS

*Work with a partner. Reread the quotations in Make Inferences. Discuss whether you agree or disagree with each one. Give reasons for your opinion. Then share your ideas with the class.*

**1** *Now read "A Decision to Leave." It is the true story of Isaac Schlabach, a young man who left his Amish community before baptism. Discuss the questions with the class before you read.*

1. For what reasons do you think Isaac Schlabach left his family and community?

2. Do you think Isaac has any regrets? Can you guess which ones?

3. Do you think Isaac will come back to his Amish community some day? Why do you think so?

## THE AMISH

1    North America is a land of immigrants, many of whom left their home countries to escape religious **persecution**. In the early 1700s, a group of Christians from Switzerland came to the United States and Canada. **Pious** and hard-working, they **established** farming communities. These people, known as the Amish, still live in Ontario, Canada, and in several states in the U.S., including Pennsylvania, Ohio, and Indiana. Avoiding the use of modern technology such as computers, their goal has always been to **maintain** the simple farming life that they had in Europe.

2    The Amish people are considered "reclusives" because they live separately from other people. They speak Pennsylvania Dutch, a form of German. Children learn English at school and complete their formal education by the end of the 8th grade. Because the Amish have traditionally worked on family farms, they see no need for higher learning. Working on farms and small family-owned businesses allows fathers, mothers, and children to remain together all day. Men dress in dark suits and wear full beards, while women wear plain long dresses and head coverings. The Amish work hard on their farms without using modern farm equipment or electricity. They normally do not drive cars or keep telephones in their homes. While the Amish pay taxes, they neither vote nor serve in the military.

3    As farming has **declined** in the United States, more Amish have recently entered the outside world as factory and restaurant workers. This means that more young people are spending time away from the Amish community and becoming familiar with the "English" way of life. While Amish people

## A DECISION TO LEAVE

1    It is estimated that 80–90% of Amish youth in *rumspringa* decide to stay in their Amish communities. Isaac Schlabach is a young man who represents the 10–20% of Amish youth who decide to join the outside world. As a boy growing up on an Amish farm, Isaac became determined not to live as his parents did, struggling all day with labor and chores for very little financial reward. Two weeks before his baptism, which would mark his commitment to the Amish way of life, he decided to leave his family and friends for an uncertain life in the outside world. His older brother had already left, and Isaac knew that he would face a lifetime of regret if he did not try, at least once, to see what life was like in the world of television, cars, and computers. In the back of his mind, Isaac was secure in the knowledge that if he wanted to return to the farm, there would always be a place for him.

still use the horse and buggy in their daily lives, many learn about the outside world through contact with car and taxi drivers who are hired to provide them with transportation. One Amish woman, Ruth Irene Garrett, left her community to marry her family's driver. In her book *Crossing Over* she describes how difficult it was to leave her family and friends. After Garrett left her community, family and friends stayed away from her. Because the Amish have a custom of *shunning*, or staying away from, people who leave the Amish way of life, the choice to leave means losing the opportunity to stay in touch with family and friends.

4    One very important Amish custom is adult baptism. Through baptism, a person becomes a full member of the Amish church and is expected to follow all church rules. The period before baptism is known as *rumspringa*, which can be translated as "running around." At age 16, young people are **allowed** to leave their parents' homes and meet together in youth groups for singing and playing games. In some communities, young people are allowed to attend parties, drive cars, and **socialize** in the outside world. Most Amish youth in rumspringa decide to join the Amish church, **settle down**, marry and raise families. However, some choose to live in the outside world, a decision which usually leads to a permanent separation from their Amish family and friends. It is estimated that 80–90% of Amish youth decide to remain within their communities. The **bonds** of family and religion are very strong. According to Dr. Donald Kraybill, author of *The Riddle of Amish Culture*, the Amish way of life meets important social and psychological needs, providing its members with "identity, meaning, and belonging."

5    Those who consider leaving the Amish community face a very difficult decision: leaving their family and friends to join the modern world with all its **conveniences** and opportunities. Joe Keim, the oldest of 14 children, left the Amish as a young man. Since leaving, he and his wife have helped hundreds of other Amish people in their decision to join the outside world. Still, after more than 20 years, he and other former Amish sit together at their "English" church on Sundays. "After all this time, we still need community," he explains. "We feel most comfortable when we're together."

6    Joe Keim's comment shows how the closeness shared by Amish people continues even after individuals have left their Amish communities. Despite all the changes of technology and society, the Amish way of life has survived and continues to grow.

2    He left a simple note for his parents, wishing to avoid their shock and tears. His parents soon followed him to Ohio, where they told him that he would soon be forced to serve in the military if he remained in the outside world. Isaac simply didn't care. He had gotten a modern-style haircut and exchanged his Amish clothing for jeans. As a 17-year-old, he was eager to test his skill in a world of opportunity. Looking ahead, he decided to invest in real estate with his brother, hoping to achieve financial security for the rest of his life. The two moved to Texas and managed to buy a house. They gradually acquired more and more houses, which brought them rental income and allowed them to continue investing.

3    Today Isaac works full-time, attends college, and manages his properties. He has found a busy and satisfying life in a world that he had been taught to believe was dangerous and evil. Looking back on his Amish childhood, he recognizes the value of his upbringing, which included hard physical work and neighborly concern for others. He also appreciates the fact that his parents never argued in front of their 14 children, despite all the stresses of raising a large family on a limited budget. His only regret is the loss of contact with his Amish relatives, especially his mother, whom he contacts once or twice a year. At the same time, he enjoys all the rewards that have come as a result of his success in the modern world of business.

**2**  *Write short answers to the questions.*

1. Why didn't Isaac want to live as his parents had lived?

   _____

2. What was his reason for choosing a career in real estate?

   _____

3. What had Isaac been taught about the outside world?

   _____

4. What does he regret about his choice to leave?

   _____

## C  INTEGRATE READINGS ONE AND TWO

### ◖STEP 1: Organize

*Read the outline. Add information from Reading Two to provide details that support the main ideas from Reading One.*

> **I.** Amish people are hard-working.
>
>   **A.** Isaac's father _____
>
>   **B.** Isaac's mother _____
>
> **II.** Amish people are considered reclusives because of their lifestyle and clothing.
>
>   **A.** When Isaac left, he _____
>
>   **B.** When Isaac left, he _____
>
> **III.** The decision to leave the Amish is difficult.
>
>   **A.** Isaac left his parents _____
>
>   **B.** When Isaac left, his parents _____
>
> **IV.** Leaving the Amish means losing contact with loved ones.
>
>   **A.** Isaac regrets _____
>
>   **B.** Isaac only contacts _____
>
> **V.** Leaving the Amish means gaining modern conveniences and opportunities.
>
>   **A.** Isaac wanted to _____
>
>   **B.** Now Isaac _____

*Imagine that you are a young person who has left the Amish. You are writing a letter in response to Readings One and Two. Use information from both readings to complete the letter.*

Dear *American Religion* Magazine,

    I recently read your articles on the Amish, and I found them extremely interesting. I left the Amish five years ago during my *rumspringa*. It was a very difficult decision for these reasons: _____

_____

_____

_____

    On the other hand, I really wanted to leave because_____

_____

_____

I also wanted to leave because _____

_____

_____

    Since I left, I have really enjoyed _____

_____

_____

But I have also regretted some things. For example, _____

_____

_____

I've tried to accept this and move on with my life.

    I would like to thank you for your articles on the Amish. I think it's important to let other people know about the Amish religion and way of life.

Sincerely,

_____

    *(your name)*

*Homework*

# 3 FOCUS ON WRITING

## A VOCABULARY

### ◖ REVIEW

*Cross out the word in each group that has a different meaning from the boldfaced word.*

| 1. bond | connection | closeness | ~~separation~~ |
| 2. convenience | ease | ~~commitment~~ | helpfulness |
| 3. decline | ~~improve~~ | decrease | lessen |
| 4. establish | found | ~~equalize~~ | start |
| 5. maintain | keep | preserve | ~~change~~ |
| 6. persecution | ~~acceptance~~ | abuse | mistreatment |
| 7. pious | godly | religious | ~~rewarding~~ |
| 8. allowed | accepted | ~~stopped~~ | permitted |
| 9. settle down | stabilize | take root | wander |
| 10. socialize | converse | ~~shun~~ | hang out |

**1** *Read more about the true story of Ruth Irene Garrett, a woman who left the Amish to marry her "English" driver. Pay attention to the boldfaced phrases.*

Ruth Irene Garrett was the daughter of an Amish church leader. A few years after her baptism at age 16, she met an "English" driver, Ottie Garrett. He had been hired to drive people in her community who, as Amish, were not allowed to drive themselves. As she and Ottie developed a friendship, she had to think about **(1) the pros and cons** of being close to an outsider. While she really liked Ottie, she knew that if she followed him into the outside world, she would lose her Amish relationships. She was really **(2) stuck between a rock and a hard place.** One morning he told her that he was moving to another state and asked if she wanted to come with him. **(3) If she turned** Ottie **down,** she might never see him again. Her parents were away from home that day, so she wrote them a note, took a few dresses, and left. Ruth Irene was not **(4) up in the air** about her decision. She knew that she wanted to marry Ottie. The **(5) deciding factor** was her love for him. Soon, they were married. This **(6) opened up a can of worms**—Ottie was divorced. Not only had she married a non-Amish but she had broken an important church rule—not to marry a divorced person. What made the situation even worse was the fact that, as the daughter of a church leader, Ruth Irene was expected to be an example of good behavior to all. In the end, despite her doubts and worries, Ruth Irene is a happily married woman and the author of several books, including *Crossing Over*.

**2** *Read the sentences. Choose the correct definition of the boldfaced phrase.*

1. When you consider **the pros and cons** of a decision, you think about the _____.
   **a.** good and bad sides     **b.** most important sides

2. When you are **stuck between a rock and a hard place**, you are dealing with a / an _____.
   **a.** easy choice          **b.** difficult choice

3. When you **turn** people **down,** you _____ to them.
   **a.** say "no"          **b.** say "yes"

4. To be **up in the air** about a decision is to be _____.
   **a.** unable to decide       **b.** able to decide

5. When you have to make a decision, the **deciding factor** is the _____.
   **a.** most important reason   **b.** least important reason

6. To **open up a can of worms** is to _____.
   **a.** solve a problem        **b.** make a problem more complicated

*Work with a partner. Ask your classmate about a difficult decision that he or she has made. Write a one-paragraph summary of your partner's decision. Use at least five to six words or phrases from Review (page 132) and Expand (page 133).*

Example

> My classmate is Chen. He moved from Shanghai to Hong Kong three years ago. He was **up in the air** about his decision because he had a very good job in Shanghai. However, he had the opportunity to start his own business in Hong Kong. This was the **deciding factor** for him. Now he lives in Hong Kong and owns a small business there. Like all business owners, he faced many risks, but now he has successfully **established** his company. However, living in Hong Kong has **opened a can of worms** for Chen—he misses his parents and his girlfriend very much. He's trying to **maintain** his **bonds** with them by using the Internet, but living far away has still been difficult.

## B  GRAMMAR: Noun Clauses with *Wh-* Words

**1**  *Read the paragraph. Look at the boldfaced phrases. Can you find any similarities in their structure?*

> My friend grew up in an Amish community. She saw **how her parents worked hard** every day, and she wanted a different kind of life. Even though it was difficult to leave her friends and family, she decided to go to college and become an attorney. It is easy to understand **why this was a good choice for her**. Working as an attorney has allowed her to live very comfortably, and now she knows **what she wants to do in the future**: retire at age 50 and live in the Bahamas.

**2**  *Look at the sentences. Label the boldfaced parts of the sentences as **Wh-** for the Wh- word, **S** for the subject, and **V** for the verb.*

```
        Wh-  S   V
```
- Isaac knew **when he needed to leave his Amish community**.

- Isaac and his brother discussed **what they wanted to do**.

- He understood **why his parents were worried about him**.

# NOUN CLAUSES WITH *WH-* WORDS

| | |
|---|---|
| **1.** A **noun clause** follows the main verb of a sentence. It is the object of this verb. | [S]    [V]        [O = NC]<br>Isaac understood [**why his parents were worried about him**]. |
| **2.** A noun-clause is a subject-verb combination. It begins with a **wh-** word (***who, what, when, where, why,*** and ***how***) and is followed by a subject and verb. |           [S]    [V]<br>He knew [**why** he wanted to leave].<br>           [S]    [V]<br>He planned [**what** he would do in Texas]. |
| **3.** The **verb in the noun clause** does not always have to be the same tense as the verb in the main clause. | He **understands** [why his parents **didn't want** him to leave]. |
| **4.** *Wh-* **questions** can be changed into noun clauses. To make this change, drop the auxiliary verb and use subject-verb order in the noun clause. |   [AUX]<br>**Why did** Isaac **want** to leave?<br>           [S]   [V]<br>They asked [**why** Isaac **wanted** to leave]. |
| **5.** *Yes / No* **questions** can also be changed into noun clauses. To make this change, use ***whether*** or ***if***[1] in the noun clause. You can add ***or not*** at the end of the sentence or after *whether*.<br><br>In a question with a **be-** verb, move this verb after the subject of the noun clause.<br><br><br><br>If there is an **auxiliary** verb, drop this verb and use subject-verb order in the noun clause. | **Were** his parents worried?<br>She asked [**whether** his parents **were** worried].<br><br>She asked [**whether** his parents **were** worried **or not**]. OR<br>She asked [**whether or not** his parents **were** worried].<br>  [AUX]<br>**Does** he still **see** his parents?<br>I want to know [**if** he still **sees** his parents]. OR<br>I want to know [**if** he still **sees** his parents **or not**]. |

[1] ***Whether*** and ***if*** have the same meaning. The only difference is that ***whether*** is more formal and is used more often in writing.

**3** Two tourists from Spain are visiting Ontario, Canada. They are very surprised to see Amish people riding in buggies and wearing Amish-style clothing. Read the dialogue.

JUAN: Look at those people over there. Are they wearing costumes?

MARÍA: I don't think so. I think they might be Amish.

JUAN: Who are they?

MARÍA: I read in the tour book that the Amish don't wear modern clothing or drive cars. They use buggies instead.

JUAN: Why?

MARÍA: It's part of their religion. They believe in living separately from the rest of the world.

JUAN: Hmm, I don't really understand. What else did the book say?

MARÍA: They don't use electricity . . . they have lots of kids.

JUAN: Do they speak English like other Canadians?

MARÍA: I'm not sure. The book says they came from Switzerland.

Complete the sentences with a noun clause. Use the words in parentheses and pay attention to the verb tense.

1. Juan wants to know whether / if _____.
   (costumes)

2. Juan doesn't know who _____.
   (Amish)

3. Juan asks why _____.
   (clothing / cars)

4. Juan doesn't understand why _____.
   (live separately)

5. María tells Juan what _____.
   (believe in)

6. María explains how _____.
   (electricity)

7. María isn't sure whether / if _____.
   (English)

**4** Work with a partner. Discuss questions that you have about the Amish and their way of life. Then complete the sentences with noun clauses expressing your questions. Share your questions with the class.

1. We want to know why _____.

2. We're not sure how _____.

3. We don't know where _____.

4. We want to know when _____.

5. We don't understand who _____.

6. We wonder whether _____.

In this unit, you learned how difficult it is for some of the Amish to leave their communities.

Now you will **write an essay explaining your own difficult decision—a personal decision, career decision, or a decision involving your family or friends.** You will explain why the decision was difficult, and describe the pros and cons. Use the vocabulary and grammar from the unit.*

### ◖ PREPARE TO WRITE: Asking Yourself Questions

*Write answers to the questions.*

1. What are some difficult decisions that you have made?

2. Which decision do you think might be a good writing topic? Answer these questions about the decision.
   - What were the pros and cons of this decision?
   - Was there anything that opened up a can of worms (made your decision more complicated)?
   - What was the deciding factor that finally helped you to make this decision?
   - Do you have any regrets about this decision?
   - What kind of rewards have you enjoyed as a result of this decision?

### ◖ WRITE: An Outline

An **outline** is a plan for how you will write an **essay.** Use outlines to help organize the main ideas and details that you want to include in each paragraph. Use your outline to organize your thesis statement, main ideas, and supporting details.

> **I. Introductory Paragraph**
>
> Thesis statement
>
> **II. Body Paragraph**
>
> Main idea    ← Benefic pro
>
> 1. Supporting detail    ← cours
>
> 2. Supporting detail    *(continued on next page)*

*For Alternative Writing Topics, see page 142. These topics can be used in place of the writing topic for this unit or as homework. The alternative topics relate to the theme of the unit, but may not target the same grammar or rhetorical structures taught in the unit.

*decision*

**1** Read this essay about a difficult decision. Then discuss the questions on the next page with a partner.

### Moving to Rio

1    I was born in Vitória da Conquista, Brazil. This is a city located in the interior of my country. When I graduated from high school, I had the opportunity to move to Rio de Janeiro and work in a large hotel. This may sound exciting, but it was really hard for me to decide what to do. In fact, I think moving to Rio was one of the toughest decisions of my life.

*most*

2    There were several wonderful reasons for moving to Rio and settling down there. First of all, I love the beach, and Rio is famous for having one of the most beautiful beaches in the world. I knew how much I would enjoy living in a place where I could take long walks in the sand and smell the ocean air. Second, the hotel offered to pay me more money than I was making at home. I needed the extra money to help my family. The final reason was my career. Working in a hotel would give me the experience I needed to establish my own hotel someday. I have always wanted to own a hotel and work in the tourist business.

3    On the other hand, moving to Rio had some disadvantages and risks. The first one was not having a place to live. I didn't know anyone, and I wasn't sure who I could live with. Another problem was the cost of living. I would earn more money, but I would also have to pay more to live in such a famous area. Finally, what really made it difficult was leaving my family and friends. I knew that I would be working many hours at the hotel, and I didn't know how often I could return home for visits.

4    I was up in the air for a long time, and I thought about turning the hotel down. But I finally made a decision. I signed a one-year contract to work at the hotel. I promised my family and friends that I would come home for a visit after one year. I knew that if I didn't like living in Rio, I would be able to come home. Now I am very happy with my new job. I am learning more about the hotel business every day. In addition, I really enjoy living in such a scenic and exciting place. Of course, I miss my loved ones, but I understand that every decision has pros and cons. For now, I am happy with my choice.

1. What was the writer's decision?

2. What were some of the pros?

3. What were some of the cons?

4. What was the deciding factor in the writer's decision?

**2** *Complete the outline with information from the essay above.*

I. **Introductory Paragraph**

   Thesis statement: _Moving to Rio was one of the toughest_
   _decisions of my life._

II. **Body Paragraph**

   Main idea: _There were good reasons for moving to Rio._

   Supporting details: _Rio has a beautiful beach._

   _____

   _____

III. **Body Paragraph**

   Main idea: _____

   Supporting details: _____

   _The cost of living is higher in Rio._

   _____

IV. **Concluding Paragraph**

   Conclusion: _____

**3** *Look at your answers from Prepare to Write, page 137. Organize your ideas into an outline. Then use your outline to write the first draft of your essay. Be sure to include:*

- An introductory paragraph providing background information about your decision and a thesis statement about the difficulty of your decision

- Two or three body paragraphs focusing on the pros and cons of your decision (you may add a third body paragraph describing a situation that opened a can of worms)

- A concluding paragraph explaining the deciding factor and stating how you now feel about your decision

### ◖REVISE: Using Parallel Structure

**1** *Read the sentences about a difficult decision. Label the subjects and verbs.*

- My parents carefully listened as I slowly explained the reasons why I wanted to move into my own apartment.
- I knew that I would stay in touch with my parents and would always maintain a good relationship with them.

---

**PARALLEL STRUCTURE**

Writers use **parallel structure** when they put two or three words or phrases of the same part of speech (noun, verb, adjective, adverb) together in sentences. The use of parallel structure allows writers to express several ideas in one sentence.

- I think my feelings of **wanting to move out** and **wanting to stay home** made my decision more **difficult** and **painful**.
- Finally, I decided to **get my own apartment** and **visit my parents** once a week.

Two ideas can be expressed in one sentence:

- When I **explained** my reasons, my parents listened.
- When I **expressed** my love, my parents listened.
- When I **explained** my reasons and **expressed** my love, my parents listened.

A third idea can be added:

- When I **promised** to stay in touch, my parents listened.
- When I **explained** my reasons, **expressed** my love, and **promised** to stay in touch, my parents listened.

    (Notice that *explained, expressed,* and *promised* are all past tense verbs.)

Look at two more examples:

    [ADV]     [V]                    [ADV]       [V]

- I **clearly explained** my reasons and **strongly expressed** my love.

    (The phrases are parallel because they both contain an adverb and a verb.)

                           [ADJ]   [N]     [ADJ]    [N]

- I thanked my parents for all the **generous help** and **valuable advice** they had given me.

    (The phrases are parallel because they both contain an adjective and a noun.)

---

**2** *Use parallel structure to combine each pair of sentences.*

1. Rio is well-known for lovely beaches.
   Rio is well-known for exciting nightlife.

   _____

2. The hotel will help me develop my career.
   The hotel will help me earn more money.

   _____

3. If I go to Rio, I will have to leave my beloved family.
   If I go to Rio, I will have to leave my dear friends.

   _____

4. When I received the job offer, I couldn't believe my good luck.
   When I received the job offer, I couldn't believe what the new job would pay.

   _____

5. My boss has a lot of experience in the hotel business.
   My co-workers have a lot of experience in the hotel business.

   _____

6. When I told my mother I was leaving, she cried.
   When I told my mother I was leaving, she said she was proud of me.

   _____

7. At the hotel, I will develop my job skills.
   At the hotel, I will develop my career opportunities.

   _____

8. I will try to help hotel guests cheerfully.
   I will try to do my job efficiently.

   _____

**3** *Describe your dream job, a job that you would like to have. Complete the paragraph. Use parallel structure.*

---

**My Dream Job**

I would like to work as a / an _____. This job is
                                        (name of the job)

_____, _____, and _____. People
     (ADJ)              (ADJ)                (ADJ)

who do this job are talented because they can _____ and
                                                      (V)

_____. I respect these people because they work so
      (V)

_____ and _____. I would like to have this job
     (ADV)                (ADV)

because of its _____ _____ and
                     (ADJ)              (N)

_____ _____.
     (ADJ)              (N)

---

**4** *Look back at the first draft of your essay. Rewrite at least three to four sentences using parallel structure.*

◀ **EDIT:** Writing the Final Draft

*Write the final draft of your essay. Carefully edit it for grammatical and mechanical errors, such as spelling, capitalization, and punctuation. Make sure you used some of the vocabulary and grammar from the unit. Use the checklist to help you write your final draft. Then neatly write or type your essay.*

## ✔ FINAL DRAFT CHECKLIST

○ Does your essay clearly describe the pros and cons of a difficult decision?

○ Does it contain an introductory paragraph, two or three body paragraphs, and a concluding paragraph?

○ Does the introductory paragraph contain a thesis statement stating the main idea of the essay?

○ Does each body paragraph focus clearly on one main idea?

○ Does each body paragraph include details that support the main idea?

○ Does the concluding paragraph restate the main idea expressed in the thesis statement?

○ Does the essay use parallel structure?

○ Are noun clauses used correctly?

○ Do you use vocabulary from the unit?

## ALTERNATIVE WRITING TOPICS

*Write about one of the topics. Use the vocabulary and grammar from the unit.*

1. Imagine that a friend has invited you to share an apartment in a big city. Write a letter to your friend explaining your preference: to live in a big city or to live a family-oriented life in a rural area.

2. What is another group that has faced persecution? What was the cause of persecution? How did the group respond? Write a report.

3. What are the advantages and disadvantages of living in the modern world? Do you prefer to live in the modern world or would you like to live in the past? Write an essay to explain your reasons.

## RESEARCH TOPICS, see page 214.

# Finding a Spouse

## 1 FOCUS ON THE TOPIC

### A PREDICT

*Read the joke and discuss the questions with the class.*

"Marriage has three rings: an engagement ring, a wedding ring, and suffering."

1. What do you think this joke means?

2. In your home culture, do men or women wear wedding or engagement rings? In what other ways do they show that they are engaged or married?

3. Do you agree that suffering is a part of marriage? Why or why not?

*People choose marriage partners for various reasons. Which of these reasons is important to you? Mark each one from 1 (very important) to 6 (not important). Discuss your choices with a classmate.*

_____ **a.** ability to have children      _____ **d.** religion

_____ **b.** partner's age      __1__ **e.** love

_____ **c.** parents' choice      _____ **f.** money

## C BACKGROUND AND VOCABULARY

**1** *Work in a small group. Test your knowledge of past and present marriage customs around the world. Look at the list of cultures in the box. Choose a culture that you think practices or has practiced the custom described in each sentence. Write the letter on the line. There may be more than one correct choice. Pay attention to the boldfaced words.*

| | | |
|---|---|---|
| **a.** Arab | **d.** Vietnamese | **g.** modern European |
| **b.** old Bavarian | **e.** traditional Chinese | **h.** early Mormon |
| **c.** traditional Hopi | **f.** Oneida community | |

_____ **1.** Parents try to find someone who has the right **background**, someone who has gone to school, and who has an honorable mother and father.

_____ **2.** Girls are allowed to choose a marriage partner. Their favorite boyfriend can become their **spouse**.

_____ **3.** Parents use a matchmaker to find a spouse with the right **characteristics**, for example, someone who is honest, intelligent, and hard-working.

_____ **4.** Young women used to invite men to visit them at night by leaving their windows open.

_____ **5.** Men and women can usually follow their **romantic** feelings and get married for love rather than just the advice from their parents.

_____ **6.** The goal of marriage is to **produce** sons, and these sons will take on a **leadership** position by making the important decisions for the family.

_____ **7.** If a woman can become **pregnant**, the man will ask her to marry him. Having children is very important.

_____ **8.** Getting pregnant allowed a woman to show the community her **fertility**.

_____ **9.** In this community, group marriage was approved so that everyone could be treated equally.

_____ **10.** All the people in the community **raised** the children, not just the mother and father.

_____ **11.** The bride's hands and feet are painted with henna, a reddish-brown dye, before the wedding.

_____ **12.** This group practiced **polygamy**, following the example of their leader, Joseph Smith.

**2** *Match the words on the left with the definitions on the right.*

__b__ **1.** background

__i__ **2.** spouse

__h__ **3.** characteristics

__g__ **4.** romantic

__j__ **5.** produce

__f__ **6.** leadership

__a__ **7.** pregnant

__e__ **8.** fertility

__c__ **9.** raise

__d__ **10.** polygamy

**a.** having a baby that has not been born yet growing in your body

**b.** past experience, including family life and education

**c.** to take care of and educate

**d.** the custom of having more than one wife at a time

**e.** the ability to have children

**f.** the ability to direct other people

**g.** related to strong feelings of love between a man and a woman

**h.** special features or qualities that make each person or thing different from others

**i.** a husband or wife

**j.** to make or create

# 2 FOCUS ON READING

## A READING ONE: Finding a Spouse

*The following article comes from a journal for students of anthropology (the study of how human beings live together in communities). Read the first paragraph of the article and answer the questions. Compare your answers with a classmate's.*

What about you?

1. If you are already married, how did you find your spouse?

2. If you are single, what do you think is the best way for you to find a spouse or partner?

# Finding a Spouse

1   All human beings are born into families, and families begin with the joining together of a man and a woman in marriage. All societies have their own form of marriage. The ideas that we have about marriage are part of our cultural **background**; they are part of our basic beliefs about right and wrong. As we study marriage, we find that different cultures have solved the problem of finding a **spouse** in different ways. Finding a marriage partner has never been easy for people, no matter when or where they have lived.

2   In traditional Chinese culture, marriage decisions were made by parents for their children. Parents who wanted to find a spouse for their son or daughter asked a matchmaker to find someone with the right **characteristics**, including age and educational background. According to the Chinese way of thinking, it would be a serious mistake to allow two young people to follow their **romantic** feelings and choose their own partners. The all-important decision of marriage was made by older family members who understood that the goal of marriage was to **produce** healthy sons. In traditional Chinese society, sons were important because they would take positions of **leadership** in the family and keep the family name alive.

3   As part of our cultural background, beliefs about marriage can be as different as the cultures of the world. While the traditional Chinese did not believe that young people should be free to choose their own marriage partners, the Hopi, a native people of North America, had a very different idea about freedom. The Hopi allowed boys to leave their parents' home at age thirteen to live in a *kiva*, a special home for young males. Here they enjoyed the freedom to go out alone at night and secretly visit young girls. Most boys tried to leave the girl's home before daylight, but a girl's parents usually did not get angry about the night visits. They allowed the visits to continue if they were impressed that the boy was someone who would make a good marriage partner. After a few months of receiving visits, most girls became **pregnant**. As a consequence, they could choose their favorite boy for a husband.

4   The Hopi culture is not the only one that allowed young people to visit each other at night. Some Bavarian people of southern Germany once had a "windowing" custom that took place when young women left their windows open at night so that young men could enter their bedrooms. When a woman became pregnant, the man usually asked her to marry him. But women who did not manage to get pregnant after windowing were often unable to find a husband. This was because **fertility** was a very important requirement for women in this culture, and the windowing custom allowed them to prove their fertility to others in the community. Some people are surprised when they learn of this unique custom because they expect the people of southern Germany to follow the rules of the Catholic religion, which teach that it is wrong for unmarried women to become pregnant. But the windowing custom is only one example of the surprising views of marriage that are found around the world, even among people whose religious beliefs require more common marriage practices.

5   One view of marriage that surprises most of us today was held by John Noyes, a religious man who started the Oneida Community in the state of New York in 1831. He began it as an experiment of a different way of living. Noyes decided that group marriage was the best way for men and women to live together. In this form of marriage, men and women changed partners frequently. They were expected to love all members of the community equally. Children belonged to all members of the community, and all the adults worked hard to support themselves and shared everything they had. Members of the Oneida Community

succeeded in this lifestyle for a while without any serious problems; however, this way of life ended when John Noyes left the community in 1876. Without his leadership and unique way of thinking, members of the community quickly returned to the traditional marriage of one woman and one man.

6  A more famous example of a different style of marriage is found among the early Mormons—a Christian sect that was founded in New York State in 1830 and migrated to Utah in 1847. The group's first leader, Joseph Smith, believed in **polygamy**. As the Mormon Church grew, many of the men followed Smith's teaching and married a number of wives. The Mormons believed that it was a woman's duty to marry at a young age and **raise** as many children as possible. For example, in 1854, one Mormon leader became a father nine times in one week when nine of his wives all had babies. In 1890, however, polygamy was officially banned by the church. Today, while the Mormon Church teaches that marriage should be a partnership of one man and one woman, there are some smaller groups which have left the main group and still practice polygamy.

7  In these modern times, there are some men who might agree with the custom of allowing a man to have as many wives as he chooses. Many young lovers today dream of the freedom of the Hopi, and some of us wish that a matchmaker would help us find the perfect mate. Finding a spouse with whom we can commit to spending a lifetime has always been an important concern. Despite all the different ways of finding a marriage partner, one idea is the same throughout the world: Marriage is a basic and important part of human life.

## ◀ READ FOR MAIN IDEAS

*Work in a small group. These sentences describe cultural beliefs. Match each belief with the correct culture.*

**a.** traditional Hopi     **c.** Oneida Community     **e.** early Mormon

**b.** old Bavarian     **d.** traditional Chinese

____ **1.** Young people are not capable of making the right marriage choices for themselves.

____ **2.** Getting pregnant shows that you will be a good wife.

____ **3.** Women should have as many children as possible.

____ **4.** A girl should be free to choose her own husband.

____ **5.** It is better for society if people are not limited to one marriage partner.

## ◀ READ FOR DETAILS

*Briefly answer the questions. Check your answers with a classmate.*

**1.** Who helped Chinese parents choose a spouse for their sons or daughters? How did this person help?
help to find a man with right characteristics (background)

**2.** What was the Chinese idea of a successful marriage?
The goal of marriage was to produce healthy sons

**3.** At what age did young Hopi boys leave their homes?

*thirteen*

**4.** Why did Hopi parents sometimes stop night visits?

*when most girls become pregnant.*

**5.** How did Bavarian women catch a man?

*when ~~the~~ the women left their windows open.*

**6.** What happened to a woman in Bavaria if she did not become pregnant?

*~~She/the~~ the women don't find a husband*

**7.** What do people in some Catholic countries believe about unmarried women?

*it's wrong for unmarried women to become pregnant*

**8.** Why didn't the Oneida Community continue to exist?

*when John Noxes left the community in 187*

**9.** What happened to the Mormon church in 1890?

*poligamy was officially banned by church, eighteen seventy si*

## ◖ MAKE INFERENCES

*Look at the number line. According to what you learned in Reading One, give each of the cultures a number. Discuss your choices in a small group.*

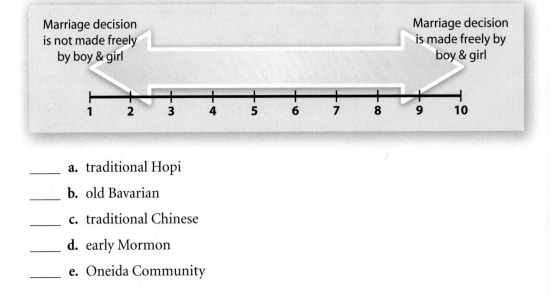

Marriage decision is not made freely by boy & girl ← → Marriage decision is made freely by boy & girl

1  2  3  4  5  6  7  8  9  10

_____ **a.** traditional Hopi

_____ **b.** old Bavarian

_____ **c.** traditional Chinese

_____ **d.** early Mormon

_____ **e.** Oneida Community

*With a classmate, discuss the pros and cons of each marriage custom. Which do you like the most? The least?*

- arranged by parents
- girls choosing their favorite boy after becoming pregnant
- the "windowing" custom
- group marriage
- one man having multiple wives
- choosing your own spouse because you are in love with him or her

## B READING TWO: What's Wrong with Tradition?

**1** *Read a letter to the editor taken from the student newspaper of an American university. It was written by an international student who believes strongly in his culture's traditional way of choosing a spouse.*

Dear Editor:

1 I am a twenty-seven-year-old student from Vietnam. My purpose in coming here is to get a business degree. I am extremely grateful to have the chance to get an education in a country of such great business leadership. However, I am tired of the questions that people ask me about my personal life. American students seem to think that their way of dating romantically before marriage is the only way, but I disagree. Let me give you an example from my own life.

2 My parents have been married for thirty-five years. Their marriage has all the characteristics of a happy one: deep friendship, love, and trust. They have six children, and I am the second son. Because of their help, I am able to study in the United States. They have always worked hard to raise their children in the right way. When I finish my degree, I will go back to my country and help them.

3 American people are always surprised when I tell them that my parents met for the first time on their wedding day. Americans can't believe that an arranged marriage could be happy, but I have seen my parents with my own eyes. They love each other faithfully, and they are proud of the children that their marriage has produced. They learned to love each other slowly, as time passed. I believe they share a true and everlasting love.

*(continued on next page)*

4  When people ask, "Are you looking for a girlfriend?" I tell them no. For me, studying comes first. When I go back to my country and start working, my parents will help me find a good wife. She will be someone with a good family background, someone I can trust. Good apples come from good trees. If I marry a good apple, we can make a beautiful, growing tree together: no divorce, no AIDS, no broken heart.

5  I want a peaceful, happy life just like my parents have. Why can't Americans understand this?

Paul Nguyen

**2**  *Read the statements and mark them **T** (true) or **F** (false).*

_F_  **1.** Paul Nguyen thinks dating romantically is the best way to find a marriage partner.

_T_  **2.** Paul thinks a happy marriage includes deep friendship, love, and trust.

_F_  **3.** His parents were in love with each other before the marriage.

_F_  **4.** Paul wants a different life than his parents.

_T_  **5.** Paul thinks his parents can help find him a good wife.

## C  INTEGRATE READINGS ONE AND TWO

### STEP I: Organize

*Look at the chart on the next page. It shows ways of choosing a spouse in the different cultures mentioned in Readings One and Two. Fill in the chart. Check (✓) the appropriate boxes.*

C = traditional Chinese     OC = Oneida Community

H = traditional Hopi     M = early Mormons

B = old Bavarian     V = Vietnamese

| WAYS OF CHOOSING A SPOUSE | C | H | B | OC | M | V |
|---|---|---|---|---|---|---|
| 1. Parents choose the spouse because young people aren't able to make a good decision by themselves. | ✓ | | | | | ✓ |
| 2. Family background is important in choosing a spouse. | | | | | | |
| 3. Educational background is important in choosing a spouse. | | | | | | |
| 4. A girl must become pregnant to demonstrate her fertility before she can marry. | | | | | | |
| 5. Marrying young is an important factor in choosing a spouse. | | | | | | |
| 6. The boy and girl had a relationship before they married. | | | | | | |
| 7. The goal of marriage is to produce sons who will become leaders in the family. | | | | | | |
| 8. If the girl becomes pregnant, she can choose the boy she likes best to marry. | | | | | | |
| 9. If the girl becomes pregnant, the boy will ask her to marry him. | | | | | | |
| 10. Men and women practice group marriage in which they change partners frequently. | | | | | | |
| 11. This group used to practice polygamy, a custom in which the man can have more than one wife at a time. | | | | | | |
| 12. If a woman can't get pregnant, she probably can't marry. | | | | | | |

*Imagine that you are taking a sociology class. Your professor has given you a study guide for next week's quiz about "Marriages and Cultures." Use information from Step 1 to fill in the chart.*

| MARRIAGES AND CULTURES | | |
|---|---|---|
| **Week** | **Topic** | **Summary** |
| **Week 9** | **Arranged Marriage:** Traditional Chinese | Marriage was arranged by the parents because young people weren't able to make good decisions by themselves. Age and educational background were important in choosing a spouse. The goal of marriage was to produce sons who would become leaders in the family. |
| | Vietnamese | Marriage is arranged by the parents because young people aren't able to make good decisions by themselves. Family background  is important in choosing a spouse. |
| **Week 10** | **Fertility-Based Marriage:** Traditional Hopi | Boys were encouraged to visit girls at night. _____ |
| | | If the girl became pregnant, _____ _____ |
| | Old Bavarian | The "windowing" custom was the custom of letting boys come into girls' bedrooms at night through their windows. _____ _____ |
| **Week 11** | **Plural Marriage:** Oneida Community | Founded by John Noyes, _____ _____ |
| | Early Mormon | Founded by Joseph Smith, _____ _____ |
| | | Currently, it teaches that marriage is a partnership between one man and one woman. |

# (3) FOCUS ON WRITING

## A VOCABULARY

### ◀ REVIEW

*Read the paragraph about traditional courtship. Then, decide if the sentences below are related to courtship (**C**), the wedding ceremony (**W**), or married life (**M**), and mark them appropriately. Share your choices with the class.*

> **Courtship** refers to the period of time when a man and a woman get to know each other before marriage. In some cultures, they spend time together alone. In other cultures, they spend time together with friends and relatives. During this time, a couple may decide whether or not to marry.

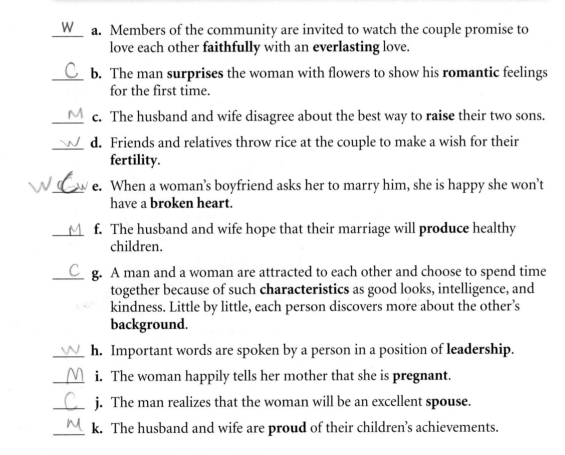

__W__ **a.** Members of the community are invited to watch the couple promise to love each other **faithfully** with an **everlasting** love.

__C__ **b.** The man **surprises** the woman with flowers to show his **romantic** feelings for the first time.

__M__ **c.** The husband and wife disagree about the best way to **raise** their two sons.

__W__ **d.** Friends and relatives throw rice at the couple to make a wish for their **fertility**.

__W C w__ **e.** When a woman's boyfriend asks her to marry him, she is happy she won't have a **broken heart**.

__M__ **f.** The husband and wife hope that their marriage will **produce** healthy children.

__C__ **g.** A man and a woman are attracted to each other and choose to spend time together because of such **characteristics** as good looks, intelligence, and kindness. Little by little, each person discovers more about the other's **background**.

__W__ **h.** Important words are spoken by a person in a position of **leadership**.

__M__ **i.** The woman happily tells her mother that she is **pregnant**.

__C__ **j.** The man realizes that the woman will be an excellent **spouse**.

__M__ **k.** The husband and wife are **proud** of their children's achievements.

◀ **EXPAND**

*taste       valantine       recept*

*advantages*

Work in pairs. Read the chart. Then analyze the relationships between the vocabulary
words given below. First, circle the word that best completes each comparison. Be sure
that the second pair of words has a similar relationship to the first pair. Second, label
each comparison with the letter of the correct category.

| CATEGORY | DEFINITION | EXAMPLE |
|---|---|---|
| Synonym (**S**) | The words have a very similar meaning. | mistake : error |
| Antonym (**A**) | The words have opposite meanings. | modern : traditional |
| Cause / effect (**C / E**) | One word is the result of another word. | mistakes : experience |
| Degree (**D**) | One word has a stronger meaning than the other. | different : unique |
| Related (**R**) | The words are connected by similar ideas. | tough : suffering |

*duro      sufrimiento*

**S**  1. characteristics : features = make : _____
   a. raise          **b.** produce          c. grow

**S**  2. spouse : husband = romantic : _____
   a. characteristic     b. infertility     **c.** attracted to

**A**  3. marriage : divorce = pregnancy : _____
   **a.** infertility       b. commitment       c. traditional

**C**  4. pregnancy : baby = romance : _____
   **a.** love marriage     b. arranged marriage     c. group marriage

**C/D** 5. surprised : shocked = enduring : _____
   a. lasting        b. continuing        **c.** everlasting
   *perdurable*

**C/D** 6. group : leader = marriage : _____
   **a.** partner          b. produce          c. characteristics

**D**  7. usually : always = hurt : _____
   a. brokenhearted     **b.** loved     c. trusted

**S**  8. engagement : marriage = fertility : _____
   a. miracle          b. proof          **c.** pregnancy

_____  9. custom : tradition = society : _____
   a. country          **b.** culture          c. organization

**A**  10. honesty : dishonesty = hard-working : _____
   **a.** lazy          b. trustworthy          c. thoughtful
   *dignos de          Pensativo*
   *confianza*

_____ **11.** faith : religion = support : _____

    **a.** carry         **b.** take care of         **c.** help

_____ **12.** wife : husband = bride : _____

    **a.** partner         **b.** mate         **c.** groom

**◀ CREATE**

*Describe five different courtship traditions in your culture. Write one or two paragraphs using at least five of these words.*

| | | | |
|---|---|---|---|
| arranged marriage | custom    *compromiso* | leadership | spouse |
| attracted to — *atraído* | engagement | modern | traditional |
| background | faithfully — *fielmente* | produce | unique |
| characteristics | fertility | romantic | |

**B**   **GRAMMAR: Definite and Indefinite Articles**

*Language Language Language Language*

**1**   *Look at this passage from "Finding a Spouse." Underline the definite articles (**the**). Circle the indefinite articles (**a/an**).*

A more famous example of a different style of marriage is found among the early Mormons—a Christian sect that was founded in New York State in 1830 and migrated to Utah in 1847. The group's first leader, Joseph Smith, believed that a man should be allowed to have several wives. This type of marriage is called polygamy. As the Mormon Church grew, many of the men followed Smith's teaching and married a number of wives. The Mormons believed that it was a woman's duty to marry at a young age and raise as many children as possible. For example, in 1854, one Mormon leader became a father nine times in one week when nine of his wives all had babies. In 1890, however, polygamy was officially banned by the church. Today, while the Mormon Church teaches that marriage should be a partnership of one man and one woman, there are some smaller groups which have left the main group and still practice polygamy.

## DEFINITE AND INDEFINITE ARTICLES

| | |
|---|---|
| 1. Use the **definite article *the*** when you have a specific person, place, or thing in mind. | **The** group's leader, Joseph Smith, believed a man should be allowed to have several wives.<br><br>As **the** Mormon Church grew, many of **the** men followed Smith's teaching and married a number of wives. |
| 2. Use the **indefinite article *a*** when you do not have a specific person, place, or thing in mind.<br><br>Use the **indefinite article *an*** before words that begin with vowel sounds. | The group's leader, Joseph Smith, believed **a** man should be allowed to have several wives.<br><br>He began it as **an** experiment of a different way of living. |
| 3. Use the indefinite article *a* the first time you mention a person, place, or thing.<br><br>Then use the definite article *the* when you refer to that same thing again. | Some Bavarian people of southern Germany once had **a** "windowing" custom that . . .<br><br>. . . and **the** windowing custom allowed them to prove their fertility to others in the community. |
| 4. Use the definite article *the* in forming the **superlative** of an adjective. | Noyes decided that group marriage was **the best** way for men and women to live together. |

**2**  *Complete the paragraph with the definite article **the** or the indefinite article **a(n)**.*

### Planning a Wedding

An American bride often looks in _____ bridal magazine for advice about
**1.**
planning her wedding. Every bride has her own idea of _____ most perfect
**2.**
wedding. For most brides, this includes flowers, music, and _____ delicious
**3.**
wedding cake. Most magazines also provide information about planning _____
**4.**
romantic trip. Some brides dream of going to _____ warm beach, while others
**5.**
wish to travel to _____ distant country. Bridal magazines also give advice about
**6.**
following traditional American wedding customs. For example, _____ bride
**7.**
will sometimes give _____ piece of wedding cake to her friends. Each friend
**8.**
takes _____ piece of cake home and places it in a bag underneath her pillow.
**9.**
According to tradition, if a woman does this, she will dream of her future husband
that night. _____ woman will see his face in her dreams.
**10.**

**3** Read each statement, paying special attention to the boldfaced phrase. Then circle the correct explanation of its meaning.

1. I went to **a wedding** last week.
   a. We don't know exactly which wedding.
   b. We know exactly which wedding.

2. **The bride** carried beautiful roses.
   a. This is a specific bride.
   b. This is not a specific bride.

3. The groom wore **a black hat**.
   a. We know exactly which hat.
   b. We don't know exactly which hat.

4. **The hat** reminded me of one I'd seen in movies.
   a. This is the same hat mentioned before.
   b. This is a different hat.

**4** Write a paragraph about a wedding that you have attended. Be careful with the use of **the** and **a(n)**. Share your paragraph with a classmate.

## C  WRITING

In this unit, you read an article about world customs related to finding a spouse. You also read a letter in support of parents helping their children find a spouse.

Now you are going to **write an essay about the characteristics that you think are important in a spouse or partner**. Use the vocabulary and grammar from the unit.*

### ◖ PREPARE TO WRITE: Categorizing

**Categorizing** is a way of organizing your ideas by putting them into **logical groups.**

**1** In a small group, think of characteristics that are important in a spouse or partner. Have one person in the group write down all the ideas. Think of as many ideas as you can.

Example

| | | | |
|---|---|---|---|
| athletic | honest | nice smile | wealthy |
| good-looking | kind | tall | well-educated |

---

*For Alternative Writing Topics, see page 161. These topics can be used in place of the writing topic for this unit or as homework. The alternative topics relate to the theme of the unit, but may not target the same grammar or rhetorical structures taught in the unit.

**2** *Choose the characteristics from the list in Exercise 1 that are most important to you. Put these characteristics into categories such as appearance, personality, beliefs, family background, and education / occupation.*

Example

| Appearance | Personality |
|------------|-------------|
| nice smile | honest |
| tall | kind |

**3** *Check the two categories from Exercise 2 that are most important to you. Check (✓) the three most important characteristics in each category.*

◀ **WRITE: A Point-by-Point Paragraph**

In **point-by-point organization**, the **points (ideas)** in a paragraph are **discussed one by one.** In this essay, each paragraph you write will describe one category, or group, of characteristics that are important in a spouse or partner (personality, background, education, and so on). You will discuss the characteristics in each category one by one.

**1** *Read the paragraph. Then discuss the questions with a classmate.*

> My spouse's personality is very important to me. Most importantly, I want to marry someone who is kind. Kindness is important because it affects everyone in the family. It is difficult to live with someone who is mean or critical of others. This is especially important if we have children. It is also important for my spouse to be honest. I want my spouse to tell me the truth. I don't want to be married to someone who hides things from me. Finally, my spouse should have a good sense of humor. I believe that life is easier and more fun with laughter. Even when bad things happen, we should find a way to laugh. For all these reasons, my spouse's personality matters a lot to me.

1. What is the topic sentence? Underline it.

2. What category is discussed in the paragraph?

3. What characteristics are included in that category?

4. What reasons does the writer give for choosing each characteristic?

**2** *In point-by-point organization, some points may be more important than others. Writers use **transition words** to show the degree of importance. Look at the paragraph in Exercise 1 again. Notice the transition words **most importantly**, **also**, and **finally** that introduce each characteristic. Which characteristic is most important to the writer?*

**3** *Look back at your list of categories and characteristics in Prepare to Write (see above). Number the characteristics in each category by order of importance. Then make notes on your reasons for choosing these characteristics.*

**4** *Use your list from Prepare to Write, page 158, and your notes from this section to write the first draft of your essay. Include the following:*

- An introductory paragraph including a thesis statement about what is important to you in choosing a spouse or partner
- Two or three body paragraphs, each one focusing on one category of characteristics (personality, background, beliefs, and so on)
- Reasons and examples to describe each characteristic
- A concluding paragraph summarizing your main ideas and adding a final comment

## ◖ REVISE: Using Related Word Forms for Cohesion

In a well-written text, the ideas are cohesive; that is, they fit together clearly. When your **ideas fit together clearly**, you are using **cohesion**.

**1** *Look at these paragraphs about marriage. Can you identify what makes them cohesive?*

1.

> Some people are surprised when they learn of this unique custom because they expect the people of southern Germany to follow the rules of the Catholic religion, which teach that it is wrong for unmarried women to become pregnant. But the windowing custom is only one example of the surprising views of marriage that are found around the world, even among people whose religious beliefs require more common marriage practices.

2.

> A more famous example of a different style of marriage is found among the early Mormons—a Christian sect that was founded in New York State in 1830 and migrated to Utah in 1847. The group's first leader, Joseph Smith, believed that a man should be allowed to have several wives. This type of marriage is called polygamy. As the Mormon Church grew, many of the men followed Smith's teaching and married a number of wives. The Mormons believed that it was a woman's duty to marry at a young age and raise as many children as possible. For example, in 1854, one Mormon leader became a father nine times in one week when nine of his wives all had babies. In 1890, however, polygamy was officially banned by the church. Today, while the Mormon Church teaches that marriage should be a partnership of one man and one woman, there are some smaller groups which have left the main group and still practice polygamy.

Writers use **related word forms** to gain more **cohesion** in their writing.

- In **Paragraph 1**, the ideas fit together clearly because the writer uses such related word forms as *religion* and *religious, unmarried,* and *marriage.*
- In **Paragraph 2**, some related word forms are *marriage, married, marry.* There are also many repetitions of the words *Mormon* and *wives.*

The use of **related word forms** helps the writer move smoothly from one idea to the next. The writer is able to keep the reader's focus on the main idea without repeating the same exact words again and again. Look at this example:

- Other pregnant women believe that they are quite **beautiful** during pregnancy. Their **beauty** comes from the joy of becoming a mother. There is a light in their eyes, and their skin shines **beautifully**.

**2** *Complete the paragraph with the appropriate word forms. Choose words from the box.*

| | | | | |
|---|---|---|---|---|
| court | marriage | romance | ~~similar~~ | tradition |
| courtship | married | romantic | similarity | traditional |

Many social scientists agree that it is important to marry someone whose background is ___similar___ to your own. One example of this idea is expressed
**1.**

when Americans talk about marrying "the boy (or girl) next door." When we get

_____ to the boy or girl next door, we are joining our lives with a partner
**2.**

who shares our lifestyle, income, and educational level. According to most social

scientists, this type of _____ is likely to be successful because the spouses
**3.**

will understand each other more easily. One practical advantage of marrying the

boy or girl next door is that it is easy to _____ someone who lives near
**4.**

you. During the _____ period, the two partners can get together easily. If
**5.**

they come from _____ families, their parents can watch their relationship
**6.**

develop and give them advice. Of course, there is also the possibility that the

_____ will not be accepted by parents, and the young couple may not be
**7.**

able to participate in the _____ of having a wedding ceremony. They may
**8.**

elope, or run away to get married secretly. For some couples, this is a _____
**9.**

way to begin their lives together. But whether or not they elope, many experts

believe that people who marry the boy or girl next door will be happy. This is

because of the _____ of their backgrounds.
**10.**

**3** *Look back at the first draft of your essay. Find at least one place in each paragraph where you can use related word forms to give your writing more cohesion.*

◖ **EDIT: Writing the Final Draft**

*Write the final draft of your essay. Carefully edit it for grammatical and mechanical errors, such as spelling, capitalization, and punctuation. Make sure you used some of the vocabulary and grammar from the unit. Use the checklist to help you write your final draft. Then neatly write or type your essay.*

---

### ✔ FINAL DRAFT CHECKLIST

○ Does your essay clearly describe the characteristics that you think are important in a spouse or partner?

○ Does it contain an introductory paragraph, two or three body paragraphs, and a concluding paragraph?

○ Does the introductory paragraph contain a thesis statement stating the main idea of the essay?

○ Does each body paragraph focus on one category of characteristics?

○ Does each body paragraph contain reasons and examples describing the importance of each characteristic?

○ Does the concluding paragraph restate the main idea expressed in the thesis statement?

○ Does your essay use related word forms for cohesion?

○ Are definite and indefinite articles used correctly?

○ Do you use vocabulary from the unit?

---

## ALTERNATIVE WRITING TOPICS

*Write about one of the topics. Use the vocabulary and grammar from the unit.*

1. What are the characteristics of a happy marriage? Do these characteristics change as a couple gets older? Write an essay to explain. Describe a happy marriage of a couple that you know. What is special about it?

2. Do you believe that using a matchmaker (including online services) can be a good way to find a spouse or partner? Why or why not? Write your opinion in a blog.

3. You are taking a quiz in your sociology class. This is one of the questions: Describe a marriage or courtship custom with which you are familiar. How is this custom related to religion and/or traditions? Write an essay to answer the question.

---

**RESEARCH TOPICS, see page 215.**

# UNIT 9

# Is Our Climate Changing?

# 1 FOCUS ON THE TOPIC

## A PREDICT

*Look at the photograph of the Earth. Discuss the questions in a small group.*

1. What are some ways in which the Earth is changing?

2. How responsible are humans for changes on the planet?

3. Are these changes making the world better or worse?

163

Write **A** *(agree) or* **D** *(disagree) next to each statement.  Discuss your answers with a classmate.*

_____ 1. The Earth goes through warming and cooling periods, and the warming period happening now is just part of those natural changes.

_____ 2. The weather has become more dangerous in recent years.

_____ 3. The hole in the ozone layer[1] is causing climate change.

_____ 4. New fuels will solve the problem of pollution.

_____ 5. Some people are frightening us with "global warming" so they can make money from it.

---

[1] **ozone layer:** a layer of ozone above the Earth that prevents harmful radiation from the sun reaching the Earth's surface

**C** **BACKGROUND AND VOCABULARY**

**1** *Look at the pictures and read the texts.  Pay special attention to the boldfaced words.*

### How Greenhouse Gases Cause Climate Change

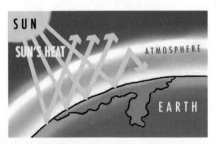

Most of the sun's heat hits the Earth and **escapes** back into space. Some is trapped by the **atmosphere** and warms the Earth.

**Fossil fuels** (coal, gasoline) are burned and **carbon dioxide** ($CO_2$) is released. Released $CO_2$ and other **gases** are called greenhouse gas **emissions**.

Greenhouse gases make the atmosphere thicker. As the sun's heat hits the Earth, more and more of the heat is trapped and warms the Earth. As $CO_2$ increases, so does the temperature. This shows that there is a **link** between $CO_2$ and temperature. This connection is **evidence** that climate change is caused by humans.

## **Signs** of Climate Change

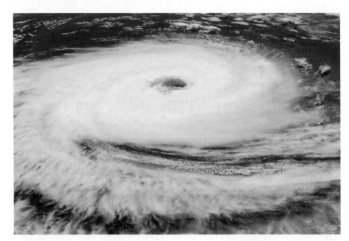

More **energetic** weather

Increasing drought

Rising sea levels and floods

## Can we **adapt** to these changes?

**2** *Choose the best definition for each word or phrase.*

_____ 1. escape
   a. to get out
   b. to change

_____ 2. atmosphere
   a. mixture of gases that surround the Earth
   b. half of a sphere

_____ 3. fossil fuels
   a. substances that are buried in the ground and can be burned for power
   b. solar energy

_____ 4. carbon dioxide ($CO_2$)
   a. colorless gas breathed out by people and animals
   b. gas we use in our cars

_____ 5. gases
   a. hot air
   b. air-like substances

_____ 6. emissions
   a. sending out of something
   b. representatives

_____ 7. link
   a. effect
   b. connection holding two things together

_____ 8. evidence
   a. interest in something
   b. information that proves something

_____ 9. sign
   a. an event that shows that something is happening or will happen in the future
   b. an idea that something is happening or will happen in the future

_____ 10. energetic
   a. visible
   b. powerful

_____ 11. adapt
   a. to change something to be more useful
   b. to move something

# FOCUS ON READING

## A  READING ONE: Our Climate Is Changing . . .

*Read the article adapted from a New Zealand government brochure.*

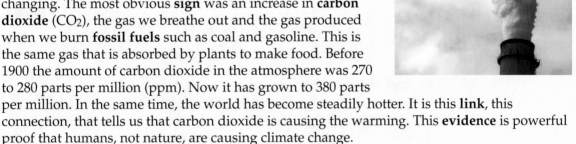

# Our Climate is Changing and It is Going to Keep Changing

### Climate Change

1   It's getting hotter. Our climate is changing, so you'd better get used to it. It's changing because of what we humans do and the **gases** we have put into the **atmosphere**. We have already put so much gas into the atmosphere, the climate will keep changing for a long, long time. Some of the changes may be good (at least in the short term) and some may be bad. But change is a near certainty.

2   We have known for 25 years that the atmosphere was changing. The most obvious **sign** was an increase in **carbon dioxide** ($CO_2$), the gas we breathe out and the gas produced when we burn **fossil fuels** such as coal and gasoline. This is the same gas that is absorbed by plants to make food. Before 1900 the amount of carbon dioxide in the atmosphere was 270 to 280 parts per million (ppm). Now it has grown to 380 parts per million. In the same time, the world has become steadily hotter. It is this **link**, this connection, that tells us that carbon dioxide is causing the warming. This **evidence** is powerful proof that humans, not nature, are causing climate change.

### Not Just Hotter

3   Since the atmosphere is getting hotter, it is also getting more **energetic**. This means that in some places it will be windier, in some places wetter, in some places drier. In some places it may even be cooler. That's why we talk about "climate change" rather than "global warming." Although on average it will be warmer, it won't necessarily be warmer everywhere.

### Can We Stop It?

4   No. We can slow it, but we can't stop it for a long, long time. We have already made the greenhouse gas **emissions** that will keep the atmosphere changing for decades to come. If we could keep the world's greenhouse gas emissions from growing, the temperature would continue to grow as fast as it is growing now. If we could cut emissions by half, the world would still keep getting hotter for a hundred years or more. But if we act soon, we can make sure the changes can be managed and kept to a minimum, and we can **adapt** to them.

*(continued on next page)*

### The Greenhouse Gases

5    Our activities release gases that contribute directly to climate change—key gases are carbon dioxide, methane, and nitrous oxide. We call these gases "greenhouse gases" because of the warming they cause. Carbon dioxide has a bigger total effect than all the other gases we make put together. But methane matters, too. Carbon dioxide is released when we burn fossil fuels like coal and gasoline. All these gases—the ones we produce, and the water vapor in the atmosphere—warm the Earth because they let the sun's heat through but block some of the heat **escaping** back out to space.

### The Bottom Line

6    It seems that the climate is changing and is going to keep changing. Almost every country wants to reduce its emissions. If all the countries of the world act, and act soon, the risks from climate change can be reduced.

*Source:* Adapted from "Gentle Footprints Boots 'n' All," a New Zealand Government online publication. www.mfe.govt.nz/publications/ser/gentle-footprints-May06. May 16, 2007. Reprinted with the permission of the Ministry for the Environment, New Zealand.

*Read also this short article about some possible results of climate change.*

## Some Predictions and Results of Climate Change

Most of the world's land mass is north of the equator, the middle of the Earth. The farther north you go, the warmer and drier it will become. For example, Siberia has always been harsh and cold, but climate change could cause it to become temperate (not too warm and not too cold). It might then be an attractive vacation spot. Since the soil of Siberia has never been farmed because it was always covered by snow, it would probably be excellent for farming. Agriculture and real estate could make Russia richer than any other country in the world. In contrast, Pakistan may become too hot for its inhabitants. Temperatures in the Punjab are often over 100°F now, but what if climate change causes the temperature to stay above 120 or 130°F? Another example is the Qori Kalis glacier in Peru. As it melts, big pieces have broken off and caused flooding in the valley. So now the valley often has too much water. Eventually, however, the glacier will disappear. When it does, the people in the valley will not have enough water and it will be drier. Finally, Western Europe could experience much colder temperatures as a result of changing ocean patterns.

*Now read the information and the chart about $CO_2$ emissions.*

## WORLD EMITTERS[1] OF CARBON DIOXIDE

In order to understand how big the problem of gas emissions is, it's helpful to look at how much is being produced and by which countries. The chart below shows how many metric tons of carbon dioxide emissions were being produced by the top 15 emitters in 2004.

### TOP 15 EMITTERS OF CARBON DIOXIDE

| Rank | Country | Annual $CO_2$ emissions (in thousands of metric tons[2]) | Percentage of total emissions |
|------|---------|------------------------|-------------------------------|
| 1 | United States | 6,049,000 | 22.2% |
| 2 | China | 5,010,000 | 18.4% |
| 3 | Russia | 1,525,000 | 5.6% |
| 4 | India | 1,343,000 | 4.9% |
| 5 | Japan | 1,258,000 | 4.6% |
| 6 | Germany | 809,000 | 3.0% |
| 7 | Canada | 639,000 | 2.3% |
| 8 | United Kingdom | 587,000 | 2.2% |
| 9 | South Korea | 466,000 | 1.7% |
| 10 | Italy | 450,000 | 1.7% |
| 11 | Mexico | 438,000 | 1.6% |
| 12 | South Africa | 437,000 | 1.6% |
| 13 | Iran | 434,000 | 1.6% |
| 14 | Indonesia | 378,000 | 1.4% |
| 15 | France | 374,000 | 1.4% |

*Source:* Wikipedia, 2007 (www.en.wikipedia.org)

Note that New Zealand is not in that group of top emitters of carbon dioxide. In fact, in 2004, New Zealand was ranked as the 69th emitter, with only 0.2% of emissions.

---

[1] **emitters:** countries that make emissions
[2] **metric ton:** unit for measuring weight, equal to 1,000 kilograms or about 2,205 pounds

## ◀ READ FOR MAIN IDEAS

*Based on the reading, mark each statement **T** (true) or **F** (false). Rewrite the false statements to make them true. Share your answers with the class.*

global warming

__F__ **1.** The increase in carbon dioxide is related to ~~our temperature changes.~~

_____ **2.** All places on Earth are getting warmer.

_____ **3.** We can stop global warming if we act now.

_____ **4.** Human activity contributes to the warming of the Earth.

Is Our Climate Changing? **169**

Match the beginning of each sentence on the left with the best ending on the right.
There may be more than one correct answer.

_f_  **1.** Our climate is changing
because . . .

_____  **2.** An increase in $CO_2$ was . . .

_____  **3.** If we could reduce greenhouse
gases by 50%, . . .

_____  **4.** The largest emitters of $CO_2$
are . . .

_____  **5.** We know that . . .

_____  **6.** Water vapor and greenhouse
gases warm the Earth because . . .

_____  **7.** Since 1900, . . .

_____  **8.** Greenhouse gases are released
into the atmosphere when . . .

_____  **9.** It will be warmer on average,
but . . .

**a.** the U.S., China, and Russia.

**b.** they allow the heat of the sun in,
but block some of the heat from
escaping.

**c.** we burn coal and gasoline.

**d.** the most obvious sign that our
atmosphere was changing.

**e.** it won't be warmer everywhere.

**f.** the amount of $CO_2$ in the
atmosphere has increased.

**g.** the atmosphere is getting more
energetic.

**h.** humans have put a lot of gases
into the atmosphere.

**i.** the world would continue
heating for about another 100
years.

◖ **MAKE INFERENCES**

Based on your understanding of the text, choose the best ending for each of these
statements. Share your answers with a partner.

**1.** The primary purpose of the New Zealand brochure is to _____.
  **a.** educate New Zealand's citizens about climate change
  **b.** educate the citizens of the world about climate change

**2.** The priority of the government of New Zealand is to _____.
  **a.** make its country cooler
  **b.** get its citizens to support reducing greenhouse gases

**3.** This country wants to _____.
  **a.** buy more oil
  **b.** buy less oil

**4.** The New Zealand government thinks _____.
  **a.** the climate change situation is dangerous
  **b.** that other countries of the world are not doing enough to slow climate
change

*Discuss the questions with the class.*

1. Some of the climate changes may be good (at least in the short-term) and some may be bad. What do you think the good and bad changes will be?

2. The text says: "If we could cut emissions by half, the world would still keep getting hotter for a hundred years or more. But if we act soon, we can make sure the changes can be managed and kept to a minimum, and we can adapt to them." In your opinion, what changes should be made immediately?

3. Look at the World Emitters chart. Is your country on the chart? If so, is it near the top, around the middle, or near the bottom? If not, where do you think it would be? How much does your country contribute to this problem?

---

**B** ┃ **READING TWO: Climate Change: Making Informed Decisions**

**1** *Read the editorial about climate change.*

---

# CLIMATE CHANGE: MAKING INFORMED[1] DECISIONS

1    For the past decade, there have been angry debates about whether our planet is heating up and whose fault it is. Now the debate cannot be avoided. TV reporters, scientists, famous actors and singers are all delivering the message that our planet is in trouble and that human beings are the cause. They say we must act now to reduce our use of fossil fuels, before it is too late. At the same time, a few governments and some scientists argue there is no clear evidence that humans are causing recent changes in climate and weather. Clearly, the experts can't agree. So, what is the average person supposed to think, or do, about this issue?

2    *Can carbon dioxide produced by humans cause climate change?* This question was first studied in the early 1900s. For the next sixty years, most scientists did not think that the daily actions or lifestyles of humans could really change the Earth's temperature. Since then, however, many scientists have come to believe that our actions *do* make a difference. In 1988, a group of scientists called the International Panel on Climate Change (IPCC) met to discuss three critical issues: 1) how our lifestyles affect the Earth's climate, 2) how climate change would affect us in the future, and 3) how exactly to deal with climate change. Later, the IPCC recommendations were used to write the Kyoto Protocol, a 1997 agreement that addressed our role in the Earth's changing atmosphere and set international limits for gas emissions.

3    A few governments, including the United States and Saudi Arabia, and some companies don't support the Kyoto Protocol. They think achieving the limits recommended by the Protocol would cost too much money and be bad for business. Scientists retained[2] by these governments and companies argue that recent climate change is not actually caused by

---

[1] **informed:** involving a lot of knowledge or information
[2] **retained:** paid to work for a company now and in the future

*(continued on next page)*

humans. These scientists don't think we really need to change our lifestyles, that is, we should continue to drive, fly, and live normally. They present evidence they say proves that the Earth is going through a normal heating and cooling cycle, as it has done throughout its history.

4  So, is there a link between humans and climate change or not? Who should we believe? The IPCC or the governments and companies that disagree with it? To reach an educated opinion, it is important to think about the people who make scientific claims and what their purposes may be. For example, some say the scientists who warn about global warming are trying to scare people in order to get attention and money for their research. According to Petr Chylek, Professor of Physics and Atmospheric Sciences at Dalhousie University in Nova Scotia, scientists can only get this attention and money "by making things bigger and more dangerous than they really are."

5  And what about the other experts who say our use of fossil fuels is *not* causing climate change? Well, some of *them* receive money from companies that produce these fossil fuels. For example, ExxonMobil, one of the world's biggest oil companies, spends $2 million a year to support groups that discredit[3] the idea of global warming. Both the Union of Concerned Scientists, a group of watchdog[4] scientists in the United States, and the Royal Society, Britain's top scientific academy, have accused ExxonMobil of trying to confuse people with incorrect and dishonest information about climate change.

6  Clearly, scientific information can be affected by the interests of individual scientists. When we hear reports on climate change, we must use good judgment and ask ourselves where the facts are coming from. We must interpret the research, make informed decisions, and most importantly, continue to actively participate in the debate.

---

[3] **discredit:** to criticize someone or something so that they are not respected
[4] **watchdog:** a person or group that makes sure other people follow the rules

**2** *Answer the questions.*

1. Whose recommendations were used to write the Kyoto Protocol?

_____

2. What limits were set by the Kyoto Protocol?

_____

3. Why does Petr Chylek say scientists want to make things more dangerous than they are?

_____

4. Why does ExxonMobil spend $2 million a year?

_____

5. Why do the Union of Concerned Scientists and the Royal Society criticize ExxonMobil?

_____

**STEP 1: Organize**

*A causal chain helps you to see the relationships between causes and effects. Look at the causal chain below describing the information in Readings One and Two. The green indicates information from Reading One; the purple indicates information from Reading Two. Look back at the readings to fill in the missing causes and effects.*

ExxonMobil produces fossil fuels → (1) Fossil fuels (coal and gasoline) are burned → Greenhouse gases are put into the atmosphere → (2a) _____ → (2b) _____ →

→ The atmosphere gets warmer → (3a) _____ → (3b) _____ → Climate Change → The IPCC meets to discuss climate change issues. →

→ (4) _____ → The Kyoto Protocol sets international limits for gas emissions → (5) _____ → (6a) _____ → (6b) _____

**STEP 2: Synthesize**

*Complete a summary of the cause-and-effect relationships of ExxonMobil, scientists, and climate change. Use information from Step 1.*

There is an interesting relationship between oil companies, scientists, and climate change. ExxonMobil is a company that produces fossil fuels. When fossil fuels such as coal and gasoline are burned, greenhouse gases are put into the atmosphere.

_____

_____

_____

_____

_____

_____

_____

*(continued on next page)*

As the climate began to change, a group of scientists called the International Panel on Climate Change (IPCC) began to study the effects of climate change.

_____

_____

_____

_____

_____

Hopefully, we will be able to slow climate change by using less of the fossil fuels in the future.

# 3 FOCUS ON WRITING

## A VOCABULARY

### ◖ REVIEW

*Read this story about a group called the Global Climate Coalition. Complete it with words from the box. Use each word only once.*

| | | | |
|---|---|---|---|
| adapt | ~~emissions~~ | evidence | link |
| atmosphere | energetic | fossil fuels | reduce |
| carbon dioxide | escaped | limited | sign |
| climate | | | |

**The Global Climate Coalition**

The Global Climate Coalition (GCC) was founded in 1987. It was a group that

included some of the most powerful oil companies. Among its members were

British Petroleum (BP), Royal Dutch Shell, Dupont, and the Ford Motor Company.

In 1997, just before the Kyoto Conference on Climate Change, it started a massive

advertising campaign. The purpose of this campaign was to stop the United States

from agreeing to reduce gas _____emissions_____ . The ads tried to frighten
                                          1.

Americans. One of the things these ads said was that if the use of

_____ was _____, the price of gasoline would go up
    **2.**               **3.**

50 cents a gallon. There was no truth to this, but the campaign was successful.

Even though the public image of the GCC was good, there were problems.

The Chairman of BP announced in May 1997 that the _____
                                                               **4.**

between greenhouse gases and climate change was too strong to ignore. BP

withdrew from the Global Climate Coalition. Dupont and Royal Dutch Shell also

left. In 1999, Ford _____ from the sinking ship of the GCC. Ford's
                         **5.**

decision was another _____ that fossil fuel industries were changing.
                                 **6.**

In 2000, DaimlerChrysler, Texaco, and General Motors left the Coalition. Leading

companies left the Global Climate Coalition because there was more and more

_____ that the _____ was really getting warmer and
      **7.**                    **8.**

more _____, and that _____ was the cause. The GCC
            **9.**                **10.**

represented old thinking, while the companies leaving were the companies trying to

_____ to the new information about climate change science. These
      **11.**

companies joined a new group called the Business Environmental Leadership

Council, as did Toyota and Boeing. Companies that joined the Council had to have

their own programs to _____ carbon emissions.
                        **12.**

The GCC closed in 2002. The organization which successfully stopped the U.S.

from agreeing to the Kyoto Protocol in 1997 has stopped influencing the global

_____ debate.
      **13.**

◀ EXPAND

*Look at this list of nouns taken from Readings One and Two. Which of these nouns can be used with the adjectives below? Some nouns can be used more than once.*

| | | | | |
|---|---|---|---|---|
| agreement | climate | doubt | fossil fuels | production |
| atmosphere | coal | emissions | gas | public |
| carbon dioxide | confusion | evidence | government | |

1. successful: _agreement, government, production_
2. clear: _____
3. warm: _____
4. powerful: _____
5. energetic: _____
6. harmful: _____
7. increasing: _____
8. national: _____
9. obvious: _____
10. massive: _____

◀ CREATE

*Write a paragraph explaining different views of climate change science. Use at least five of these words.*

| | | | | |
|---|---|---|---|---|
| agreement | climate | emissions | gas | public |
| atmosphere | confusion | evidence | government | purpose |
| carbon dioxide | doubt | fossil fuels | production | sign |

**B  GRAMMAR: Future Possibility: *May, Might, Could***

**1** *Read the paragraph. Underline the words **may, might,** and **could.***

Computers are used to make models of how the climate might respond to more carbon dioxide in the atmosphere. Some of the changes may be good and some may be bad. Since the atmosphere is getting more energetic, some places will be warmer, some places will be wetter, and some places will be drier. Some places may even be cooler. Many of the changes will cause shortages of drinking water and food for people and animals, especially poor people. But if we could cut emissions by half, we could manage the changes and adapt to them.

# FUTURE POSSIBILITY: *MAY, MIGHT, COULD*

| | |
|---|---|
| **1.** Use *may, might,* and *could* to talk about **future possibility.** | It **may** be windier.<br><br>It **might** be drier.<br><br>It **could** be managed. |
| **2.** Use *may not* and *might not* to express the possibility that something will not happen.<br><br>Use *couldn't* to express the idea that something is impossible.<br><br>**BE CAREFUL!** We usually do not contract *might not,* and we never contract *may not.* | There are a lot of clouds, but it **might not rain.**<br><br>We **couldn't** stop carbon dioxide emissions completely, but we could reduce them.<br><br>USE: If we develop new fuels, we **may not need** oil in the future.<br><br>NOT: If we develop new fuels, we ~~mayn't~~ need oil in the future. |
| **3. Questions** about possibility usually do not use *may, might,* or *could.* Instead, they use the future (*will, be going to,* the present progressive) or phrases such as *Do you think . . . ?* or *Is it possible that . . . ?*<br><br>The **answers** to these questions often use *may, might,* or *could.*<br><br><br>In **short answers** to yes / no questions, use *may, might,* or *could* alone.<br><br><br>**USAGE NOTE:** If *be* is the main verb, it is common to include *be* in the short answer. | Q: When **will** CO₂ levels **come down?**<br>A: They **might start** coming down in 100 years.<br><br>Q: **Are** we **going to be able** to adapt?<br>A: We **might adapt** if we limit emissions soon.<br><br>Q: When **will** the temperature **stop rising?**<br>A: It **may stop** in 100 years.<br><br>Q: **Do you think** developing countries **will reduce** gas emissions?<br>A: They **could reduce** them if it's not too expensive.<br><br>Q: Is ExxonMobil going to continue to pay for skeptical global warming reports?<br>A: It **might.**<br><br>Q: Will emissions **be** reduced quickly?<br>A: They **might be.** |

**2** Complete the questions and answers to express future possibility. There may be more than one correct answer.

   **1. Q:** How much are sea levels going to rise in the next 100 years?

   **A:** Sea levels _____ rise from seven inches to two feet.

   **2. Q:** What will the weather be like in Siberia?

   **A:** It _____ be warm and comfortable.

*(continued on next page)*

**3. Q:** Will some places be wetter?

   **A:** They _____ be.

**4. Q:** When will sea levels stop rising?

   **A:** They _____ stop rising in 100 years.

**5. Q:** _____ coastal areas flood?

   **A:** They might.

**6. Q:** _____ some places _____ colder?

   **A:** They might be.

**7. Q:** How much stronger do you think hurricanes could get?

   **A:** They _____ get up to Category 5½.

**3** Work with a partner. Make questions about climate change in your country or a country that you're interested in. Share your questions with the class.

## C WRITING

In this unit, you read a brochure and an editorial about climate change.

Now you are going to **write an essay about how climate change is affecting your home country or another country**. What changes have already occurred? What is changing now? What changes are predicted for the future? Explain the causes and effects of these changes. Use the vocabulary and grammar from the unit.*

### ◀ PREPARE TO WRITE: Using a Causal Chain

**1** Look at the causal chain below. A causal chain helps you to see the relationships between causes and effects. The arrows show how one or more causes leads to one or more effects.

_____ → _____ → _____ → _____ →

_____ →

_____ → _____ → _____ → _____

**2** Think of the causes and effects you will be writing about. Draw a causal chain to help you organize the cause-and-effect relationships.

*For Alternative Writing Topics, see page 183. These topics can be used in place of the writing topic for this unit or as homework. The alternative topics relate to the theme of the unit, but may not target the same grammar or rhetorical structures taught in the unit.

# ◖ WRITE: A Cause-and-Effect Essay

In a **cause-and-effect essay**, you explain the **relationships** between the causes and effects of a situation. Often, there are many causes which result in one effect, or one cause which results in many effects.

**1** *Read the essay and complete the activities that follow.*

1    The future of climate change does not look very good for our Earth. There will be flooding of coastlines, water shortages, and food shortages. The areas near the middle of the world will suffer the most because they will become hotter and experience more storms and dry weather. The poor will become poorer and the wealthy will become wealthier. Africa will experience the worst effects of climate change due to irregular weather, the rising temperature of the atmosphere and water, and rising sea levels.

2    Africa's climates have always been irregular, and now climate change is causing more irregular weather. Dry areas are becoming drier and wet areas are becoming wetter. In the future, this will hurt people who grow their own food since the time of the growing season and the amount of food they get will decrease. Since 70 percent of Africa's people grow their own food, they will not have enough. In some countries, the amount of food grown could decrease by 50 percent.

3    Another problem is the rising temperature of the atmosphere and water. Africa is an average 0.5°F hotter than it was 100 years ago. In some areas, however, it is as much as 3.5°F hotter. As a result, the earth in Africa is becoming drier. Another result is that the glaciers are melting. The snows of Kilimanjaro are expected to disappear in the next 10 years. Also, rising water temperatures in lakes will result in fewer fish, another important food. In addition, the rising temperature of the North Atlantic will cause rain to occur further and further north, so that northern Africa will experience less and less rain. This will cause more drought. Consequently, by 2020, 75–250 million people in Africa will not have enough water.

4    In the next 50 to 100 years, there will be flooding of coastlines since sea levels will rise. Many people live along the coastlines of Africa, and these people will become homeless. They will have to move away from the coastline. For most of them, there will be little help from the government. In addition, some of the best farmland will be under water. This will result in more food shortages.

5    The latest studies of climate change show that Africa may be in a more dangerous situation than any other continent. According to Andrew Simms of the New Economics Foundation, "Global warming is set to make many of the problems which Africa already deals with much, much worse." Unless the rich countries of the world reduce gas emissions now, we will see millions of Africans die of hunger and sickness.

1. What is the topic sentence? Underline it.

2. Read paragraph 2 and draw a cause-and-effect map for it.

3. Read paragraph 3 and draw a cause-and-effect map for it.

4. Read paragraph 4 and draw a cause-and-effect map for it.

**2** *Look back at the causal chain you wrote in Prepare to Write, page 178. Add notes about reasons, examples, and facts to support your causes and effects.*

**3** *Use your causal chain and notes to write the first draft of your cause-and-effect essay. It will have the following:*

- An introductory paragraph including a thesis statement about how climate change is affecting the country of your choice
- Three body paragraphs, each one focusing on one set of cause-and-effect relationships
- Each body paragraph will give reasons, examples, and facts to support your causes and effects
- A concluding paragraph summarizing your main ideas and adding a final comment

◀ **REVISE: Using Cause-and-Effect Transitions**

**1** *Look at the sentences taken from Reading One. What do the boldfaced words mean?*

- All these gases—the ones we produce, and the water vapor in the atmosphere—warm the Earth **because** they let the sun's heat through but block some of the heat escaping back out to space.

- **Since** the atmosphere is getting hotter, it is also getting more energetic.

- Carbon dioxide has a bigger total effect than all the other gases we make put together. **Consequently**, it is very important to decrease carbon dioxide.

- We have already made the greenhouse gas emissions that will keep the atmosphere changing for decades to come. **Therefore**, even if we stop the emissions now, the Earth will continue to warm.

*Because, since, consequently,* and *therefore* are **transitions**. Writers use transitions to help the reader move from one idea to the next. These words or phrases prepare the reader for what type of information will come next. *Because* and *since* show **cause**. *Consequently* and *therefore* show **effect**.

**Different transitions** are used to show **cause and effect**. Transitions used to show **cause** are also called **adverbial conjunctions**. Notice that these transitions are used with a complete sentence containing a subject and verb.

## ADVERBIAL CONJUNCTIONS USED TO SHOW CAUSE

**because     since     as**

- It's changing **because** humans have put gases into the atmosphere.
- In the next 50 to 100 years, there will be flooding of coastlines **since** sea levels will rise.
- We know that the atmosphere is getting more energetic **as** it is getting hotter.

## TRANSITIONS USED TO SHOW EFFECT

**Therefore,     Consequently,     Thus,     As a result,**

- **Therefore,** ExxonMobil thought of a good way to avoid this problem.
- **Consequently,** it has only one goal: to make money by selling fossil fuels.
- The atmosphere is getting hotter and more energetic. **Thus,** in some places it will be windier, in some places wetter, in some places drier.
- The climate is changing. **As a result,** every country in the world will be affected.

**2**  *Read this report about climate change around the world. Complete the sentences with the best choice of transitions. You may need to add commas to some sentences.*

According to the IPCC, climate change in the next century could bring both benefits and problems to different parts of the world. In Africa, 75 to 250 million people will not have enough water. _____Since_____ this will hurt
<u>1. (Since / As a result,)</u>
agriculture, or farming, there will not be enough food. _____
<u>2. (As a result, / Because)</u>
more people in Africa will be malnourished. The water temperature of lakes will increase. _____ there will be less and less fish to eat.
<u>3. (Consequently, / As)</u>

In Asia, the melting of glaciers will first cause flooding. Later,

_____ the glaciers get smaller, the rivers will dry up. In some areas
<u>4. (therefore, / as)</u>
of Asia, agriculture will improve 20 percent, while in other areas it will decrease by 30 percent.

There will be less rain in Australia and New Zealand. _____
<u>5. (As a result, / Since)</u>
there will be less water and less clean water. In southern and eastern Australia there will be drought and fires. In some areas of New Zealand, however, farming will improve because it will be warmer and there will be more rain.

_____ the coastal areas will have more and bigger storms, there
**6. (Because / Consequently,)**
will be more flooding.

In northern Europe, it will be warmer. _____ agriculture will
**7. (Therefore, / As)**
increase and forests will grow. In southern Europe, there will be drought and water

shortages _____ it will be warmer.
**8. (therefore, / since)**

In North America, it will be warmer and drier. _____ there
**9. (As a result, / As)**
will be more fires and disease, and problems with insects. _____
**10. (Because / Thus,)**
some areas will be drier, Latin America will have a decrease in agriculture.

_____ sea temperature will rise, there will be fewer fish in some
**11. (As a result, / As)**
places. These things will result in food shortages.

**3** *Look back at the first draft of your essay. Add cause-and-effect transitions to help the reader move from one idea to the next. Don't forget to use commas where needed.*

◀ **EDIT: Writing the Final Draft**

*Write the final draft of your essay. Carefully edit it for grammatical and mechanical errors, such as spelling, capitalization, and punctuation. Make sure you used some of the vocabulary and grammar from the unit. Use the checklist to help you write your final draft. Then neatly write or type your essay.*

---

## ✔ FINAL DRAFT CHECKLIST

- ○ Does your essay clearly explain the causes and effects that you think are important for your topic?
- ○ Does it contain an introductory paragraph, three body paragraphs, and a concluding paragraph?
- ○ Does the introductory paragraph contain a thesis statement stating the main idea of the essay?
- ○ Does each body paragraph focus on one set of cause-and-effect relationships?
- ○ Does each body paragraph contain reasons, examples, and facts to support the causes and effects?
- ○ Did you use cause-and-effect transitions to help the reader move from one idea to the next?
- ○ Does the concluding paragraph restate the main idea expressed in the thesis statement?
- ○ Did you use *may, might,* or *could* to express future possibility?
- ○ Did you use vocabulary from the unit?

# ALTERNATIVE WRITING TOPICS

*Write about one of the topics. Use the vocabulary and grammar from the unit.*

1. Think about how your life will change in 20 years as a result of climate change. Write an essay discussing the positive and negative changes in your life.

2. Imagine you work for a government organization that provides help to victims of disasters. Write a report about a natural disaster that you know about. What caused the disaster? What were the results of the disaster? Who helped the victims after it happened? Did the government provide most of the help (relief)? Did international organizations help? How long did it take for this area to recover?

3. What will you do personally to slow down climate change? How much action are you willing to take? What do you think you will achieve? Write a journal entry about your reaction to information about climate change.

## RESEARCH TOPICS, see page 215.

# Crime and Punishment

## ① FOCUS ON THE TOPIC

### Ⓐ PREDICT

*First, look at the photograph and discuss the questions: What is this? What is it used for? Then, look at the list of words and circle the words that are the most closely related to the photograph.*

| | | | |
|---|---|---|---|
| agreement | doctor | government | opinion |
| crime | education | justice | protest |
| disagreement | execution | murder | punishment |

185

*Discuss the following questions in a small group.*

1. Capital punishment (the death penalty) means taking the life of someone who has committed a crime. How many forms of capital punishment do you know about?

2. In the United States, capital punishment is allowed in some states. Do you know of any other societies in which capital punishment is allowed?

3. Why do some people believe that capital punishment is fair? Why do others think that it is unfair?

## C  BACKGROUND AND VOCABULARY

**1**  *Read the fact sheet about capital punishment. Pay special attention to the boldfaced words.*

- In Belarus, the only country in Europe that uses the death penalty, it is the punishment for **murderers** who have killed one or more people.

- Italy abolished[1] the death penalty in 1994. In 2007, 310 prisoners serving life sentences wrote to the President. They asked him to give them the death penalty because life in prison was too **cruel**.

- Iraq has been asked to end capital punishment because its prisoners do not receive **justice**. Some prisoners are killed for **revenge**—someone kills the prisoner because the prisoner hurt them before. The people who want **revenge** do not have forgiveness for the prisoners.

- Switzerland abolished the death penalty because it takes away the **right** to life and dignity.

- In Rwanda in 1994, Hutus killed 800,000 Tutsis. Many Tutsis today want justice; they want the Hutus to be punished. Rwanda abolished the death penalty in 2007. It wanted to show the world that its people **respect** the right to life, even for murderers.

- The president of Kyrgyzstan abolished the death penalty in 2007. The new law says that no one with Kyrgyz **citizenship** can be deprived of life.

- The number of **executions** in China is a state secret. Amnesty International estimates the number in 2006 was 7,500 to 8,000.

- Spain abolished the death penalty in 1995, stating that the death penalty should not be a part of advanced **societies**.

---

[1] **abolished**: ended the existence of something

- Since 1900, in the United States, there have been 426 prisoners sentenced to death who were later found to be **innocent**. Unfortunately, 23 had already been executed.
- In the United States, states that do not have the death penalty have fewer **violent** crimes. The murder rate in states with the death penalty is 37 percent higher than the murder rate in states that do not have the death penalty.
- Here is a summary of capital punishment around the world: During 2006, 3,861 people who were found **guilty** were sentenced to death in 55 countries, and more than 1,591 prisoners were executed in 25 countries.

**2** *Match the words on the left with the definitions on the right.*

_____ 1. murderer

_____ 2. cruel

_____ 3. justice

_____ 4. revenge

_____ 5. forgiveness

_____ 6. right

_____ 7. respect

_____ 8. citizenship

_____ 9. execution

_____ 10. society

_____ 11. innocent

_____ 12. violent

_____ 13. guilty

a. doing something bad to someone because they did something bad to you

b. to be careful not to do something against someone's rights or wishes

c. having broken a law

d. the act of killing someone legally as punishment

e. all the people who live in the same country and share the same laws and customs

f. letting go of anger towards someone who hurt you

g. a person who kills someone

h. not having broken a law

i. something you are allowed to do or have because of the law

j. meant to hurt someone by using force

k. causing pain or suffering because you want to

l. right and fair treatment

m. the legal right of belonging to a certain country

**A** **READING ONE: Two Points of View**

A newspaper **editorial** gives the **writer's opinion** about a topic. As with any news article, an editorial begins with a headline or title.

*Look at the headlines of the two editorials. Get into a small group and discuss what you expect to find. Choose one person to take notes for the group. Be prepared to discuss the topics with the whole class. Then read the editorials.*

**Editorial 1**

# Life in Prison Is Still Life: Why Should a Killer Live?

1    Murder is totally unfair; the victims of murder are gone forever. Their hopes and plans have ended permanently, and the pleasures they enjoyed in life have been destroyed. They will never see their friends again and will never hear the voices of parents, brothers, and sisters who cry, "How could this have happened?" But the **murderer** is still alive. Without capital punishment, murderers are allowed to participate in and enjoy life.

2    Today there are murderers in prisons all over the world. Most of them would rather spend their lives in prison than die. This is not surprising since the desire to live is normal and natural. In prison there are many small pleasures that one can enjoy every day: the feeling of warm sunshine, the taste of a hot meal, the comfort of sleep. The lifestyle in prison is not always harsh and **cruel**; many prisoners have the opportunity to continue their education, play sports, enjoy movies, and receive visits from their loved ones.

3    There is no reason why a killer, a destroyer of life, should live. **Justice** requires that each person **respect** the **rights** and freedoms of every other person, or be punished for not doing so. The people who commit murder give up their rights to **citizenship** and life itself. Why should the tax money of citizens, including the victim's family, keep the killer alive? The only fair punishment is **execution**. Execution puts the killer away from **society** forever, stops him from killing again, and sends a strong message to others who might kill: Killers will not be allowed to live.

4    Let sunshine fall on those who respect life—not on those who destroy it.

# Why Do We Kill People to Show That Killing People Is Wrong?

1    There are times when murder is not committed because of cruelty. People may kill for many other reasons such as anger, misunderstanding, and fear. Everyone has made mistakes because of such feelings. For society, it is a serious mistake to take the life of someone who has killed because it teaches everyone that **forgiveness** is unnecessary.

2    The government has the difficult job of deciding who is **innocent** and who is **guilty**, and this job can never be done perfectly. If capital punishment is allowed, there always exists the possibility that an innocent person will be executed by mistake. When that happens, an even worse crime has been committed—the killing of an innocent person by the government. Then there is the fact that the poor and minorities get the death penalty more often than whites do. Furthermore, the idea that capital punishment stops criminals from committing murder is doubtful; studies have been unable to show that the fear of capital punishment stops someone from committing murder more than other punishments. And let us not forget that murdering the murderer is a **violent** act in itself; it is **revenge**.

3    The United States government once followed the example of Germany, Britain, France, and other nations that no longer execute their citizens. However, since 1977, our society has been allowing capital punishment again, at a high cost. We cannot imagine the pain of family members who have been waiting for years for the government's decision to execute or not execute their loved ones. It also costs the taxpayer millions of dollars more to execute a criminal than to imprison that criminal for life. The *Los Angeles Times* reported that it costs California taxpayers $136 million to keep a murderer in prison for life, but more than $250 million if that criminal is executed. Prison is a better form of punishment because it protects society and punishes criminals by taking away their freedom.

4    People can change, even people who have made terrible mistakes. Life in prison gives people the chance to change. Caryl Chessman is an example of someone who became a better person in prison. He taught other prisoners how to read, and he wrote several books. Before his execution, he wrote that he had finally learned not to hate. Jaturun Siripongs is another example. He had murdered two liquor store employees, but while he was on death row, he became a Buddhist monk.

5    Chessman and Siripongs learned this important lesson in prison. But a dead man learns nothing, and an executed person will never change. When a government kills, it is murdering hope.

# ◖ READ FOR MAIN IDEAS

The two editorials express different opinions about capital punishment.

**Opinion A:** Execution is a better form of punishment than life in prison.

**Opinion B:** Life in prison is a better form of punishment than execution.

*Look at the main ideas below. Which were used to support Opinion A and which were used to support Opinion B? Match them correctly by writing **A** or **B**. Look at Reading One again to make sure that your answers are based on information from that reading.*

__B__ **1.** Execution may cause an innocent person to die.

_____ **2.** Prisoners are able to enjoy life, and this is not fair.

_____ **3.** Not all people who kill are cruel.

_____ **4.** Capital punishment is revenge.

_____ **5.** A prisoner is no longer free.

_____ **6.** People naturally want to live.

_____ **7.** Racial prejudice affects capital punishment.

_____ **8.** Prison can sometimes improve a person.

_____ **9.** Execution may teach other people not to commit crimes.

_____ **10.** Execution is more expensive than life imprisonment.

# ◖ READ FOR DETAILS

*Match the main ideas from the previous exercise with the details below. Write the number of the main idea next to the detail. Note that some of these details support the same main idea.*

__3__ **a.** Some murders are mistakes, caused by anger or fear.

_____ **b.** The government spends millions of tax dollars on execution decisions.

_____ **c.** Most people would rather go to prison than be executed.

_____ **d.** Caryl Chessman learned not to hate while in prison.

_____ **e.** The message of execution is that murderers will not be allowed to live.

_____ **f.** The government can make mistakes when it decides if a person is guilty or not.

_____ **g.** Prisoners have the basic pleasures of eating and sleeping.

_____ **h.** Executing the murderer is a violent act.

_____ **i.** Jaturun Siripongs became a Buddhist monk while in prison.

_____ **j.** Murderers lose their rights of citizenship.

# ◖ MAKE INFERENCES

*Imagine the people who wrote the two editorials in Reading One are having a debate about capital punishment. Some of their arguments are in the chart. Use specific quotes from the two editorials to refute the ideas.*

| CAPITAL PUNISHMENT | |
|---|---|
| **PRO: Arguments from Editorial 1** | **CON: Arguments from Editorial 2** |
| **1.** | "Prison is a better form of punishment because it protects society and punishes criminals by taking away their freedom." |
| **2.** "The people who commit murder give up their rights to citizenship and life itself." | |
| **3.** | "Furthermore, the idea that capital punishment stops criminals from committing murder is doubtful: studies have been unable to show that fear of capital punishment stops someone from committing murder more than other punishments." |
| **4.** "Why should the tax money of citizens, including the victim's family, keep the killer alive?" | |
| **5.** "There is no reason why a killer, a destroyer of life, should live." | |

# ◖ EXPRESS OPINIONS

*Choose which editorial you agree with. Then, on a separate piece of paper, write a paragraph that gives your opinion on capital punishment. Use the information from Make Inferences. Then discuss your opinion with a classmate.*

1. A killer should not be allowed to live.

2. It is wrong to kill anyone—even a killer.

Look at the five charts. Titles, captions, and notes near a chart contain important information. Study this information in order to interpret the charts correctly. Then work with a classmate to answer the questions below each chart.

## CHART 1

### Death Penalty Facts

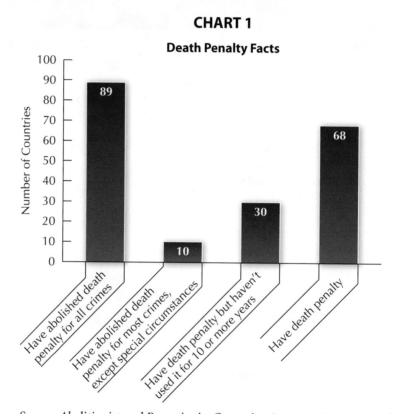

Source: *Abolitionist and Retentionist Countries,* Amnesty International Index, April 27, 2007 www.amnesty.org.

1. When were these facts published?

2. How many countries have definitely not used the death penalty for the last 10 years? Why do you think this is so?

3. Are most of these countries for or against the death penalty? Explain.

4. Can you use these facts to explain how the death penalty is used in a country you know well?

5. What do you think "except special circumstances" means?

In May 2006, the Gallup Poll surveyed United States voters with the following results, as shown in Charts 2 and 3.

## CHART 2

**Do you support or oppose capital punishment for murderers?**

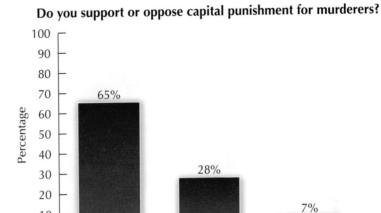

*Source:* The Gallup Poll, May 2006.

## CHART 3

**Do you support capital punishment or life imprisonment with absolutely no chance of parole for murderers?**

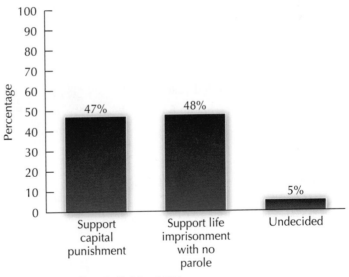

*Source:* The Gallup Poll, May 2006.

6. Why do you think the number of voters who support capital punishment dropped from 65 percent in Chart 2 to 47 percent in Chart 3?

7. What conclusion can you make from these charts?

# CHART 4

### Execution of the Innocent in the United States 1900–2007

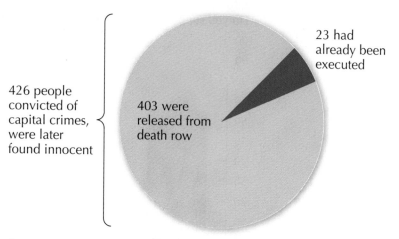

426 people convicted of capital crimes, were later found innocent

403 were released from death row

23 had already been executed

*Source:* From *In Spite of Innocence* by Michael Radelet et al., 1994, as on Amnesty USA website and "The Innocence List" on www.deathpenaltyinfo.org., May 11, 2006.

**8.** What does this information show about the capital punishment system in the United States?

**9.** Can anything be learned from this information? Explain.

# CHART 5

### Executions by Country in 2006

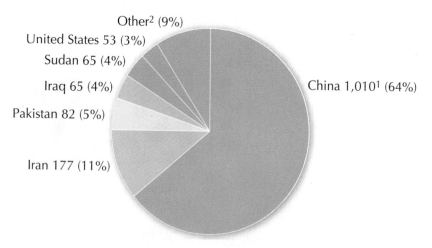

Other[2] (9%)

United States 53 (3%)

Sudan 65 (4%)

Iraq 65 (4%)

Pakistan 82 (5%)

China 1,010[1] (64%)

Iran 177 (11%)

[1] Credible sources estimate more: 7,500–8,000

[2] This represents the other 62 countries that have capital punishment and use it, but do very few executions as compared with the 6 countries listed above.

*Source:* "Facts and Figures on the Death Penalty" (January 1, 2007) as on Amnesty International website.

**10.** Can you think of anything these six countries have in common?

◀ **STEP 1: Organize**

*Below are some statements about capital punishment. Mark each statement as either*
*F (fact) or O (opinion).*

<u>O</u>   **1.** Execution costs too much money.

_____   **2.** Prisoners have basic pleasures such as eating and sleeping.

_____   **3.** Although 65% of Americans say they support the death penalty, if they are given the option of life imprisonment without parole, that number drops down to 47%.

_____   **4.** Most countries of the world disagree with capital punishment because they know it is wrong.

_____   **5.** Murder victims can no longer enjoy the basic pleasures of life.

_____   **6.** Americans want life imprisonment, not capital punishment.

_____   **7.** Execution is a warning: Don't murder or you will pay with your life.

_____   **8.** From 1900–2007, 426 people who were convicted of capital crimes were later found to be innocent.

_____   **9.** It is unfair that a victim's family, who has lost their loved one's life, must support the murderer's life.

_____   **10.** Americans want the death penalty, not life imprisonment.

# STEP 2: Synthesize

*Writers often need to support their opinions with facts and data. A debate is being held at a local university. Below are the notes that each team is writing in preparation for the debate. Use information from Step 1 to fill in opinions and facts. Note that the Roman numerals (I, II, III, IV) are the opinions and the letters (A, B) are the facts to support the opinions.*

Debate Team X—PRO: Death Penalty

I. It is unfair that a murderer should enjoy life while the victim cannot.

A. _____

B. _____

_____

II. _____

A. According to an article in the *Los Angeles Times*, California taxpayers pay more than $136 million to keep a murderer in prison for life.

III. _____

IV. _____

A. The U.S. government once followed the example of Germany, Britain, France, and other nations that no longer execute their citizens—but since 1977, our society has been allowing capital punishment again.

Debate Team Y—CON: Death Penalty

I. Execution may cause an innocent person to die.

A. _____

II. _____

A. According to an article in the *Los Angeles Times*, California taxpayers pay $136 million to keep a murderer in prison for life, but more than $250 million if that same criminal is executed.

III. _____

A. One hundred and nineteen countries have either abolished capital punishment, or haven't used it for 10 years.

B. Only a minority of countries, 69, have the death penalty.

IV. _____

A. _____

# ③ FOCUS ON WRITING

## Ⓐ VOCABULARY

### ◀ REVIEW

*Complete the student essay with words from the box. Use each word only once.*

| | | | | |
|---|---|---|---|---|
| abolished | forgiveness | justice | ~~revenge~~ | support |
| citizens | guilty | oppose | rights | violent |
| cruel | innocent | respects | | |

STUDENT ESSAY CONTEST WINNER

**Why I Personally Oppose the Death Penalty**

"An eye for an eye" is an expression that is used to support ____revenge____. It
**1.**

means to hurt someone because they hurt you. It is always _____. This is
**2.**

what the United States government does when it uses capital punishment.

Unfortunately, those who are executed are often executed because of their race or

lack of money, or for political reasons. If we are a nation that believes in equality,

shouldn't the death penalty be used fairly? And yet, it is not. This is why the death

penalty is a terrible thing. What should citizens who _____ the death
**3.**

penalty do? The death penalty should be _____ because it is morally,
**4.**

economically, and socially wrong.

On the Supreme Court building in Washington, D.C. it says "Equal

_____ Under Law" because Americans have always believed every person
**5.**

should be treated fairly. Yet, non-white murderers get the death penalty much more

often than white murderers. In addition, the Supreme Court has decided that it's

*(continued on next page)*

OK to execute _____ people if they have had a fair trial. But this is not
                    **6.**

justice. We must also not forget that when an innocent person is found

_____ the real killer is still free! This should not continue.
        **7.**

The death penalty uses a lot of the state's money. According to the *Miami Herald,* it costs two to six times more to execute a criminal than to imprison him or her for life. Furthermore, life in prison is better because it gives two benefits: Society is protected from future crime and the murderer can think about what he or she has done. Even if the killer doesn't change, the government has saved a lot of money.

Many people believe that capital punishment is a deterrent, that murderers won't murder if they know they could be punished with the death penalty. But executions do not discourage others from committing murder. Actually, studies show that murders increase after an execution that has been in the news. States that do not have executions have lower murder rates. Countries that do not have capital punishment have lower murder rates. This shows that killing only results in more

_____ behavior.
        **8.**

The death penalty not only encourages killing, but it is also morally and economically wrong. The government puts innocent people to death and justifies it by saying the person had a fair trial. The community loses a friend and keeps a killer. The death penalty does not reflect a nation that _____ the
                                                                        **9.**

_____ of the individual and believes in equality for all. What should
        **10.**

_____ who oppose the death penalty and _____ life
        **11.**                                          **12.**

imprisonment do? Speak out against an eye for an eye. Be a person who practices

_____.
        **13.**

**1** Some nouns refer to ideas or feelings. They refer to things that cannot be seen or touched, such as love and peace. These nouns are called **abstract nouns**.

*Look at the following nouns, and mark the abstract nouns with **A**. Discuss your answers with the class.*

_____ **1.** prison        _____ **9.** citizenship

_____ **2.** friends       _____ **10.** innocence

__A__ **3.** misunderstanding       _____ **11.** person

_____ **4.** anger        _____ **12.** government

_____ **5.** punishment       _____ **13.** guilt

_____ **6.** justice        _____ **14.** society

_____ **7.** family        _____ **15.** rights

_____ **8.** food

**2** When writers use abstract nouns, they often use **examples** to help the reader understand more clearly what they mean.

*Match the abstract nouns on the left with the examples on the right.*

__c__ **1. forgiveness**

_____ **2. cruelty**

_____ **3. innocence**

_____ **4. society**

_____ **5. citizenship**

_____ **6. fairness**

_____ **7. immigration**

_____ **8. punishment**

_____ **9. opposition**

_____ **10. crime**

_____ **11. support**

_____ **12. guilt**

_____ **13. abolition**

**a.** cutting off the hand of a person who steals

**b.** agreeing with an opinion

**c.** deciding not to stay angry when someone has hurt you

**d.** considering a person innocent until proven guilty

**e.** choosing to do something that breaks the law

**f.** ending a custom because it's not good for people

**g.** carrying the passport of a particular country

**h.** a court has proof that someone is a murderer

**i.** a court has proof that someone did not rob a bank

**j.** people moving from Mexico to California

**k.** relatives, friends, and neighbors

**l.** strong disagreement with something someone says

**m.** hurting an animal for no reason

**3** In editorial writing, writers **choose their words carefully.** They want to present their opinions as strongly as possible so that the reader will agree with them.

*Look at the pairs of sentences. Complete each sentence **b** by choosing one word to replace the underlined word in sentence **a**. Then, circle the strength of meaning of the new word. Discuss the variation in meanings with the class.*

1. **a.** A government is wrong when it <u>kills</u> its citizens.

   **b.** A government is wrong when it _____*executes*_____ its citizens.
   (punishes / executes)

   **New meaning:** Weaker /(Stronger)/ Neither

2. **a.** Why should we keep a <u>murderer</u> alive?

   **b.** Why should we keep a _____ alive?
   (criminal / guilty person)

   **New meaning:** Weaker / Stronger / Neither

3. **a.** Life in prison is not always <u>bad</u>.

   **b.** Life in prison is not always _____.
   (fair / cruel)

   **New meaning:** Weaker / Stronger / Neither

4. **a.** Prisoners hope to receive visits from the <u>people who care about them</u>.

   **b.** Prisoners hope to receive visits from their _____.
   (loved ones / relatives)

   **New meaning:** Weaker / Stronger / Neither

5. **a.** Men and women who follow the laws of their country are usually good <u>people</u>.

   **b.** Men and women who follow the laws of their country are usually good

   _____.
   (adults / citizens)

   **New meaning:** Weaker / Stronger / Neither

6. **a.** <u>Immigrants</u> are sometimes the victims of crime.

   **b.** _____ are sometimes the victims of crime.
   (Strangers / Foreigners)

   **New meaning:** Weaker / Stronger / Neither

7. **a.** Many people fear prison because they believe it will <u>hurt</u> their future.

   **b.** Many people fear prison because they believe it will _____
   (change / destroy)
   their future.

   **New meaning:** Weaker / Stronger / Neither

8. **a.** The murder was done out of <u>anger</u>.

   **b.** The murder was done out of _____.
   (passion / revenge)

   **New meaning:** Weaker / Stronger / Neither

9. **a.** Many people want to <u>abolish</u> abortion.

   **b.** Many people want to _____ abortion.
   (end / reduce)

   **New meaning:** Weaker / Stronger / Neither

10. **a.** This woman is <u>violent</u>.

   **b.** This woman is _____.
   (passionate / tough)

   **New meaning:** Weaker / Stronger / Neither

11. **a.** You need to <u>respect</u> her things.

   **b.** You need to _____ her things.
   (recognize / protect)

   **New meaning:** Weaker / Stronger / Neither

◀ CREATE

*On a separate piece of paper, write one paragraph to answer the questions below about crime and punishment in the United States or in the world. Use at least five of the words from the box.*

| | | | |
|---|---|---|---|
| cruel | innocent | punishment | rights |
| forgive | justice | respect | society |
| guilty | murder | revenge | violent |

1. What do you predict will happen in the future with murderers?

2. Will punishment be more or less severe?

## B GRAMMAR: Present Perfect and Present Perfect Progressive

**1** *Read these two paragraphs taken from the two editorials in Reading One. Look at the two different verb tenses in bold. How are these tenses similar? How are they different?*

**Paragraph I**

Murder is totally unfair; the victims of murder are gone forever. Their hopes and plans **have ended** permanently, and the pleasures they enjoyed in life have been destroyed. They will never see their friends again and will never hear the voices of parents, brothers, and sisters who cry, "How could this **have happened**?" But the murderer is still alive. Without capital punishment, murderers are allowed to participate in and enjoy life.

**Paragraph 2**

The United States government once followed the example of Germany, Britain, France, and other nations that no longer execute their citizens. However, since 1977, our society **has been allowing** capital punishment again, at a high cost. We cannot imagine the pain of family members who **have been waiting** for years for the government's decision to execute or not execute their loved ones. It also costs the taxpayer millions of dollars more to execute a criminal than to imprison that criminal for life. The *Los Angeles Times* reported that it costs California taxpayers $136 million to keep a murderer in prison for life, but more than $250 million if that criminal is executed. Prison is a better form of punishment because it protects society and punishes criminals by taking away their freedom.

## PRESENT PERFECT AND PRESENT PERFECT PROGRESSIVE

| | |
|---|---|
| **1.** We often use the **present perfect** to talk about an action that started in the past, continues into the present, and may continue into the future. | She **has visited** him almost every day. |
| **2.** We often use the **present perfect** to indicate that an action was recently completed. | Their hopes and plans **have ended** permanently. (*completed action*) |
| **3.** We often use the **present perfect progressive** to show that an action that began in the past is still continuing. | We cannot imagine the pain of family members who **have been waiting** for years for the government's decision to execute or not execute their loved ones. (*continuing action*) |
| **4. Non-action verbs,** such as **be,** and verbs that refer to mental states or emotions (**believe, wish, trust**), are not used in the present perfect progressive. | For most prisoners, life in prison **has been** difficult.<br><br>Many prisoners **have wished** they could be free. |
| **5.** You can use the **present perfect** and the **present perfect progressive** with the time expressions **for** and **since**.<br><br><br>Both tenses can be used with adverbs such as **always** and **recently**. | However, *since* 1977, our society **has allowed** capital punishment again.<br><br>We cannot imagine the pain of family members who **have been waiting** *for* years for the government's decision to execute or not execute their loved ones.<br><br>Amnesty International **has** *always* **worked** to protect human rights throughout the world.<br><br>*Recently*, most Americans **have been supporting** life imprisonment without parole. |

**2** *Read this passage, which describes the life of a prisoner. Complete it with the present perfect or the present perfect progressive forms of the verbs in parentheses.*

Wayne Paulson _____ in prison since 1992. For many years he
                          **1. (be)**

_____ for the government's decision whether or not to execute him.
  **2. (wait)**

Lately, he _____ letters because he wants to make sure that his loved
              **3. (write)**

ones understand that he is innocent. He _____ very lonely in prison.
                                            **4. (be)**

Only a few people _____ him. But one person _____
                      **5. (visit)**                          **6. (come)**

to see him nearly every day—his mother. She will visit him as long as he remains in

prison because she _____ that her son is innocent. Wayne's mother
                      **7. (always / believe)**

_____ everyone that her son is a good citizen. She will continue to
  **8. (tell)**

do this because she _____ her son since the day he was born.
                        **9. (love)**

**3** *Describe the information about the charts in Reading Two (page 192). Make complete, grammatical sentences with the words and phrases in parentheses. Use the present perfect or the present perfect progressive.*

1. (Recently / 119 countries / not / use / death penalty.)

   _____

2. (30 countries / not / use / death penalty / 10 years.)

   _____

3. (China / execute / more than / 1,000 / annually.)

   _____

## C  WRITING

In this unit, you read two editorials about capital punishment: one pro and one con. You also read some charts about capital punishment in the United States and in the world.

Now you are going to **write an essay giving your opinion about capital punishment.** You will write an essay in which you try to convince the reader of your point of view. Use the vocabulary and grammar in the unit.

*For Alternative Writing Topics, see page 210. These topics can be used in place of the writing topic for this unit or as homework. The alternative topics relate to the theme of the unit, but may not target the same grammar or rhetorical structures taught in the unit.

1. Work in a small group. List reasons for and against capital punishment. Use ideas from the readings and your own ideas.

2. Decide whether you are for or against capital punishment. Put a check mark next to the reasons you agree with on your list from Question 1.

◀ **WRITE:** A Persuasive Essay

The purpose of a **persuasive essay** is to convince the reader to agree with your point of view. You give **reasons to support** your opinion. You also **refute** (argue against) the opposing point of view. In addition, you use concrete details such as examples, quotations, and statistics to support your reasons.

**1** *Read the essay. Then discuss the questions that follow in a small group.*

1    In some places, murderers get life sentences for their crimes. In others, they get the death penalty. There is a lot of disagreement about how murderers should be punished. However, I believe that people should get life sentences for murder, not the death penalty.

2    One reason I support life sentences for murder is that death is not the worst punishment. It is worse to have to sit in jail for the rest of one's life. Life imprisonment is hard. According to Lt. Vernall Crittendon, the public information officer at San Quentin Prison in California, every time the prisoner is out of his cell he is wearing chains and an officer is standing next to him with his hands on him. Prisoners never get to do what they want. All they can do is think about their crimes. They know that they will never be able to get out of prison. Therefore, life imprisonment is an effective punishment.

3    Another reason is that sometimes people change. Some people commit murder when they are addicted to drugs or have other bad influences in their lives. With time, people can change in jail. Many convicted criminals start studying or learn about religion when they are in jail. Some of them start to really think about what they did wrong. They even try to help other prisoners by teaching or counseling them. Stanley "Tookie" Williams is an example of this. He was in prison for the killings of four people in 1979. In 2001, he was nominated for the Nobel Peace Prize after writing eight children's books about not being violent. But prisoners like Williams cannot change if they are dead.

4    Some opponents of life sentences for murder say that it is too expensive to keep murderers in jail and it would be cheaper to execute them. However, capital punishment can also be very expensive. The courts are very careful before they execute people, so there are many court hearings before they decide to execute them. Sometimes the hearings will continue for years. The government has to pay for the court hearings, the criminal's lawyer, and many other expenses. In California, for example, it costs more than $250 million for each execution. It is clear that capital punishment is not always cheaper than life in prison.

5    In conclusion, there are many good reasons to give life sentences to murderers instead of the death penalty. Life sentences are an effective punishment, they give criminals a chance to change, and they do not involve a lot of expensive court hearings. For these reasons, I think that life sentences are a better punishment for murder than the death penalty.

1. Which sentence is the thesis statement? What is the writer's opinion?

2. What two reasons support the writer's point of view?

3. What specific examples support each reason?

4. What opposing point of view does the writer mention?

5. How does the writer refute that point of view?

6. Find one example, one quotation, and one statistic used as concrete details to support the reasons and refute the opposing point of view. Underline each one.

**2**  *Look again at what you checked in your list either for or against capital punishment in Prepare to Write, page 204.*

1. Choose the two reasons that most strongly support your point of view.

2. Choose the reason that most strongly argues against your point of view.

3. Make notes about examples that support your reasons.

4. Make notes about examples that refute the opposing point of view.

**3**  *Now plan the first draft of your essay by completing this outline. Use your notes.*

I. **Introductory paragraph**

Thesis statement (your opinion of capital punishment):

_____

_____

II. **Body Paragraph**

Topic sentence for reason 1:

_____

Supporting details:

_____

_____

_____

*(continued on next page)*

**4** *Use your outline to write the first draft of your persuasive essay.*

◀ **REVISE: Using Sentence Variety**

**1** *Read the paragraph. Look at the sentences carefully. How are they similar? How are they different?*

> Murder is totally unfair because the victims of murder are gone forever. Their hopes and plans have ended permanently, and the pleasures they enjoyed in life have been destroyed. They will never see their friends again and will never hear the voices of their parents, brothers, and sisters. But the murderer is still alive. If we stop capital punishment, murderers will still be allowed to participate in life.

Writers often use different **sentence types** to make their writing more interesting. The three basic **sentence types** are **simple**, **compound**, and **complex**.

1. A **simple sentence** includes one subject and one verb.

   A simple sentence can also include a **compound subject**. This is a subject with two or more nouns.

               [S]           [V]
   - The victims of murder are gone forever.

          [S]     [S]    [V]
   - Their hopes and plans have ended permanently.

2. A **compound sentence** consists of two independent clauses (subject-verb combinations). They are often joined with **coordinating conjunctions** (*and, but, or, so*).

   A **comma** is used before the coordinating conjunction.

   [S]  [V]
   - I believe in capital punishment,

           [S]    [V]
   **but** my sister doesn't.

   [S]  [V]
   - You are either in favor of the

              [S]  [V]
   death penalty, **or** you are against it.

3. A **complex sentence** includes two clauses: independent and dependent. The independent clause (I.C.) is a complete sentence. It can stand alone. The dependent clause (D.C.) begins with a **subordinating conjunction** (*because, if, since, when, although*). The dependent clause is an incomplete sentence. It cannot stand alone.

   A **comma** is used when the sentence begins with a dependent clause. It is not used when the sentence begins with an independent clause.

   [I.C.]           [D.C.]
   - Murder is unfair **because** the victims of murder are gone forever.

   [D.C.]
   - **If we stop capital punishment,**
   [I.C.]
   murderers will still be allowed to participate in life.
   [I.C.]
   - Murderers will still be allowed to
                [D.C.]
   participate in life **if we stop capital punishment.**

**2** The sentences describe the life of Wayne Paulson. Combine each pair of sentences into one compound or complex sentence. Use coordinating conjunctions (**and, but, or, so**) in compound sentences. Use subordinating conjunctions (**because, if, since, when, although**) in complex sentences. Be sure to use subject pronouns and commas where appropriate.

Example: **a.** Wayne reads books in prison.
**b.** Wayne sometimes exercises.

<u>Wayne reads books in prison, or he sometimes exercises.</u>
(or)

1. **a.** Wayne was the kind of guy that was never noticed at school.
   **b.** Wayne wasn't the kind of guy that got into trouble.

   _____
   (and)
   _____

2. **a.** The police came to his house and arrested Wayne for murder.
   **b.** His life has never been the same.

   _____
   (since)
   _____

3. **a.** Wayne was found guilty at the end of his trial.
   **b.** He was given the death penalty.

   _____
   (because)
   _____

4. **a.** Wayne said that he is innocent.
   **b.** The jury didn't believe Wayne.

   _____
   (but)
   _____

5. **a.** Wayne still remembers his life before jail.
   **b.** Wayne's life in jail is very different now.

   _____
   (although)
   _____

6. **a.** Wayne's mother doesn't want him to feel lonely.
   **b.** She visits him almost every day.

   _____
   (so)
   _____

7. **a.** Wayne's lawyer visits him.
   **b.** Wayne asks about getting a new trial.

   _____

   (when)

   _____

**3** *Read a letter by an American college student taking a criminal justice class. On a separate piece of paper, rewrite the letter to use a variety of sentences: simple, compound, and complex. Make at least five changes, and change the sentence structure as much as you like.*

Dear Anne,

I'm taking a criminal justice class right now. We've been discussing capital punishment. I have really been shocked by some of the statistics we've learned! My classmates have really been shocked by some of the statistics we've learned! Did you know that in 1998 only four countries accounted for 80 percent of all executions worldwide? And did you know that the country which carried out the most executions of child criminals was the United States? It's true. The United States has executed ten since 1990. The United States plans to continue to execute child criminals. I used to agree with capital punishment. I always thought that the fear of the death penalty stopped some criminals. That is false. Here is a quote I discovered. "Research has failed to provide proof that executions stop murders more than life imprisonment." But the fact that is the most difficult for me to accept is that between 1900 and 2007, 426 criminals who were sentenced to death were later found to be innocent. Twenty-three of those criminals were actually executed. That is a problem that always exists with capital punishment. Some of the prisoners are innocent. They get executed. There is no perfect way to find out if someone is guilty. I now disagree with capital punishment.
   What do you think?

Your friend,
Katie

**4** *Look back at the first draft of your essay. Make sure you use a variety of sentence types (simple, compound, and complex) to make your writing more interesting.*

◀ EDIT: Writing the Final Draft

*Write the final draft of your essay. Carefully edit it for grammatical and mechanical errors, such as in spelling, capitalization, and punctuation. Make sure you use some of the vocabulary and grammar from the unit. Use the checklist to help you write your final draft. Then neatly write or type your essay.*

## ✓ FINAL DRAFT CHECKLIST

- ○ Does your essay clearly explain the reasons to support your opinion on capital punishment?
- ○ Does it contain an introductory paragraph, three body paragraphs, and a concluding paragraph?
- ○ Does the introductory paragraph contain a thesis statement stating the main idea of the essay?
- ○ Do the first two body paragraphs focus on reasons?
- ○ Does the third body paragraph use refutation?
- ○ Does each body paragraph contain reasons, examples, and facts to support your opinion?
- ○ Does the concluding paragraph restate the main idea expressed in the thesis statement?
- ○ Did you use sentence variety to make your writing more interesting?
- ○ Are present perfect and present perfect progressive used correctly?
- ○ Did you use vocabulary from the unit?

## ALTERNATIVE WRITING TOPICS

*Write about one of the topics. Use the vocabulary and grammar from the unit.*

1. Imagine that in your local area, capital punishment has been illegal for several years. Now the government plans to begin using it again. Write a letter to the editor of your local newspaper expressing your opinion of capital punishment.

2. Write a letter to Wayne Paulson. Explain what you have learned about the question of capital punishment. Give him some advice about what he might do in prison to make the best possible use of his time.

3. At times, people who visit foreign countries have trouble with the law. When they are  punished, they sometimes receive stronger punishments than they would in their home countries. Do you believe that certain countries give punishments that are too strong? Write a persuasive essay and include a refutation of the opposing point of view.

## RESEARCH TOPICS, see page 216.

# RESEARCH TOPICS

## UNIT 1: The World of Advertising

*In a small group, compare advertisements and select one to present to the class. Follow these steps:*

**Step 1:** Look at advertisements in a magazine. Find one that you think is convincing.

**Step 2:** Complete the following worksheet with information about one convincing advertisement.

Name of product: _____

Type of product: _____

Message (pictures, words, or both): _____

_____

Possible markets: _____

_____

Why is the ad convincing?_____

_____

_____

**Step 3:** Work in a small group to compare your advertisements. Which ones are the most convincing? Are there any ads that might not be successful globally? How could you change these ads?

**Step 4:** Within your group, select an advertisement to present to the class.

## UNIT 2: Fraud

*In a small group, research recent cases of fraud. Compare your findings and write a report. Follow these steps:*

**Step 1:** Choose one of these types of fraud:
- Internet fraud
- medical fraud
- identity theft
- (*your own idea*)

Go to your local school library or public library. Look for news articles that provide more information about this type of fraud.

**Step 2:** Read two or more articles describing one recent case of fraud. Answer these questions:

- When did this fraud take place?
- What happened?
- How many people were involved?
- What were the financial consequences?
- What were the emotional and psychological consequences?

**Step 3:** Work in a small group to compare your findings. Prepare a report for the class.

## UNIT 3: Going to Extremes: Sports and Obsession

*Choose an athlete or dancer famous in your community. Write a report about his or her life and accomplishments. Follow these steps:*

**Step 1:** Find a person in your community who has had significant accomplishments in sports or dance. Interview the person. You may also gather information about the person by reading local newspaper articles and/or websites.

**Step 2:** Use the information to write a factual report about this person's life and accomplishments. Refer to the following questions in writing your report.

- WHO is this person? What kind of early life and education did he or she have? Who are other important people related to this person?
- WHAT are the greatest accomplishments of this person? What kind of problems have been faced?
- WHEN did this person become well-known? When and where did this person's accomplishments take place?
- WHERE did this person first become involved in dance or sports? Where has this person traveled?
- WHY has this person become so successful? How much practice and training has been involved? Has obsession helped them in any way?

**Step 3:** Read your report to a small group of classmates.

## UNIT 4: Speaking of Gender

*In this unit you learned about gender differences in the United States. These differences are often reflected in TV programs. Investigate some TV programs for gender-specific language. Write a report summarizing your findings. Follow these steps:*

**Step 1:** Select a 30-minute drama or sitcom (situation comedy) program to watch. Listen for language and watch for behavior that you think is gender-specific. You might find it helpful to record the program so that you can listen to it more than once. Complete the following questionnaire.

1. Name of TV program:

   _____

2. Type of TV program:

   _____

3. List the main characters with a few words to describe each one.

   _____

   _____

4. Summarize the plot, or story, in one or two sentences.

   _____

   _____

5. List and identify any behaviors that you noticed were gender-specific.

   _____

   _____

6. List any language that you noticed was gender-specific.

   _____

   _____

**Step 2:** Write a one-paragraph report summarizing your findings. If there is time, you may want to show a clip of the TV program to the class.

## UNIT 5: Ecotourism

*Investigate tourism in the Arctic. Write a letter to an organization protecting the Arctic environment. Share what you learn with your classmates. Follow these steps:*

**Step 1:** Go to a travel agency or use the Internet to get information about visiting the Arctic.

**Step 2:** Use the Internet or go to the library to find the name of a local, national, or international organization that is working to protect the Arctic environment. Write to the organization, and ask these questions:

- Have any accidents occurred because of tourists?
- How have local people responded to tourists? Are they happy to have visitors?
- Is the Arctic ecosystem* endangered in any way because of the presence of tourists?

**Step 3:** Share the letter you receive with the class.

---

\* **ecosystem:** all the animals and plants in a particular area, and the way in which they are related to each other and to their environment

# UNIT 6: The Metamorphosis

*Choose one of the research topics. Follow the directions.*

### 1. Animal or insect story

Go to the library or a local bookstore and find a short story about an animal or insect to read. Draw or paint a large illustration of the story. Give an oral presentation about the story you have chosen. You might like to explain the title, say what country the story comes from, and then tell the story.

### 2. Metamorphosis of an insect or a frog

Read about the metamorphosis of an insect, such as a butterfly, or an amphibian, such as a frog. Write about the metamorphosis process by paraphrasing, not copying, the information. Make a diagram of the metamorphosis process. Submit a copy of the original text with your report so your teacher can check your paraphrasing. Give a presentation of your information to the class.

# UNIT 7: The Choice to Be Amish

*The Amish community is not the only reclusive group in the United States. There are many others. There are also many examples of reclusive individuals. Investigate one such community or individual and write a report. Follow these steps:*

**Step 1:** Use the library or Internet to research another reclusive community or individual. Listed below are some possible choices.

- Branch Davidians
- People's Temple
- Hutterites
- Shakers
- The Carthusian Order
- The Sabaean Mandeans of Iraq
- Howard Hughes
- Theodore Kaczynski
- Henry David Thoreau
- J. D. Salinger

**Step 2:** Answer these questions about the community or individual that you have chosen.

- Why did this community or individual choose to live reclusively?
- How are these reasons similar to or different from the reasons of the Amish?
- Describe the lifestyle of this community or individual: work, leisure activities, standard of living.
- Would you consider this community or individual dangerous to society or helpful to society? Explain.
- In what other ways can this community or individual be compared to the Amish?

**Step 3:** Use your notes from Step 2 to write a report on this community or individual. Share your report with the class.

## UNIT 8: Finding a Spouse

*Investigate courtship and marriage in your community. Write a summary of your findings. Follow these steps:*

**Step 1:** Look at several newspapers and magazines. How much information can you find that is related to courtship and marriage? Use these questions to organize the information that you find.

1. How many wedding announcements did you find? _____

2. How many of the following types of advertisements did you find?
   - matchmaking services _____
   - wedding fashions/jewelry _____
   - honeymoon travel _____
   - *other (describe):* _____

3. How many articles on marriage did you find? _____

4. How many advice columns* were related to courtship or marriage? _____

**Step 2:** Use these questions as a guide to write a summary of your research. Share your summary with the class.

- Which articles were the most interesting? Why?
- What kinds of advertisements did you see most often? How convincing were these advertisements? Did these advertisements make you want to buy the product or service?
- What kinds of problems did you find in the advice columns? Were any of these problems related to information in this unit? Explain.

_____

* **advice column:** a special section in a newspaper or magazine where people ask for and get advice on their problems

## UNIT 9: Is Our Climate Changing?

*Investigate one aspect of the climate change problem. Write a report about your findings. Follow these steps:*

**Step 1:** Use the library or Internet to research other aspects of climate change science. Listed below are some choices:
- the "hockey stick"
- cylinders of ice cores taken from glaciers
- measurements of $CO_2$ in the atmosphere
- the ocean's temperatures, especially in the North Atlantic
- melting glaciers

*(continued on next page)*

- the increase in frequency and strength of storms
- rising sea levels
- migrations of species
- the Kyoto Protocol
- the International Panel on Climate Change

**Step 2:** Answer the following questions about the topic you have chosen.

1. Who is responsible for initiating this study?

2. How long have people been studying this?

3. Why is this information important?

4. How will this information help us in the future?

5. Is this a major or minor part of climate change?

**Step 3:** Use your notes from Step 2 to write a report. Prepare a visual aid for your report. Share your report with the class.

## UNIT 10: Crime and Punishment

*Find out about a specific country and its laws relating to the death penalty. (See the information in the box about some countries.) Write a report about your findings. Follow the steps below:*

---

- Cote d'Ivoire, Liberia, Canada, Mexico, Paraguay, Bhutan, Samoa, Nepal, Philippines, Armenia, Bosnia-Herzegovina, Cyprus, Montenegro, Cambodia, Timor Leste, and Turkey are countries which have recently abolished the death penalty for all crimes.
- Since 1985, 55 countries have abolished the death penalty. During this same period 4 countries reintroduced it: Nepal, Philippines, Gambia, and Papua New Guinea. Nepal and Philippines have now abolished it again.
- Congo, Iran, Nigeria, Saudi Arabia, and Sudan execute child offenders who were under the age of 18 years old at the time of the crime.

---

**Step 1:** Choose a country. Go to the library to research the history of its death penalty laws.

**Step 2:** Answer these questions.

- During what period did the death penalty exist?
- Was it used for all crimes, or was it used only for exceptional crimes such as wartime crimes?
- When was it abolished?
- What is the current situation? For example, does the death penalty still exist, or has it been abolished? If it still exists in the law books, is it being used?

- Are there any plans to change the current death penalty laws? (Note: France has abolished the death penalty, but surveys show that 50 percent of the citizens would support bringing it back.) Add three questions of your own.

- _____
  _____

- _____
  _____

- _____
  _____

**Step 3:** Work in a small group to discuss the information that you found. Write a one- to three-paragraph report to explain what you learned from this fieldwork. Then read your report to the class. You could also have your research published.

# GRAMMAR BOOK REFERENCES

| NorthStar: Reading and Writing Level 3, Third Edition | Focus on Grammar Level 3, Third Edition | Azar's Fundamentals of English Grammar, Third Edition |
|---|---|---|
| **Unit 1**<br>Simple Present and Present Progressive | **Unit 1**<br>Present Progressive and Simple Present | **Chapter 1**<br>Present Time: 1-1 |
| **Unit 2**<br>Simple Past and Past Progressive | **Unit 4**<br>Past Progressive and Simple Past | **Chapter 2**<br>Past Time: 2-8 |
| **Unit 3**<br>Ability: *Can, Could, Be able to* | **Unit 11**<br>Ability: *Can, Could, Be able to* | **Chapter 7**<br>Modal Auxiliaries: 7-2 |
| **Unit 4**<br>Comparative Adverbs | **Unit 26**<br>Adverbs: *As . . . as,*<br>Comparatives, Superlatives | **Chapter 9**<br>Comparisons: 9-3 |
| **Unit 5**<br>*Because* and *Even though* | **Part VIII**<br>**From Grammar to Writing**<br>Combining Sentences with *Because, Although, Even though* | **Chapter 8**<br>Connecting Ideas: 8-6, 8-7 |

| NorthStar: Reading and Writing Level 3, Third Edition | Focus on Grammar Level 3, Third Edition | Azar's Fundamentals of English Grammar, Third Edition |
| --- | --- | --- |
| **Unit 6**<br>Infinitives of Purpose | **Unit 30**<br>Infinitives of Purpose | **Chapter 13**<br>Gerunds and Infinitives: 13-9 |
| **Unit 7**<br>Noun Clauses with *Wh-* Words | | **Chapter 14**<br>Noun Clauses: 14-2, 14-3, 14-4 |
| **Unit 8**<br>Definite and Indefinite Articles | **Unit 22**<br>Articles: Indefinite and Definite | **Chapter 11**<br>Count/Noncount Nouns and Articles: 11-8 |
| **Unit 9**<br>Future Possibility: *May, Might, Could* | **Unit 36**<br>Future Possibility: *May, Might, Could* | **Chapter 7**<br>Modal Auxiliaries: 7-3, 7-4 |
| **Unit 10**<br>Present Perfect and Present Perfect Progressive | **Unit 20**<br>Present Perfect Progressive and Present Perfect | **Chapter 4**<br>The Present Perfect and the Past Perfect: 4-3, 4-5, 4-6, 4-7 |

# CREDITS

**Photo Credits: Page 1** Oliver Berg/dpa/Corbis; **Page 4** Eveready Battery Company, Inc.; **Page 8** AFP/Getty Images; **Page 39 (left)** Pascal Tournaire/Corbis, **(middle)** Doug Pensinger/Getty Images, **(right)** Shutterstock; **Page 40** Tim Rue/Corbis; **Page 42** Duomo/Corbis; **Page 46** John G. Zimmerman/Getty Images; **Page 49** Bettman/Corbis; **Page 59** Shutterstock; **Page 60** Nonstock/Jupiterimages; **Page 63** Peter Cade/Getty Images; **Page 68** Datacraft/age fotostock; **Page 79** Steve Bloom/Getty Images; **Page 82** Roger Mear/Getty Images; **Page 83** Maurice Joseph/Alamy; **Page 85** Alan White/Alamy; **Page 86** Danita Delimont/Alamy; **Page 87** Tim Davis/Corbis; **Page 99** Kathie Atkinson/Oxford Scientific/Jupiterimages; **Page 100** Bettmann/Corbis; **Page 121** Three Lions/Getty Images; **Page 127** H. Mark Weidman Photography/Alamy; **Page 128** Herman Schlabach; **Page 132** Robert Sciarrino/Star Ledger/Corbis; **Page 143** Dave Bartruff/Corbis; **Page 146** Eddie Shih/AP Images; **Page 150** Michael Newman/PhotoEdit; **Page 163** Shutterstock; **Page 165 (top)** Purestock/Getty Images, **(middle)** Marc Schlossman/Getty Images, **(bottom)** Shutterstock; **Page 167 (top)** Shutterstock, **(bottom)** Shutterstock; **Page 175** Shutterstock; **Page 185** Joe Raedle/Getty Images; **Page 187** Shutterstock; **Page 188** Shutterstock; **Page 189** Shutterstock; **Page 195** Index Stock Imagery.

**Illustration Credits:** Paul Hampson, **Pages 19, 164**; Mapping Specialists Limited, **Page 122**; Dusan Petricic, **Page 32**.

# Notes

# Notes

# Notes

# Notes

# Notes

# Notes

study verb or nouns

woo hookendon

- Chicago is know for its beauty (nouns)

- chicago is a (Ads) beautiful city.

- Many city leaders beautify (verb) chicago by planting trees and flowers